THE JOY OF

JAMS, JELLIES,
AND OTHER SWEET PRESERVES

ALSO BY LINDA ZIEDRICH

The Joy of Pickling, Revised Edition

THE JOY OF
JAMS, JELLIES,
AND OTHER SWEET PRESERVES

200 Classic and Contemporary Recipes

Showcasing the Fabulous Flavors of Fresh Fruits

LINDA ZIEDRICH

The Harvard Common Press

Boston, Massachusetts

The Harvard Common Press
535 Albany Street
Boston, Massachusetts 02118
www.harvardcommonpress.com

Printed in the United States of America
Printed on acid-free paper

Library of Congress Cataloging-in-Publication Data
   Ziedrich, Linda.
   The joy of jams, jellies, and other sweet preserves : 200 classic and contemporary recipes showcasing the fabulous flavors of fresh fruits / Linda Ziedrich.
      p.   cm.
   ISBN 978-1-55832-406-0 (pbk.) —— ISBN 978-1-55832-405-3 (hardcover)
      1. Jam.   2. Jelly.   I. Title.
   TX612.J3Z54 2009
   641.8'52——dc22   2008036447

Cover design by Night & Day Design
Interior design by Ralph Fowler / rlf design

10 9 8 7 6 5 4 3 2 1

5|14

FOR REBECCA,

MY INTREPID FORAGER

CONTENTS

Preface . . . ix

Introduction . . . xi

PRESERVER'S PRIMER . . . 1

THE FRUITS

Apple . . . 35

Apricot . . . 51

Banana . . . 57

Blackberry . . . 60

Blueberry and
   Huckleberry . . . 75

Cantaloupe and
   Muskmelon . . . 82

Carrot . . . 87

Cherry . . . 90

Coconut . . . 107

Cranberry . . . 110

Currant . . . 118

Eggplant . . . 127

Elderberry . . . 130

Feijoa (Pineapple Guava) . . . 138

Fig . . . 140

Flowers . . . 150

Garden Huckleberry . . . 161

Ginger . . . 163

Gooseberry . . . 166

Grape . . . 168

Grapefruit . . . 177

Kiwi . . . 180

Kumquat . . . 184

Lemon and Lime . . . 188

Mango . . . 196

Medlar . . . 199

Nuts . . . 203

Orange . . . 213

Oregon Grape . . . 225

Papaya . . . 227

Peach . . . 230

Pear, European and
    Asian . . . 237

Pepper . . . 253

Pineapple . . . 259

Plum . . . 264

Pomegranate . . . 283

Pumpkin and
    Winter Squash . . . 286

Quince . . . 291

Raspberry . . . 309

Rhubarb . . . 319

Strawberry . . . 325

Strawberry Tree . . . 335

Tomatillo and Ground
    Cherry . . . 337

Tomato . . . 341

Watermelon . . . 348

Zucchini (Marrow) . . . 353

Measurement Equivalents . . . 355
Select References . . . 357
Index . . . 359

PREFACE

I have been working on this book for so long that I can't remember why I started. But my inspiration must have come partially from a Yugoslavian immigrant I knew when both of us were barely into our twenties. On a hike he picked some blackberries or plums, and he made them into jam simply by cooking them with sugar, as he remembered his mother and grandmother doing. There was no trip to the supermarket for a package of pectin, no unfolding the long page of instructions and searching for the relevant ones—which had to be followed *exactly*, the manufacturer always warned, or else the jam wouldn't set. My friend's success got me wondering how people made jams and jellies before pectin was packaged and sold in stores. I soon learned that many people still make jams and jellies the old-fashioned way, and that there are many traditional ways of preserving fruit that don't require gelling at all. For nearly three decades before writing this book, I researched and experimented with traditional preserving methods.

Because I am a native of California now living in western Oregon, most of the fruits and nuts I know come from these two states. For anyone who wants to explore North American fruits, the fecund Pacific states, and particularly California, are probably the best place to start. But because I want this book to be as valuable as possible to as many people as possible, I've also experimented with fruits from elsewhere, especially the tropics. If I've neglected fruits you know and love, or if I've left out your favorite ways of making them into sweet preserves, please feel free to write me in care of The Harvard Common Press, and I will keep your suggestions in mind for a second edition.

For their support in this project, I thank Bruce Shaw, Valerie Cimino, Karen Wise, and the whole staff at The Harvard Common Press; my family, who have had to taste everything in this book; and all the people who have patiently answered my questions about what they put into jars.

INTRODUCTION

Occasionally I'm asked why anyone in this modern world would still do home preserving. If you've picked up this book, you probably have many answers to that question. Even if you live in the middle of a big city, a bounty of free fresh fruit may sometimes fall into your hands—from a single tree in your tiny backyard, perhaps, or lush vines along a nearby abandoned railroad. Perhaps your eyes prove bigger than your stomach at the farmers' market, and you can't bear to waste the precious, lovely fruit you've emptied your pockets for. You may despair at the bland taste of commercial preserves and challenge yourself to do better. Maybe you want to avoid the corn syrup or other questionable ingredients in supermarket products, or duplicate costly preserves in pretty jars from a fancy-foods shop. You may anticipate the delight on friends' faces when they dip into one of your jars at your breakfast table or find one under a Christmas tree. You may feel the strong sense of connectedness that comes from making jams and jellies just like your mother's and grandmother's, or from exchanging recipes and jars with your neighbors or with friends around the world.

Most compelling of all may be the sensations that flood your mouth, and feelings that flood your mind, every time you taste your own well-made preserves. A jar of jam or jelly is a memory brought back to life, less bright than the original, but sweeter and mellower. The jar is also a promise—of the fresh flavors that will greet your tongue in a few short months and, if you're lucky, again every year thereafter.

PRESERVER'S PRIMER

SOME PEOPLE go about cooking by first reading recipes and then shopping for ingredients. Home preservers don't do that; they read recipes to learn what to do with the produce they already have. For this reason, this book is arranged alphabetically by type of fruit. The notes preceding each section will tell you a little about the history, varieties, growing conditions, harvest, and preparation of the particular fruit.

KINDS OF PRESERVES

This book includes recipes for several kinds of preserves, the names of which have varied over the centuries and from region to region. I have followed the most common contemporary American usage, with slight variation, as follows:

JAM. Crushed or chopped fruit that is cooked with sugar until the mixture gels, or "sets." I include in this category preserves made from pureed fruit, when the mixture is cooked quickly and without spices.

JELLY. A gelled mixture of sugar and juice, acidified if necessary. The kind of jelly that wins prizes at a county fair is clear, and it holds its shape when turned out of its container onto a dish. When the dish is moved, the jelly quivers. When the jelly is sliced, it retains the angle of the cut. Personally, I like softer, more spreadable jellies. Opaque jellies, such as milky-pink flowering-quince jelly, can also be very attractive.

MARMALADE. Jelly, usually soft and clear, in which are suspended pieces of fruit or citrus peel or both. Marmalade is often made entirely with citrus fruit. Because of the inclusion of the peel, citrus marmalades are usually bitter in flavor.

CONSERVE. Jam made from several ingredients, which may include two or more fresh fruits, nuts, and raisins.

BUTTER. Pureed fruit cooked slowly with sugar, juice, or both, usually with added spices, until the mixture is thick and dark. Butters generally have less added sugar than jams.

PRESERVES. In the narrow sense of the word, preserves are whole or sliced fruits in syrup or soft jelly. In the past, preserves were served as "spoon sweets" on their own for dessert, with or without their syrup. Today syrupy preserves are often served over cake or ice cream. For eating with bread, though, lightly gelled preserves are generally preferred. Preserves are called *conserves* in England.

SYRUP. A solution of fruit juice and sugar or honey. Syrups are usually, but not always, thick, clear, and ungelled. They are mixed with ice, water, and other liquids for drinks and poured over cake, ice cream, and other desserts.

PASTE. A mixture of pureed, pectin-rich fruit and sugar cooked until it is very thick, poured into wide dishes to dry, and served cut into pieces as a finger food. Sometimes the pieces are rolled in sugar. The most popular fruits for paste are quince and, in Latin America, guava. Quince paste was the original marmalade. The English, who make paste from many fruits, call it *cheese*.

LEATHER. Pureed fruit dried in a thin layer and usually rolled for storage. The fruit is often but not always cooked.

A VERY BRIEF HISTORY OF FRUIT PRESERVES

Our modern jams, jellies, and other fruit preserves trace their ancestry to western Asia and the Mediterranean region. There, beginning in ancient times, fruits were often preserved in honey or syrup, which was made by boiling down the juice of grapes, figs, or other fruits. After the introduction of cane sugar and its refinement, the making of sweetmeats developed into an art. In much of medieval Europe, candied fruits or fruits preserved in heavy syrup were served after dinner, as digestives. Such preserves are still regularly eaten as spoon sweets—with coffee, tea, or cold water—in the Middle East, Russia, Greece, and the Balkans.

The first gelled sweetmeats were probably made from quince—or Cydonian apples, to the Greeks. The Greek word *mēlomeli*, "apple in honey," originally referred to quinces submerged in honey and sealed in jars. Over many months the quinces softened deliciously—if they were sufficiently ripe to begin with. If not, they might be cooked first. Because quinces are rich in pectin, cooking them with honey produces a jelly. Over the centuries, honey was gradually replaced with cane sugar, the quince was juiced or mashed or pureed, and other fruits were combined with it or used on their own. But quince remained the prototypal fruit for gelled sweet preserves. *Mēlomeli* became, in Spain, *membrillo*, the name of both the fruit and the preserve, and, in Portugal, *marmelada* (the quince, to the Portuguese, was *marmelo*). After the seafaring Portuguese began shipping *marmelada* in small wooden boxes to their trading partners, *marmelada* or *marmalade* came to mean, in England and much of Europe, any fruit pureed and stewed with sugar until stiff. Marmalade was sliced and served for dessert along with preserves and candied fruits.

In England and Scotland, in the eighteenth century, orange marmalade grew particularly popular. At first it was made, like other marmalades, of beaten whole fruit—in this case usually whole bitter oranges imported from Spain or Portugal. Soon cooks began shredding the peel and suspending it in transparent jelly. But it wasn't until the nineteenth century that orange marmalade, through the addition of water and long cooking, became soft and spreadable. The Scots were probably the first to serve orange marmalade for breakfast rather than dessert, to spread on bread in place of butter or along with it.

Most other fruits are less rich in pectin than quinces and oranges are; when cooked with sugar they tend to make softer preserves even if no water is added. Beginning in the eighteenth century, non-citrus soft fruit preserves, put up in jars rather than boxes, came to be called *jam* in England and the United States. Jam might be served as a spoon sweet or used as a cake filling, but it, too, became mainly a breakfast food.

As sugar gradually became more widely available and less expensive, cooks applied their preserving skills to every tasty fruit they found growing wild or managed to cultivate in their gardens. They learned that jams and jellies gel only with adequate pectin and acid. They learned which fruits gelled most easily, and which might combine well with others for a firmer jam or jelly. They learned that just-ripe or slightly underripe fruits gel much better than overripe fruits. They learned how much sugar to use with each kind of fruit to produce the desired degree of gelling. They learned how batch size and cooking time affect gelling. Old recipes for jellies and jams reflect a long process of trial and error.

THE ADVENT OF PACKAGED PECTIN

In the nineteenth century, scientists identified the substance in fruits that causes gelling as *pectin* (from the Greek *pēktos*, "coagulated"). In the early twentieth century, pectin made from apple pomace and citrus peels became an industrial product, first in liquid and later in powder form. Throughout the twentieth century, jam and jelly makers came to rely more and more on packaged pectin and the recipes that came with it rather than on knowledge passed down from their mothers and grandmothers.

Today packaged pectin and its accompanying recipes are available in every supermarket. These products are handy when you want to make jelly solely from fruit low in pectin, such as strawberries. Packaged pectin is useful to have on hand when jelly fails to gel, as may sometimes happen even when you think your fruit has adequate pectin.

But packaged pectin has shortcomings. First, it may seem expensive, especially if you've gotten your fruit for free. It may deteriorate with age (be sure to check the expiration date on the package).

Pectin comes packaged with dextrose, a form of sugar, and other additives such as fumaric acid and sodium citrate, which you may prefer to leave out of your preserves. If the fruit you're using is uncommon, it may be left out of the recipes on the package insert. Most important, if the pectin is the conventional (high-methoxyl or high-ester) kind, which produces a gel through a reaction with sugar, you must use the amount of sugar specified, or you will likely end up with an over- or undergelled jam or jelly. Recipes that come with conventional packaged pectin require high proportions of sugar—at least one pound for each pound of fruit, and usually quite a bit more.

In recent years retailers have stocked other kinds of packaged pectin, labeled with phrases such as "no sugar needed" or "low sugar." Low-methoxyl (or low-ester) pectin gels contain less added sugar—or none at all—and no added acid. This kind of pectin, made by treating high-methoxyl pectin with a mildly acidic or alkaline solution, forms a gel in the presence of calcium, so powdered calcium is provided in a separate package or mixed in with the pectin.

Amidated pectin is a special kind of low-methoxyl pectin made by "de-esterifying" high-methoxyl pectin with ammonia. Amidated pectin needs little calcium to gel, and jam or jelly made from it will re-gel after it is heated and allowed to cool.

In my experience, low-methoxyl pectins generally make more spreadable jams, with a softer gel. If I'm going to use packaged pectin, this is the kind I generally choose. But my preference for softer gels made me wonder, about twenty years ago, whether I needed packaged pectin at all. After some reading and experimentation, I concluded that I did not. None of the recipes in this book call for it.

I have written this book so that you, too, can recover the once-common knowledge behind the art of making sweetmeats—jams, jellies, preserves, butters, syrups, pastes, and more. Following are some basic facts and principles that you should know before you begin. They will help you interpret the recipes, avoid and repair mistakes, and let your local harvests, good taste, and whims guide you as you create your own original preserves.

Jam and jelly set through a combination of evaporation and gelling. Gelling occurs through a reaction of sugar, water, acid, and pectin.

Pectin is a substance found in all land plants that helps them maintain their structure by binding water. Pectin is concentrated in the structural and rapidly growing parts of plants, including the fruits and especially the cores and peels. For humans, pectin is nonnutritive fiber, useful as a bulk-forming laxative and effective in lowering blood cholesterol. Most important for the cook, pectin is essential in gelling jellies and jams.

Pectin develops as fruit ripens. Underripe fruit contains proto-pectin, or pectose, which gradually converts to pectin. Heating also converts protopectin to pectin.

As fruits become very ripe, they lose water-insoluble pectin and gain water-soluble pectin; this causes gradual softening. At the same time, enzymes break down the pectin and convert it to pectinic acids. Overripe fruit has very little pectin that can form a gel. For good gelling, therefore, jam and jelly makers traditionally use three parts just-ripe fruit to one part underripe, and avoid overripe fruit altogether.

Pectin is best extracted through heating. You can taste the pectin in heat-extracted fruit juices. It has no flavor, but it feels mucilaginous on the tongue and coats the roof of the mouth. If you swirl a little heat-extracted fruit juice in a glass, the viscous juice coats the glass. Cold-pressed juice, such as fresh apple cider, may taste viscous if the apples were pressed soon after picking, but not nearly as viscous as heat-extracted apple juice. (Blackberries are an exception to this rule; their pectin is extracted well with cold pressing.) Heating also destroys the enzymes in fruit that break down pectin.

Sugar is present in all fruits, but additional sugar is needed to produce a gel. The sugar of choice is usually refined and granulated; this is what is meant when the recipes call for simply "sugar." Refined sugar is generally preferred because of its simple flavor; it adds sweetness but doesn't overwhelm the flavor of the fruit. Granulated sugar is easy to

Some people prefer to make all their sweet preserves with honey, because it is less processed than sugar and, arguably, more healthful. But when honey is heated it loses much of its magic—the complexity of its fragrance and flavor, and perhaps also some of its health-promoting properties. Honey comes in as many flavors as there are flowers attractive to bees, and some of these flavors are quite strong—easily strong enough to overwhelm the flavor of most fruits. Honey contains water and so may necessitate longer boiling. Honey also produces a lot of foam during cooking, and gelled preserves made with honey tend to be soft.

Although I keep bees, I tend to use honey in ways that let me enjoy its special flavors rather than as a routine substitute for sugar. Numerous recipes in this book call for honey, but I seldom use honey in recipes for gelled preserves. If you want to make your jam with honey, choose a light-colored one, such as clover (if it is light in color, it will probably be light in flavor, too). I recommend using no more than one part honey to one part refined sugar. Finally, expect to boil the mixture a little longer than you would if you used only sugar.

pour and measure; moreover, it has a consistent ratio of volume to weight, so you can measure it with a cup instead of a scale.

The amount of sugar needed depends mainly on the pectin content of your fruit or juice. High-pectin fruits can produce too-stiff gels unless you use plenty of sugar, as much as 1¼ cups per cup of fruit or juice. But using that much sugar with lower-pectin fruits could produce a sticky, moist jelly or even a syrup. Low-pectin fruits, in contrast, need as little as ½ cup sugar per cup of fruit or juice. For most fruits, the rule of thumb is to use ¾ cup sugar for each 1 cup juice or fruit.

Acid enhances the extraction of pectin. Without sufficient acid, a gel may not form at all. For this reason, as well as for flavor balance, citrus juice (usually lemon) or citric acid is often added to jellies and jams. A tablespoon of lemon juice or ¼ teaspoon of citric acid

TESTING FOR ACIDITY

If you're not sure whether your fruit or juice is acidic enough, you might compare it with a mixture of 3 tablespoons water, ½ teaspoon sugar, and 1 teaspoon lemon juice. Juice for jelly, or fruit for jam, should taste at least as tart as this mixture.

If you want a more scientific test, use pH strips or a pH test kit. The optimum pH for jam or jelly making is 3.2 to 3.4.

should suffice for 2 pounds of low-acid fruit. Slightly underripe fruit is more acidic than ripe fruit; this is another reason to seek it out for preserving.

Some people think that making jam without added pectin requires long cooking, but this isn't so. Overheating breaks down pectin. After the sugar is added, jams and jellies shouldn't be cooked for more than 15 minutes. English cooks warm their sugar in the oven before adding it to the preserving pan, to minimize the boiling time. A shorter boiling time results in a brighter color and fresher flavor.

Jams and jellies set faster and more reliably when made in small batches. Large batches slow evaporation and result in overheating, which, again, breaks down pectin and degrades color and flavor. Batch sizes in my recipes are generally much smaller than those in pectin-package recipes.

Although jams and jellies should cook fast, they don't need a roaring flame. In the recipes, I usually call for "medium-high heat." I'm not referring to a particular setting on your stove; every stove model differs, and different burners on the same stove can produce different heat levels. Turn the heat up just enough to produce a rolling boil. This might mean a medium setting on a gas-fueled restaurant-style stove or a high setting on a typical electric range. Too-fast boiling can cause the sugar to crystallize after the jam or jelly is put into jars. (This happens because the sucrose doesn't have time to convert to glucose and fructose.)

Crystallization is especially likely to occur if boiling begins before the sugar is completely dissolved in the fruit juice. To promote the dissolution of the sugar, pour it into the center of the pan and stir the mixture gently over medium heat. If sugar crystals stick to the side of the pan, wash them down with a damp pastry brush.

Depending on the fruit you're using, your jam or jelly may foam during cooking. Skim off this foam so it doesn't end up as a whitish deposit at the top of your jam or jelly jar. A wire skimmer usually works best for this purpose; the foam might fall through the holes of a slotted spoon. Some cooks add a bit of butter to the pot to reduce foaming, but if the jam or jelly is to be stored for a long time, the butter might go rancid and produce an off-flavor.

Overcooking can make jelly or jam tough, so test each batch often. I keep several stainless-steel soup spoons by the stove so I can frequently lift a bit of syrup and watch how it drips from a clean, cool spoon. When you see signs of gelling, turn off the heat and move the pot to a cold burner. If another test shows that a little more boiling is needed, just return the pan to the heat.

JAM

Jam is made by mashing cooked fruit, or sometimes chopping or pureeing it, and then cooking it with sugar. If the fruit is low in acid, an acidic ingredient, usually lemon juice, is added to produce a good gel. If the fruit is low in pectin, it might be combined with a high-pectin fruit. Typical combinations are raspberry and red currant,

DON'T DOUBLE BATCH SIZES!

Oversized batches not only tend to boil over; they also delay gelling and so require longer cooking times, which degrade color and flavor. Sometimes big batches won't gel at all. You will find that making two or three small batches is only a little more trouble than making one big batch.

PECTIN CONTENT OF FRUITS

High	Medium	Low
Apples (tart)	Apples (sweet)	Apricots
Crabapples	Blackberries	Bananas
Cranberries	Blueberries (some)	Blueberries (some)
Currants	Grapes (Concord and	Cherries
Gooseberries	some others)	Elderberries
Grapefruits	Guavas	Figs
Kiwis	Oranges (navel)	Grapes (some)
Lemons	Papayas	Mangoes
Limes	Plums (some)	Melons
Oranges (Seville,	Raspberries	Nectarines
Valencia)		Peaches
Plums (some)		Pears
Quinces		Pineapples
Tangerines		Rhubarb
		Strawberries
		Overripe fruits

elderberry and apple, and cherry and lemon. A small batch size helps ensure good gelling and a fresh flavor, so I work with no more than 4½ pounds of fruit at a time.

If you're a beginning preserver, I encourage you to start with jam. It is usually much easier to make than jelly or preserves. Because fruit pulp contains pectin, jam gels more easily than jelly does, and because the fiber in fruit pulp is an added thickener, gelling is less critical with jam. And although a firm jelly is still the ideal, most people prefer a soft jam. If your jam seems too soft, you can cook it a little more to thicken it—keeping in mind that it will thicken more as it cools, and perhaps more still in the following week or two.

ACID CONTENT OF FRUITS

High	Medium	Low
Cranberries	Apples (tart)	Apricots
Currants	Blackberries	Bananas
Gooseberries	Blueberries	Cherries (sweet)
Grapefruits	Cherries (sour)	Elderberries
Kiwis	Grapes (some)	Figs
Lemons	Guavas	Grapes (some)
Limes	Mangoes (underripe)	Mangoes (ripe)
Quinces (some)	Oranges (Valencia,	Nectarines
Oranges (Seville)	navel)	Papayas (ripe)
Pineapples	Plums (Japanese,	Peaches
Rhubarb	damson)	Pears
Tangerines	Raspberries	Plums (prune)
	Strawberries	Overripe fruits

JELLY

Because abundant pectin is needed to make a firm jelly, pectin-rich fruits such as quince, damson, crabapple, tart apple, currant, and lemon are traditionally used for this preserve. The fruit must be just ripe or slightly underripe. The juice is extracted by heating the fruit in a pot, with added water if needed, and then straining the juice through a jelly bag, or by using a steam juicer (page 14).

Steam juicers are big, so I use mine only when I'm making large quantities of juice. For small quantities, I use a covered saucepan, adding water only as needed to soften the fruit, because extra water lowers the concentration of pectin. Usually I heat the fruit on the stovetop, but some people prefer to use a low oven. I mash the fruit occasionally while the heat draws out the juice. When the fruit is soft, I pour it with its juice into a damp jelly bag set over a bowl.

A jelly bag is simply a piece of fine-woven muslin or nylon mesh stitched into a bag. Drawstring bags with metal stands for jelly making are sold in kitchenware stores. If you don't have a stand, you can suspend a closed bag from a cabinet knob (taking care to protect your cabinet from staining), faucet, or something else secure and handy. It's probably easiest, though, to simply lay a piece of muslin in a colander set over a bowl or pot. If you don't have muslin on hand, you can sub-

WHAT'S A STEAM JUICER?

A stovetop device that is best made of stainless steel, a steam juicer works much like a stovetop espresso pot. Like an espresso pot, a steam juicer has three main parts. The bottom is a pan to hold water. The middle is a juice receptacle with a raised and perforated center section through which steam rises, and a hose for draining the juice into jars. Set into the juice receptacle is a metal basket that holds fruit. You add a lid to keep the steam in, and set the juicer over high heat. As the steam cooks the fruit, the juice drains into the receptacle. You then draw off the juice through the hose.

In my experience, steam juicers generally produce clear, pectin-rich juice quickly and with minimal effort. High heat is required, though, and starchy fruits like apples and quinces require long steaming. For maximum extraction, I leave these dense fruits in the steaming basket (off the heat) overnight.

Steam juicers must be used with care. Depending on the model, the hose may be prone to coming off or even melting; you must make sure it is well attached and protected from direct heat. The outer end of the hose must be securely clamped to prevent leaks; it's wise, also, to set a pan under the end of the hose. If the fruit—for example, grapes—is very juicy and the juice isn't drained off soon enough, enough juice may accumulate in the receptacle that it drips through the perforated center section into the water pan below. If the fruit is starchy, such long steaming may be necessary that the water pan may run dry, in which case the juice will end up tasting scorched. I heat my juicer for no more than an hour before turning off the heat, carefully removing the fruit basket and juice receptacle, and adding more water.

Steam juicers are available at many farm-supply stores, at other stores that stock preserving equipment, and from Internet-based sources.

stitute four layers of cheesecloth. In any case, dampen the cloth before using it so it will absorb less juice. I pour boiling water through my jelly bag, let it cool a bit, and then squeeze out excess water before adding the fruit.

With starchier fruits and larger quantities, the dripping can take 8 hours or more. The time can be shortened by straining out the solids with a colander before pouring the juice into the jelly bag.

Your jelly bag should let pectin through but strain out starch, which is abundant in underripe fruits, especially apples. Starch can make a jelly cloudy. Cloudy jelly is certainly safe to eat, but it won't win you prizes at the county fair. Squeezing the jelly bag will let starch through. If you want a clear jelly, resist the temptation to squeeze the bag, even though this will mean a longer dripping period and some wasted juice.

You can judge the pectin content in your juice by swirling a little juice in a glass and tasting it. If the juice isn't noticeably viscous, it may be low in pectin. There are several ways to increase the pectin concentration. You can boil the juice (before adding the sugar, not afterward). You can heat the cooked fruit with water a second time to extract additional pectin and then boil down this liquid. You can boil the seeds, peels, and cores, along with the rest of the fruit or in a separate pan of water. Or you can soak the seeds in cold water for a day, as the English do with bitter oranges (this technique may not be effective with other fruits). Then add the cooking water or soaking water to the juice.

Another option is to combine the juice with the pectin-rich juice of another fruit, concentrated, if needed, by boiling. Concentrated quince, crabapple, tart apple, or orange juice, put up in canning jars or frozen, can serve as a homemade substitute for packaged pectin. For jelly, use 1 cup homemade pectin (page 17) for 1 to 2 cups of low-pectin juice. For jam, 1 cup homemade pectin should be adequate for 3 pounds of fruit.

As explained on page 10, you can judge the acidity of your juice by tasting it. If the juice is low in acid, add lemon juice, lime juice, or citric acid (which is sometimes sold in stores along with canning supplies).

TESTS FOR NATURAL PECTIN

With practice, you'll be able to identify pectin-rich juice by eye and by taste. But you can also try one of these tests:

1. Stir together 1 teaspoon cooked fruit juice and 2 teaspoons rubbing alcohol. Let the mixture stand for 1 minute. If it forms a solid mass that you can lift with a fork, the juice is high in pectin. If you see large, broken flakes, the pectin level is medium. Small flakes indicate low pectin. (Throw out your test sample, because rubbing alcohol is poisonous.)

2. Make a test batch. Combine ¼ cup cooked fruit or juice and 2½ tablespoons sugar in a small saucepan. Heat the mixture slowly, stirring until the sugar dissolves. Then raise the heat and boil the mixture until it passes the spoon test (page 18). Pour the mixture into a clean, hot glass or bowl, and let it cool. If the test batch gels, a larger batch should, too.

Too much acid is problematic, too; it can cause syrup to leak out of jelly. This "weeping," or syneresis, may not bother you at all, but it is a no-no at county fairs. When juice is very tart, combining it with low-acid juice can prevent weeping.

Cook your jelly in small batches to avoid both overboiling and the degradation of pectin (page 11). I advise using no more than 6 cups of juice in a 6-quart pan.

When your jelly begins to set, you'll want to avoid breaking the gel. Pour the syrup into jars as soon as you're sure it has reached the gel point. It's all right to process the jars; in my experience, a 5- to 10-minute boiling-water bath ensures a good seal and doesn't interfere with gelling. But don't move the jars when they are cooling. Let them stand undisturbed for at least 12 hours.

Jelly sets most reliably when it cools quickly. For this reason, jelly is usually put up in small glasses. I recommend half-pint or even half-cup canning jars.

What if your jelly fails to gel? If you're sure that the pectin and sugar were in balance and the juice was adequately tart, simply wait. Some jellies take a week or two to set. If your jelly still hasn't set after two weeks, you can gel it with store-bought powdered pectin. Empty the jars into your preserving pan. For each cup of jelly, combine 1 tablespoon sugar and 1 teaspoon powdered regular (high-methoxyl) pectin in a small bowl. Stir in 2 tablespoons boiling water. Add this mixture to the pan. If you think your jelly might not have

RECIPES FOR HOMEMADE PECTIN

Use just-ripe or slightly underripe tart apples, crabapples, or quinces for this recipe.

Homemade Apple, Crabapple, or Quince Pectin

Remove the stems and calyxes from the fruit and, if you're using quinces, rub off the fuzz. Slice the fruit, including the cores. Combine the fruit in a kettle with 2 cups water for each 1 pound fruit. Bring the mixture to a boil, cover the kettle, and simmer the mixture for 20 minutes or until the fruit is tender. Empty the pulp and juice into a jelly bag and let the juice drip into a bowl for at least 4 hours. Pour the juice into a kettle and boil it rapidly until it is reduced by half.

If you live too far south to grow apples, you might make pectin from oranges. This recipe comes from Florida.

Homemade Orange Pectin

Cut Valencia oranges in half. Squeeze out the juice and reserve it for jelly, if you like. Discard the seeds. Scrape out the membranes and some of the white pith, or albedo (a grapefruit spoon works well for this), and firmly pack these to fill a 2-cup measure. In a blender, blend the membranes and pith with 1/4 cup lemon juice and 2 cups water. Let this mixture stand for 4 hours. Add 2 more cups water, and let the mixture stand at room temperature for 12 hours. Then bring it to a boil and simmer it for 10 minutes. Strain the juice first through a colander and then through a jelly bag. You should get about 2 cups liquid. Freeze it in 1-cup portions for later use.

been acidic enough, add 1 teaspoon lemon juice for each cup of jelly. Bring the jelly to a rolling boil. Begin testing it after 30 seconds.

PRESERVES PROPER

This confusing category calls for special attention. Preserves in the narrow sense are whole fruits or pieces of fruit in syrup, which may

TESTS FOR GELLING

Also called the sheet test or drop test, the **spoon test** is best for jelly. Use a large, clean spoon. Scoop up a little of the syrup, hold the spoon high above the pan, and pour out the syrup. If the drops fall slow and thick, the jelly is almost ready. When the last bit poured from the spoon forms two drops that run together and remain suspended at the edge of the spoon for a moment—in what may or may not look like a "sheet" to you—the jelly is ready. Depending on the kind of fruit you're using, this point can be difficult to recognize. If you're making jelly from a particular fruit for the first time, I suggest checking the temperature as well (opposite page).

The **saucer test** is best for gelled preserves with fruit solids—that is, jams and marmalades. Before starting to make your jam, put a small bowl in the freezer. Take out the bowl when the fruit and syrup come together—in other words, when the mixture looks like thin jam. Remove the pan from the heat and put a drop of the jam into the chilled dish. The drop should mound slightly. When the drop has cooled, the jam shouldn't run when you tip the bowl.

A cold saucer is helpful in testing jelly, too. As well-gelled syrup cools, the surface wrinkles when the vessel is tipped.

You can also use a chilled dish to test the thickness of ungelled syrup. Put a drop of syrup onto the dish and then run your finger through the syrup. If it is thick enough, your finger will make a clear path.

A thicker syrup is indicated by the **thread test**. When you put a drop of syrup into a glass of cold water, the syrup should form a thread, about 2 inches long, as it descends through the water. If a ball forms instead, you've overheated the syrup. If

or may not be lightly gelled. Sometimes the syrup is made with added water, but usually the sugar is allowed to slowly draw water out of the fruit at room temperature. Heating dissolves any remaining sugar; with cooling the fruit reabsorbs water and plumps again. The sugar is often added gradually, because if it were all added at once the fruit might shrivel too much. Preserves are very sweet; recipes typically call for at least as much sugar, by weight, as fruit.

the syrup dissolves in the water without forming a thread, you haven't heated it enough. Fill the glass with clean water before reheating the syrup and testing it again.

If you're a beginning preserver, you might prefer to use a thermometer along with the saucer, thread, or spoon test. Sometimes you want the syrup to form a soft ball (though not a hard one). Syrup will form a thread at 230°F, a soft ball at 235°F. I recommend using an instant-read digital thermometer so you don't have to leave the thermometer in the pot, in the way of your stirring spoon.

Before you make jam or jelly, calibrate your thermometer by putting the end into a small pan of boiling water. If you're working at an altitude of less than 1,000 feet, the thermometer should read 212°F (if you use a non-digital thermometer, be sure to read it straight on, not at an angle). If the temperature reading is higher or lower than 212°F, adjust the screw beneath the face of the thermometer. When water boils at 212°F, jelly or jam should be cooked to 218° to 222°F. If your thermometer can't be adjusted or is difficult to adjust, just remember the figure on it; your gel point will be about 8 degrees higher. Because atmospheric conditions can alter the boiling point of water, some cooks check their thermometers every time they make jelly.

If you are working at a high altitude, your boiling point will be lower. Decrease the endpoint range of 218° to 222°F by 2 degrees for each 1,000-foot increase in elevation.

Syrup forms a thread beginning at 230°F, or 18 degrees above the boiling point of water.

Preserves are often cooked very slowly, for hours. Slow cooking both preserves the integrity of the fruit—which if boiled might turn to jam—and breaks down pectin. Even quince preserves may have an ungelled syrup if the cooking is long and slow enough.

Long-cooked preserves are traditional spoon sweets, but they are often served today over cake or ice cream. When drained of their syrup and allowed to dry, such preserves become candied fruit. When rolled in sugar, they become "crystallized."

Modern preserves recipes have fewer steps and shorter cooking times. These preserves turn out somewhere between jam and old-fashioned preserves. Soft-fruited, lightly gelled modern preserves are excellent for serving with warm bread.

CANNING PRESERVES

Canning is a way of preserving food by sealing it hot in airtight containers, or by heating the containers after they're filled with food. Heat raises the vapor pressure of the liquid inside the canning, or mason, jar. As the vapor pressure rises, air is forced out of the jar. As the jar and its contents cool, a vacuum forms as the vapor pressure drops, and the softened adhesive on the rim of the lid creates an airtight seal.

You don't need to can your preserves if you're making only a jarful or two at a time and planning to store the jars in the refrigerator. If the sugar content is high enough, you can even store the jars, tightly capped, on the kitchen counter for several weeks.

If you won't be canning your preserves, it's best to sterilize the jars before filling them, by immersing them in boiling water for at least 10 minutes.

Basic equipment for canning includes mason jars, which come in a variety of sizes. Because jelly sets up more reliably when it cools quickly, I recommend using half-pint or half-cup jars. For jam or preserves, you can use pint-size as well as smaller jars. Half-pint and pint mason jars come with either wide or narrow mouths.

Mason jars can be used over and over for years; some of mine are older than I am. Before each use, though, you should check the glass for cracks and the rims for nicks. Even a tiny nick could prevent a good seal.

New mason jars come with two-piece caps. The flat lids are meant for one-time use only. When you reuse the jars, you can also reuse the metal rings if they're not too rusty, but you must replace the flat lids. (You can use old lids—and jars with nicks in the rim—for storing dry foods. To avoid damaging the lid the first time you open a jar, push it up gently with the blade of a table knife.)

In place of mason jars you can use other jars, such as ones that held commercial mayonnaise, provided that the mouths fit the two-piece mason jar caps. If you use such jars, though, expect more failed seals and occasional jar breakage, since these jars have narrower rims and are less tempered. Boiling-water processing requires a large kettle with a rack at the bottom to protect the jars from overheating and breaking. Most cooks use an inexpensive enameled metal kettle made for the purpose, with a jar rack that you can raise or lower while the kettle is full of water. Many of these kettles, though, aren't quite tall enough for quart jars, and the racks quickly get rusty.

But you can use any large kettle for boiling-water processing. Internet sources sell stainless-steel racks that won't rust and may fit well into your stainless-steel stockpot. I use my pressure canner for boiling-water processing, without screwing on the lid all the way. Made entirely of aluminum and tall enough for quarts, it works very well for me, although because the rack has no handles I have to remove the jars one at a time.

Very helpful tools for canning include a jar lifter, a special kind of tongs for lifting hot jars safely; a stainless-steel or plastic canning funnel, which just fits into the mouth of a canning jar; a magnet on a stick, for lifting lids out of hot water; and a narrow plastic spatula, disposable plastic knife, or Japanese (pointed) wooden or plastic chopstick, for releasing air bubbles in a filled jar. Canning tools are available from many department stores and supermarkets as well as farm-supply stores and Internet sources.

To process jars in a boiling-water bath, you first fill the canner about halfway with water and begin heating it. Heat some more water in a tea kettle, in case the water in the canner doesn't cover the jars adequately. Have ready clean, preferably hot, jars; I wash mine in the dishwasher and leave them there until I'm ready to use them. (If you're going to process the jars for less than 10 minutes, though, you should immerse them in boiling water for 10 minutes before filling them.) Immerse the lids in hot water in a small bowl.

Unless otherwise indicated in a recipe, fill each jar to ¼ inch from the rim. A small amount of headspace means that less air will be left in the jar after processing. Air left in the jar can cause darkening of the preserves at the top of the jar.

If you're making preserves in a heavy syrup or a thick fruit butter, air bubbles may remain in the jars after you fill them. Release the bubbles by running a narrow plastic spatula or pointed chopstick along the inner surface of the jar. Move the tool up and down while slowly turning the jar.

Before covering each jar, wipe any drips from the rim with a clean, damp cloth or paper towel. Remove the lid from the hot water, using a magnet stick if you have one handy (I usually angle the edge of a lid out of the water with my spatula or chopstick, and then pick up the lid between two fingers, touching only the rim). Drain the water off of the lid, and place it gasket-down on the jar. Screw on the metal ring firmly, but not as tight as possible. Overtightening the ring can cause the lid to buckle or the jar to break, or can prevent air from venting during processing, in which case the preserves won't keep as long.

When the water in the canner is hot—about 180°F—load the jars onto the canner rack, and lower the rack if needed. (If you drop cool jars into boiling water, they are likely to break.) Add as much extra hot water as you need to cover the jars by at least 1 inch. Bring the water to a boil over high heat, and then reduce the heat. Gently boil the jars for the specified length of time, usually 10 minutes. You can cut this time to 5 minutes if you sterilize the jars first.

If you're canning at an elevation of over 1,000 feet, you should process your jars longer than the recipes specify. The higher your elevation, the lower the temperature at which water boils, and when the boiling temperature is lower, the boiling time must be increased. For jams, jellies, and butters, process the jars for 5 minutes longer than specified if you are at an elevation of 1,000 to 6,000 feet, or 10 minutes longer if you are at an elevation of more than 6,000 feet.

When the boiling time is up, remove the jars promptly. Lift them straight out of the water (if you tilt the jars so the water on top runs off, sloshing syrup might break the vacuum seal or keep it from forming). Set the hot jars at least 1 inch apart on a rack, towel, or hot pad (if you set them directly on a tile or stone counter, they will probably crack). Leave the jars undisturbed until they're completely cool. As they cool, you may hear a *pang* as each vacuum seal forms, pulling the center of the metal lid downward.

When the jars are cool, test that the lids have sealed well by pressing in the center with a finger. If the center stays down, the seal is good. If

STEPS IN BOILING-WATER CANNING

1. Fill the canner about halfway with water.

2. Heat the water to about 180°F.

3. Lower the hot jars into the canner, all together on the canner rack or individually with a jar lifter.

4. Add more hot water, if needed, so the water level is about 1 inch above the jar tops.

5. Bring the water to a vigorous boil, and begin timing the processing. Put the lid on the canner and lower the heat to maintain a gentle boil.

6. When the processing time is up, remove the jars with a jar lifter. Set them to cool on a rack, towel, or hot pad.

the center pops up, store the jar in the refrigerator, or reprocess the jar, after making sure the rim is clean and free of nicks and adding a new lid. A second processing should be done within 24 hours of the first, for the same amount of time.

If you like, you can remove the metal rings from the cooled jars. Most experienced preservers wash their rings after using them, dry them well, and store them in a dry place. This way the rings can be used over and over, although they probably won't last as long as the jars do. If left on the jars instead, rings usually rust faster.

OPEN-KETTLE CANNING

This confusing term means canning without a boiling-water bath. Many cooks, fearing a water bath will interfere with gelling or cause fruit in syrup to float, still prefer to use this older method. It generally works well if storage conditions are good and the preserves are eaten within months rather than years. There are risks, though, including a poor seal, insufficient removal of air, and the trapping of mold spores inside the jar.

If you plan to forego a boiling-water bath, I suggest sterilizing the jars, by boiling them for at least 10 minutes, and keeping them hot until you fill them. Make sure the lids are well soaked and warm when you place them on the jars. Leave no more than a ¼-inch headspace, to lessen oxidation and the possibility of mold growth.

Check your stored jars now and then. If any lids have come loose, use the preserves immediately or refrigerate the jars. If any preserves have darkened at the top, spoon off the darkened portion; it will have lost flavor as well as its original color. If mold grows in any jar—with or without a tight lid—throw out the preserves.

CLEANUP TIME

Fruit preserves have virtually no protein to stick to your pans and other cooking utensils. Sugar dissolves in water. So, when you're through making preserves, just fill the pan with water and drop smaller utensils into the pan. Wait a little while, and then rinse every-

PRESERVING EQUIPMENT

Tools that are useful in processing fruits include a vegetable peeler; a zester, a special tool for removing large or small strips of citrus rind; a corer, a heavy-duty spoon-shaped tool with sharpened edges and a pointed end, for coring apples, pears, and especially quinces; a lemon reamer or electric juicer or both; a potato masher, for jams; colanders, especially a broad, flat-bottomed one, for rinsing fruit without crushing it; strainers of various types; a stainless-steel food mill (page 26); a steam juicer (page 14), also made of stainless steel; a jelly bag and stand or piece of muslin (page 27); muslin spice bags or cheesecloth; and canning supplies (pages 20 to 21).

Because weight is much more accurate than volume in measuring fruit, most of the recipes in this book call for fruit in pounds. If you don't have a kitchen scale, I strongly advise investing in one. An inexpensive model should be accurate enough, but do make sure it can weigh at least 5 pounds at a time.

A single pan will suffice for most of the cooking involved in making preserves. A good preserving pan is heavy at the base for even heating and broad for good evaporation. The side should be moderately high, to prevent boil-overs. Evaporation is enhanced if the side flares outward from the base, but a vertical side will do. Finally, the interior surface of the pan should be made of a substance that won't react with acidic foods. This excludes iron and aluminum. Although French preserving pans were traditionally made of unlined copper—because copper *would* react with acid and thereby enhance gelling—such pans are frowned on today, at least in the United States, because copper can be toxic. I generally use a 7.5-quart enameled iron pot made by Le Creuset. Stainless steel works very well, too.

thing and put in on a rack or towel to dry. No detergent or scrubbing is needed!

STORING YOUR PRESERVES

Canned preserves will often keep a decade or longer, but their colors will darken and their flavors will deteriorate over time. High and

HARVESTING AND HANDLING FRUIT

Harvest fruit while it is cool and dry, and store it in a cool place. Tender fruit such as berries should be used right away, preferably the same day. Berries purchased at a farmers' market may have been picked the day before, so don't delay in processing them. Some fruits, fortunately, will keep well in a refrigerator for a time, and others, such as pears, should ripen gradually in a cool room. My introduction to each fruit will give you more information about harvesting and storing it.

fluctuating temperatures can cause weeping and other textural changes. Exposure to light can also cause color changes, and moisture in the air can cause metal lids to rust. For these reasons, it's always best to store canned preserves in a cool, dark, dry place, and to use them within a year or so.

Depending on the sugar content, an opened jar of preserves may keep for months at room temperature, or it may begin growing mold or fermenting within a week. Opened jars of low-sugar jam should always be stored in the refrigerator. If you have enough room in your refrigerator, I recommend storing all opened jars of preserves there.

TERMS USED IN THIS BOOK

BOILING-WATER BATH: A way of pasteurizing jarred preserves. Filled and capped mason jars are placed on a rack in a large kettle of hot water, and the water boils gently for a specified length of time (page 22).

FOOD MILL: A sieve with interchangeable screens, each perforated with holes of a different size. A blade turned by hand pushes soft food through, leaving behind skins and seeds. Other tools that can take the place of a food mill, depending on the recipe, include a sieve or strainer with a nylon or stainless-steel wire screen and, perhaps, a *champignon*, or mushroom-shaped pestle; a conical, perforated metal chinois or "China cap" sieve with a wooden pestle; or a food processor or blender, often in combination with a sieve or strainer. For use with a variety of fruits, the food mill is probably the most useful of these tools. If you're buying one, make sure it's made of stainless steel.

FULL BOIL: A boil with full, rolling bubbles.

GENTLE BOIL: A boil with small, slow bubbles.

JELLY BAG: A muslin or nylon mesh bag for straining the solids out of juice, usually in preparation for jelly making. Drawstring bags with metal stands are sold for this purpose. You can instead lay a piece of damp muslin or four layers of cheesecloth in a colander set over a bowl or pot.

KETTLE: For the purpose of making preserves, this is simply any large, deep, heavy-bottomed pot.

LEMON JUICE: I always use freshly squeezed juice, but you can substitute bottled juice if you prefer. Always strain the juice if

KEEPING COOL IN THE JAMMING SEASON

If you can, work in an outdoor kitchen, a cellar kitchen, or a screened summer kitchen. Or leave the windows and doors open at night to cool down the house. Harvest in the cool of the morning and come in when it gets too hot outside; then do your preserving during the heat of the day, with the kitchen fan running. Finish up by the time the sun goes down, open the doors and windows again, and spend the cooler evening hours outdoors.

Or do your preserving at night, if you're a night owl. This is an especially good idea if you have young children who are dangers to themselves in the kitchen.

This last idea is my favorite: Freeze your fruit, and cook it only when winter comes.

you're making jelly, syrup, or preserves; straining isn't necessary for jam. Because lemons vary greatly in their size and juiciness, I specify the volume of lemon juice in tablespoons or fractions of a cup rather than by a number of whole lemons. For shopping purposes, though, you might figure that a typical lemon holds 2 to 3 tablespoons juice. If you're using Meyer lemons, you may need a little extra lemon juice for adequate acidity.

MASON JARS: Tempered glass jars made for canning, sold by the dozen. They come with two-piece metal caps, each comprising a flat lid, with rubber around the edge of the underside, and a ring to secure the lid during processing in a water bath.

NONREACTIVE: Made of a material that won't react with acid in fruits and other foods. Stainless steel, enamel, and glass are nonreactive; iron and aluminum are reactive.

PRESERVING PAN: Any pan that is wide, fairly deep, and nonreactive, with a heavy bottom to help prevent scorching. A side that slopes outward from the base of the pan best promotes evaporation.

SIMMER: To cook just below the boiling point, with occasional small bubbles.

SKIM: To remove the foam (often called *scum*) from hot preserves during or just after cooking. A wire skimmer usually works best.

SPICE BAG: A small cloth bag for holding spices and other ingredients that are cooked with preserves, to provide flavor or pectin, and then discarded. Little muslin bags with drawstrings work well; they can be purchased or made at home. The simplest spice bag is a scrap of cheesecloth tied around the ingredients.

SPOON TEST: A test for gelling (page 18).

STEAM JUICER: A stovetop device for extracting juice from fruit with the use of steam (page 14).

STERILIZED JAR: An empty jar that has been heated in boiling water for at least 10 minutes. Sterilizing jars is unnecessary if they will be processed in boiling water for at least 10 minutes after they are filled. I recommend sterilization, however, if preserves will be stored at room temperature without processing.

SUGAR: Granulated white sugar, unless otherwise specified.

ZEST: The thin, oily outer rind of an orange, lemon, or other citrus fruit. A tool called a *zester* is used on fresh, firm fruits to remove the zest in thin shreds or long, thick strips. With softer fruits, a vegetable peeler works better; you can use a knife to cut the zest into finer bits.

TROUBLESHOOTING GUIDE FOR SWEET PRESERVES

PROBLEM	POSSIBLE CAUSES	PREVENTIVE MEASURES
Cloudy jelly	Underripe, starchy fruit	Use just-ripe or slightly underripe fruit.
	Imperfect straining	Avoid squeezing the jelly bag.
Air bubbles in jelly	Syrup stood too long before pouring	Pour the syrup as soon as it reaches the gel point.
Soft jelly	Low pectin content	Use just-ripe or slightly underripe fruit. Cook the fruit with no more water than necessary, and only until it is soft. If needed, concentrate the juice by boiling or add the juice of pectin-rich fruit.
	Too little acid	Add lemon or lime juice or citric acid.
	Too little boiling	Boil until the jelly passes the spoon test or reaches 220°F.
Tough, rubbery jelly	Too little sugar in relation to pectin	If the juice is especially rich in pectin, add 1 cup sugar for each cup of juice.
	Jelly was overcooked	Remove the pan from the heat as soon as the gel point is reached.
Sticky jelly	Too much sugar	For most juices, use 3/4 cup sugar for each cup of juice.
"Weeping" jelly (separated syrup)	High acid content	Combine high-acid juice with low-acid juice.
	Warm storage conditions (over 80°F)	Store jars in a cool place.
Crystals in jelly or jam	Too-fast boiling, or any boiling before the sugar was completely dissolved	Use medium heat until the sugar dissolves completely, and then medium-high heat.
	Undissolved sugar crystals stuck to the side of the pan	Before filling jars, wash down any crystals sticking to the side of the pan with a damp pastry brush.
	Too much sugar	Add less sugar to very sweet juice.
	Tartrate (cream of tartar) in grape juice	Refrigerate grape juice overnight to allow tartrate crystals to settle, and then strain the juice.

PROBLEM	POSSIBLE CAUSES	PREVENTIVE MEASURES
Tough or shriveled preserves	Too much sugar added at once	Syrup must be concentrated gradually.
	Too little resting time	Allow more time for the fruit to plump in the syrup.
	Overcooking	Stop cooking before syrup overthickens.
Floating fruit in jars of preserves	Haste in putting the preserves into jars	Let preserves cool for 5 minutes before putting them in jars.
	Thin syrup	Boil the syrup a little longer to thicken it.
Dark jelly or jam	Overlong cooking	Cook jelly or jam over higher heat for a shorter time.
	Overlong keeping	Try to use preserves within a year or so.
Darkening at the top of the jar	Oxidation	Leave no more than $\frac{1}{4}$ inch headspace. Use a boiling-water bath. Use preserves within a year or so. Spoon off the darkened portion before eating.
Faded jam or jelly	Exposure to sunlight or high temperatures	Store jars in a cool, dark place.
Caramel taste	Scorching	Use a pan with a heavy base, and stir frequently.
	Overlong cooking	Shorten cooking time.
Mold in a jar	Failed seal	If a lid comes loose, use the jam or jelly immediately or refrigerate it before mold can develop.
	Air and spores were sealed in the jar	Use a boiling-water bath. Store the jars in a dry place. (If mold develops, discard.)

THE FRUITS

APPLE

Apple Butter   38

Low-Sugar Apple Butter   39

Quick Apple Butter with No Sugar
    Added   40

Cider Syrup   41

Cider Jelly   42

Apple-Ginger Preserves   43

Caramel-Apple Jam   44

Crabapple Jelly with Ginger   45

Crabapple Jelly with Cloves and
    Red Wine Vinegar   47

Apple-Mint Jelly   48

Crabapple-Geranium Jelly   49

T HE GENUS *Malus* includes about 35 species, all native to Asia, Europe, or North America. *M. domestica* includes every variety of the orchard or table apple. All other *Malus* species are called wild apples, crabapples, or just crabs.

The parent species of the orchard apple, *M. sieversii*, still grows in the mountain forest in Kazakhstan where it originated. Ancient military and trade expeditions must have brought apple seeds westward to Mesopotamia, where early farmers planted the trees. (The English word *paradise* comes from a Persian word for "walled garden." Legends from many ancient cultures attest to mixed feelings about the pleasures and dangers of the orchardists' life.) Apple culture spread throughout the ancient Mediterranean region, and the Romans, inspired by their goddess of fruit trees, Pomona, took apples as far as northern continental Europe and the British Isles, where only crabapples had been previously known. The first New England apple orchards were planted around 1625, and apples continued their westward movement with the pioneers.

There is nothing as American as apple pie—except apple cider. In the eighteenth and nineteenth centuries, most households kept several large barrels of cider in the cellar. Although this cider was "hard," or alcoholic (except right after pressing), children and adults alike drank large quantities of it. When the last of the cider soured, it became vinegar for pickles and salads. Americans also valued apples, of course, for sauce, butter, and jelly.

I entered my teens when American apple consumption was at its nadir, when everyone seemed to be pitching cottony, flavorless, sadly misnamed Red Delicious apples into the trash. Since the mid-1970s, though, Washington apple growers have stopped their pursuit of the reddest, most conical apple and have begun supplying supermarkets with a few more tasty varieties, which keep better with improved commercial cold-storage methods. Still, we are not yet back to eating even an apple a day. Only a dozen or so varieties make up 90 percent of U.S. apple production. Cider sold in supermarkets is almost all sweet and made from concentrate. Chinese apple production now outstrips that of the United States by more than three times.

But some of us have never stopped loving apples. As a child, I would live for a month every summer eating little besides the world's finest apples, the Gravensteins from the abundant orchards around Sebastopol, California. I would get by the rest of the year on Newtown Pippins, which unlike Red Delicious apples are good keepers. Today American home orchardists and small farmers grow hundreds of the thousands of named apple varieties. Some are favored for cooking, others for "dessert"—that is, fresh eating. A few "bitter-sharp" varieties are grown just for cider, although most cider makers combine varieties with various characteristics: sweetness, acidity, aroma, and astringency (from tannin). Other distinguishing characteristics among apple varieties are firmness, susceptibility to browning, and dryness or juiciness of the flesh; color of the flesh (most red-fleshed varieties are crabapple crosses); russetting (leathery brown patches), color, and thickness of the skin; shape and size; ripening time (the earliest apples begin ripening in late July, the latest in November); and keeping quality (late varieties tend to store longer, and some even get sweeter in storage).

Apples don't grow true from seed but are grafted by bud or scion. Every Winesap tree, therefore, is a clone of the original Winesap seedling—although "sports," or mutations, can arise on a branch of an apple tree. "Antique" apple varieties have been cloned for at least a hundred and sometimes several hundred years. They are grown for their special characteristics or just for old times' sake, but many fruit unreliably and lack disease resistance. Current breeding programs are producing varieties, such as Liberty, that resist disease and taste good, too.

Crabapples have also been improved by breeding. Usually smaller than orchard apples, the fruits typically measure from ½ inch to about 1½ inches in diameter. They tend to be tart, tannic, and mealy, but some are fine for fresh eating or pickling. In small quantities, astringent crabapples enrich the flavor of cider. Crabapple trees are also valued because they shed their pollen over a long period and so make excellent pollenizers for orchard apples, and because their hardiness and disease resistance make them useful as rootstock. Most important, for the purposes of this book, crabs make outstanding jelly, because they are rich in pectin and, usually, color. Many varieties are red inside as well as out, and so produce a lovely dark red, clear jelly. Beware of nursery stock labeled "flowering crabapple"; the trees may be fruitless.

Apples, including crabapples, are well adapted to climates from 35° to 50° latitude, which includes most of the United States. If you want to plant an apple tree, choose a variety that reliably produces flavorful crops in your area without heavy spraying. Because apples generally aren't self-fertile, you'll need to choose a second variety that blossoms at about the same time. Pay attention to the rootstock, too: It will determine the eventual size of your tree, how soon it will begin fruiting, and whether it will need staking or trellising. Plant your tree in a sunny spot in well-drained soil. Then read up on pruning, which will be an annual chore from now on. It will be worth your trouble.

For other recipes using apples, see Blackberry-Apple Leather (page 70), Carrot-Apple Butter (page 88), Elderberry-Apple Jelly (page 135), *Cogna* (page 175), Apple–Asian Pear Paste (page 249), *Sirop de Liège* (page 251), Plum-Apple Conserve (page 276), Japanese Plum–Apple Paste (page 278), Plum-Apple Leather (page 282), Quince-Apple Paste (page 300), and Tomato-Apple Butter (page 347).

APPLE BUTTER

MAKES 3½ TO 4 PINTS

A S FAR AS I'VE BEEN ABLE to determine, this dark, spicy old-fashioned preserve is uniquely American, and it never seems to lose popularity in this country. Apple butter is a comfort food associated with warm bread, a warm fire, and rain or snow on the windowpanes. The butter is simple to make, and it's a fine use for wormy or otherwise damaged apples. Try it layered with cheddar cheese on crackers.

> 6 pounds cored and quartered apples (unpeeled)
> About 4 cups light brown sugar
> 1 tablespoon ground cinnamon
> ½ teaspoon ground mace or ground nutmeg
> ½ teaspoon ground allspice

1. In a preserving pan, cook the apples over low heat, covered, until they are soft, about 20 minutes. If they are dense, you may need to add a little water or cider at the start to keep them from scorching.

2. Using the coarse screen of a food mill, puree the apples. Measure the volume of the puree, and add half as much light brown sugar.

Add the cinnamon, mace or nutmeg, and allspice, and cook the mixture over low heat (or in an oven heated to 250°F), uncovered, until it is thick. This will probably take about 1½ hours. You'll need to stir occasionally at first and more frequently as the apple butter thickens.

3 Ladle the apple butter into pint or half-pint mason jars. Add lids and rings, and process the jars in a boiling-water bath for 10 minutes.

LOW-SUGAR APPLE BUTTER

MAKES ABOUT 5 PINTS

WHEN CANE SUGAR was a rare treat, apple butter was made from apple cider and ground apples with little or no added sweetening. This recipe is much like one I found in an old Pennsylvania Dutch cookbook. Brown sugar adds to the rich, dark color as well as to the warm, spicy flavor.

> 3 quarts apple cider, filtered or not
> 5 pounds apples, quartered (unpeeled)
> 1 cup light brown sugar
> 1 tablespoon ground cinnamon
> ½ teaspoon ground nutmeg
> ½ teaspoon ground allspice

1 In a preserving pan, boil the cider for about 20 minutes to reduce it by one-quarter.

2 Add the apples, cover the pan, and simmer the apples in the cider, stirring occasionally, until the apples are soft, 30 to 45 minutes.

3 Puree the mixture by putting it through the medium screen of a food mill or pressing it through a sieve. Put the puree into the preserving pan and add the sugar, cinnamon, nutmeg, and allspice. Cook the mixture over low heat (or in an oven heated to 250°F), uncovered, until it is thick. This will probably take an hour or two. You'll need to stir occasionally at first and more frequently as the apple butter thickens. When the apple butter is ready, it will be dark and glossy.

4 Ladle the apple butter into pint or half-pint mason jars. Add lids and rings, and process the jars in a boiling-water bath for 10 minutes.

5 This preserve is liable to get moldy if left at room temperature after opening, so plan to store each opened jar in the refrigerator.

QUICK APPLE BUTTER WITH NO SUGAR ADDED

MAKES ABOUT 4 HALF-PINTS

I DEVELOPED THIS RECIPE for a diabetic friend. Frozen apple juice concentrate makes a good substitute here for traditional boiled cider. To lessen the risk of mold growth after a jar is opened, I prefer to use half-pint jars.

Two 12-ounce containers frozen apple juice concentrate, thawed
3 pounds apples, quartered (unpeeled)
2 teaspoons ground cinnamon
¼ teaspoon ground mace or ground nutmeg
¼ teaspoon ground cloves

1. Combine the apple juice concentrate and the apples in a preserving pan. Cover the pan and bring the mixture to a boil over medium heat. Reduce the heat and simmer the apples, stirring occasionally for 30 to 45 minutes, until the apples are soft.

2. Puree the mixture by putting it through the medium screen of a food mill or pressing it through a sieve. Put the puree into the preserving pan and add the cinnamon, mace or nutmeg, and cloves. Cook the mixture over low heat, uncovered, until it is thick; this will probably take an hour or more. When the apple butter is ready, it will be dark and glossy.

3. Ladle the apple butter into half-pint mason jars. Add lids and rings, and process the jars in a boiling-water bath for 10 minutes.

4. Store each opened jar in the refrigerator, and plan to use it up within a week or two.

CIDER SYRUP

MAKES ABOUT ½ CUP SYRUP FOR EACH QUART CIDER

THE FIRST TIME I TASTED cider syrup was 1988 or thereabouts, while I was visiting Pike Place Market in Seattle. The farmer told me his method: He stored Golden Delicious apples until they were old and shriveled, and then he froze them. The aging reduced the pectin, which can turn cider syrup to jelly, and thickened the juice, so less boiling was necessary. The freezing made the juice easy to extract.

Unfiltered apple cider makes an opaque but pretty brown syrup. For a clear syrup, use filtered cider. The syrup is delicious on pancakes or waffles.

At least 2 quarts apple cider, from apples pressed several
weeks after picking

1. In a large, uncovered pot, boil the cider to a thick syrup, about one-eighth of its original volume.

2. Pour the syrup into sterilized bottles, and cap or cork them. If the syrup is sufficiently thick, you can store it in the cupboard rather than the refrigerator. It should keep for at least 6 months.

CIDER JELLY

MAKES ABOUT 2 HALF-PINTS

ALTHOUGH PEOPLE may tell you otherwise, the juice of cold-pressed apples generally contains sufficient pectin to make jelly and enough sugar that you don't have to add any. In fact, one hazard of making cider syrup is that it may turn into cider jelly.

If it's jelly you want, use cider from fresh, just-ripe apples, keep the quantity low, and boil down the cider as fast as you can.

1 gallon apple cider
(from fresh, just-ripe apples)

1. In a large, uncovered pot, boil the cider over high heat until it is reduced to about one-eighth its original volume and passes the spoon test (page 18).

2. Pour the syrup into half-pint mason jars, add lids and rings, and process the jars in a boiling-water bath for 10 minutes.

3. The jelly may not set immediately, so wait a day or so before concluding that you have made syrup instead.

APPLE-GINGER PRESERVES

T HE HOT PEPPER, along with the ginger, gives these pre-serves a little bite. They are a fine accompaniment to roast chicken or turkey, and just as good with your morning toast. Use a variety of apple that holds its shape well in cooking, such as Golden Delicious.

2 pounds peeled and cored apples, cut into vertical,
    ½-inch-thick slices
2 tablespoons strained lemon juice
Grated zest of 1 lemon
4 cups sugar
¼ teaspoon ground dried chile pepper
2 teaspoons finely grated fresh ginger
1⅓ cups water

1. Toss the apple slices with the lemon juice.

2. In a preserving pan, combine the lemon zest, sugar, pepper, gin-ger, and water. Heat the mixture over medium heat, stirring, until the sugar completely dissolves. Add the apples and cook over very low heat, uncovered, stirring only occasionally and very gently, for about 2 hours.

3. With a slotted spoon, remove the apple slices from the pan and reserve them. Boil the syrup until it reaches the thread stage (page 18) or 230°F.

4. Return the apple slices to the pan. Bring the preserves to a boil, and then ladle them into pint or half-pint mason jars. Add lids and rings, and process the jars in a boiling-water bath for 10 minutes.

CARAMEL-APPLE JAM

MAKES ABOUT 3 PINTS

R EFINED SUGAR is wonderful for preserving fruits not only because in solution it is colorless, and so lets fruits display their own beautiful colors, but also because it is nearly flavorless; it sweetens without covering up natural flavors. Cooking refined sugar beyond the syrup stage, however, changes its character entirely. It gradually darkens, and as it darkens it develops interesting and increasingly strong flavors of its own. Sometimes, as with this apple jam, caramelized sugar makes a lovely complement to natural fruit flavors.

If you have jarred applesauce in your pantry, you can make this jam quickly. Use 5 cups applesauce in place of the cooked and sieved apples in the recipe.

> 3½ pounds tart apples, cored and sliced (unpeeled)
> 3½ cups sugar
> ½ cup water
> 1 tablespoon lemon juice
> 3 tablespoons brandy (optional)
> 1 teaspoon vanilla extract

1 In a preserving pan, cook the apples over low heat, covered, until they are soft, about 20 minutes. If they are dense, you may need to add a little water or cider at the start to keep them from scorching.

2 Puree the apples by putting them through the medium screen of a food mill or pressing them through a sieve.

3 Clean and dry the preserving pan, and combine in it 2 cups of the sugar, the water, and the lemon juice. Without stirring or shaking the pan, bring the syrup to a boil and gently boil it until the water has evaporated and the syrup has turned golden brown. Remove the pan from the heat immediately, before the caramel darkens more than you'd like.

4 Add the apple puree to the caramel, which will harden at first and then begin to dissolve. Add the remaining 1½ cups sugar and stir over low heat until the sugar and caramel have completely dissolved. Raise the heat to medium-high and bring the jam to a boil. Continue boiling, stirring often, for 8 to 10 minutes, until the jam is thick enough that your spoon briefly leaves a clear track at the bottom of the pan.

5 Remove the pan from the heat. Stir in the brandy, if you are using it, and the vanilla extract. Ladle the jam into pint or half-pint mason jars, and add lids and rings. Process the jars in a boiling-water bath for 10 minutes.

CRABAPPLE JELLY WITH GINGER

MAKES ABOUT 6 HALF-PINTS

HEN MADE WITH red-fleshed crabs, these preserves look like currant jelly.

4 pounds crabapples, quartered (unpeeled)
½ cup chopped fresh ginger
½ cup water
About 5 cups sugar

1. In a preserving pan, combine the crabapples, ginger, and water. Cover the pan and simmer gently until the crabapples are soft, about 1 hour.

2. Strain the juice through a damp jelly bag for at least 8 hours. Do not squeeze the bag.

3. Measure the strained juice and put it into the preserving pan. Add 3 cups sugar for every 4 cups juice. Heat the mixture over medium heat, stirring, until the sugar is completely dissolved, and then raise the heat to medium-high. Boil the mixture until the jelly passes the spoon test (page 18). Immediately remove the pan from the heat.

4. Ladle the hot jelly into half-pint mason jars. Add lids and rings, and process the jars in a boiling-water bath for 10 minutes.

CRABAPPLE JELLY WITH GINGER, STEAM JUICER METHOD

Follow the above recipe, but make the juice by steaming the apples in a steam juicer (page 14). While the apples steam, simmer the ginger in 1 cup water in a small pan, covered, for 10 minutes. Pour the ginger liquid through a fine-mesh strainer and combine the strained liquid with the apple juice before heating the juice with the sugar.

CRABAPPLE JELLY
WITH CLOVES AND
RED WINE VINEGAR

MAKES ABOUT 6 HALF-PINTS

RY THIS SPICY JELLY with game, either as a finishing glaze or served alongside.

4 pounds crabapples, quartered (unpeeled)
½ cup water
2 tablespoons cloves, in a spice bag
½ cup red wine vinegar
About 5 cups sugar

1 In a preserving pan, combine the crabapples, water, and spice bag. Cover the pan and simmer gently until the crabapples are soft, about 1 hour. Or scatter the cloves amid the crabapples in a steam juicer, omitting the water, and heat as described on page 46 until the juice is rendered.

2 Strain the juice through a damp jelly bag for at least 8 hours. Do not squeeze the bag.

3 Add the vinegar to the strained juice, measure the mixture, and put it into the preserving pan. Add 3 cups sugar for every 4 cups liquid. Heat the mixture over medium heat, stirring, until the sugar is completely dissolved, and then raise the heat to medium-high. Boil the mixture until the jelly passes the spoon test (page 18). Immediately remove the pan from the heat.

4 Ladle the hot jelly into half-pint mason jars. Add lids and rings, and process the jars in a boiling-water bath for 10 minutes.

APPLE-MINT JELLY

....

MAKES ABOUT 5½ PINTS

ARTED UP WITH VINEGAR, mint jelly is a traditional English condiment for roast lamb. I tried several methods of making this jelly before I found one that worked. Cooking the mint along with the apples seemed to boil away the herbal flavor and aroma. Adding chopped mint to the hot jelly made a pretty product but ruined the texture of the jelly, in my opinion. I knew I could drop in a little mint extract, if I had some on hand, and even add some green dye if I wanted my jelly to look store-bought. But I decided that I like my jelly naturally colored apple-gold and flavored simply by a few swishes of some mint sprigs.

> 3 pounds apples, quartered (uncored and unpeeled)
> ½ cup water
> About 4½ cups sugar
> 1½ cups cider vinegar
> 5 mint sprigs, each 8 to 10 inches long, bruised with a rolling
>   pin or meat pounder

1. In a preserving pan, combine the apples and water. Cover the pan and simmer gently until the apples are soft, about 1 hour. Or use a steam juicer (page 14) to render the juice, omitting the ½ cup water.

2. Strain the juice through a damp jelly bag for at least 8 hours. Do not squeeze the bag.

3. Measure the strained juice and put it into the preserving pan with an equal volume of sugar. Add the vinegar. Heat the mixture over medium heat, stirring, until the sugar is completely dissolved,

and then raise the heat to medium-high. Boil the mixture until the jelly passes the spoon test (page 18). Immediately remove the pan from the heat.

4 Grasp the ends of the mint stalks and swish the stalks through the hot jelly for about 20 seconds. Ladle the hot jelly into half-pint mason jars. Add lids and rings, and process the jars in a boiling-water bath for 10 minutes.

CRABAPPLE-GERANIUM JELLY

MAKES ABOUT 6 HALF-PINTS

THIS RECIPE USES leaves of scented geraniums, which aren't true geraniums but a species of *Pelargonium*, mostly from South Africa. With insignificant flowers but very fragrant leaves, scented geraniums come in over 50 varieties, including rose, ginger, cinnamon, nutmeg, coconut, lemon, lime, peppermint, and green apple. These plants can't endure hard freezes or chronically wet soils, but fortunately they do well in pots. The leaves are used in potpourri, sachets, and infusions, and as flavorings not only for jelly but also vinegar, cakes, and even butter.

Most recipes for geranium jelly call for leaves of rose geranium, but you can use a citrus- or spice-scented variety or combine two or more types, as you like. If you're afraid of burning your fingers by swishing geranium sprigs in hot jelly, put them into a spice bag first, or cook a sprig or two along with the crabapples. In any case, you should first bruise the leaves, by crushing them with a rolling pin or meat pounder or by squeezing them in your fist or between your palms.

> 4 pounds crabapples, quartered (unpeeled)
> ½ cup water
> About 5 cups sugar
> 3 sprigs scented geranium, bruised

1. In a preserving pan, combine the apples and water. Cover the pan and simmer gently until the fruit is soft, about 1 hour.

2. Strain the juice through a damp jelly bag for at least 8 hours. Do not squeeze the bag.

3. Measure the strained juice and pour it into the preserving pan. Add 3 cups sugar for every 4 cups juice. Heat the mixture over medium heat, stirring, until the sugar is completely dissolved, and then raise the heat to medium-high. Boil the mixture until the jelly passes the spoon test (page 18). Immediately remove the pan from the heat. Gently swish the geranium sprigs through the liquid for 20 seconds or so, and then press them with a spoon against the side of the pan.

4. Ladle the hot jelly into half-pint mason jars. Add lids and rings, and process the jars in a boiling-water bath for 10 minutes.

APRICOT

Apricot Jam   53

Apricot-Pineapple Jam   54

Apricot Paste   55

Apricot Nectar   56

A DECIDUOUS TREE in the rose family, the fragrant, velvet-skinned apricot is native to China, where it was first cultivated. Like the apple, it traveled across the Persian Empire to the Mediterranean, where it thrived. (The Romans called it *precocium*, "precocious," for its early ripening; from this came the English word *apricot*.) In the eighteenth century, the Spanish brought the apricot to California and planted it in mission gardens. By 1920 apricot production was a major industry in California, and in 1935 the Santa Clara Valley alone had 18,631 acres of apricot trees. When the orchards made way for computer factories, the apricot farms moved to the San Joaquin Valley, which today produces 95 percent of the apricots grown in the United States.

This little history is misleading in several ways. First, it may cause you to think that the California apricot business is thriving as never before. Actually, production is only a third of what it was in the 1920s. Second, 75 percent of the California crop comes from trees of one species, the Patterson. This saddens older Californians, who tend to prefer varieties that were formerly popular: the perfumed, juicy Blenheim and Royal, the big, blushing Moorpark, and the late, yellow Tilton.

Finally, you might think apricots simply won't grow outside of California. In fact, apricots can grow well anywhere with moderately cool

APRICOT SORBET

To make apricot sorbet, stir ½ cup sugar into 1 quart Apricot Nectar (page 56). Freeze the mixture in an ice-cream maker according to the manufacturer's directions.

winters, mild and dry springs, warm summers, and well-drained soil. Some newer varieties have been bred to bloom later in cold regions or to produce blooms that can survive freezes following early thaws. In a Fall 2006 article in *POMONA*, the magazine of the North American Fruit Explorers, Bob Purvis discusses the best apricot varieties for every region of the United States, including Alaska and Hawaii.

Apricots ripen in June and July. When you find them in the market, keep in mind that they don't ripen off the tree. They should be free of green color, a little soft to the touch, and fragrant. To use them for jam or anything else, just cut them in half at their suture line and remove the pit; the fruit needs no peeling. The pits contain a kernel that tastes like bitter almond and can be used as a flavoring after being roasted or boiled to destroy the prussic acid.

APRICOT JAM

EVEN HARD, greenish store-bought apricots taste heavenly when made into jam. Cook the kernels along with the fruit, as directed, if you like a subtle flavor of bitter almond.

> 3 pounds ripe apricots
> ½ cup water
> 6 cups sugar
> 2 tablespoons lemon juice

1 Cut the apricots into about 8 pieces each, reserving the pits. You should have about 8 cups.

2 For a bitter-almond flavor in your jam, crack the apricot pits, remove the kernels, and blanch them in simmering water for 20 minutes. Put the blanched kernels into a spice bag.

3 In a preserving pan, combine the cut apricots, the bag of kernels (if you are using them), and the water. Simmer the fruit, covered, for 15 to 20 minutes, until the apricots are quite soft. Remove the pan from the heat.

4 Add the sugar and lemon juice to the pan. Heat the mixture over medium heat until the sugar is completely dissolved, and then raise the heat to medium-high. Boil the mixture until the jam mounds in a chilled dish. Remove the pan from the heat.

5 Press the spice bag against the side of the pan, and remove the bag. Ladle the jam into pint or half-pint mason jars, add lids and rings, and process the jars for 10 minutes in a boiling-water bath.

APRICOT-PINEAPPLE JAM

MAKES ABOUT 3 PINTS

WHEN I WAS GROWING UP, my mother made this jam every summer, with fresh apricots from the Sacramento Valley and canned crushed pineapple. In this recipe, I have substituted fresh pineapple for the canned.

1½ pounds ripe apricots, pitted and diced (about 2 cups)
1 pound peeled, cored, and chopped pineapple
   (about 2 cups, with juice)
¼ cup lemon juice (reserve the lemon seeds and pulp)
4½ cups sugar

1 In a preserving pan, combine the apricots and pineapple. Put the lemon seeds and pulp into a spice bag, and add that to the pan. Cook the mixture over medium heat, covered, for about 10 minutes, until the fruit is tender.

2 Remove the pan from the heat and add the lemon juice and sugar. Return the pan to the heat and heat the contents over medium heat, stirring often, until the sugar is completely dissolved.

3 Raise the heat to medium-high and bring the mixture to a boil. Continue boiling, skimming off any foam, until a drop of jam mounds in a chilled dish.

4 Remove the pan from the heat. Press the spice bag against the side of the pan, and remove the bag. Ladle the jam into pint or half-pint mason jars, add lids and rings, and process the jars in a boiling-water bath for 10 minutes.

APRICOT-PINEAPPLE JAM WITH GINGER

My husband suggested this alternative. Proceed as above, but add 1 teaspoon grated fresh ginger along with the sugar and lemon juice.

APRICOT PASTE

YOU CAN BUY APRICOT PASTE in some Middle Eastern markets, but it's easy to make your own. Serve it with nuts or cheese as an appetizer, snack, or dessert.

> 2 pounds ripe apricots, halved and pitted (about 5 cups)
> 2 tablespoons water
> 2 cups sugar
> 2 tablespoons lemon juice

1. In a preserving pan, combine the apricots with the water. Simmer the apricots, covered, for 10 to 15 minutes, until the apricots are tender.

2. Using the medium screen of a food mill, puree the apricots. Put the puree into the pan and add the sugar and lemon juice. Cook the mixture over low heat, stirring often at first and nearly constantly toward the end, until your spoon leaves a clear track across the bottom of the pan.

3. Pour the mixture into lightly oiled vertical-sided dishes in a layer about ¾ inch thick. Put the dishes in a warm place, such as in the sun, near a wood stove, or in a food dehydrator. Let the paste dry on the top side, and then turn it out onto a rack to dry throughout. When it is firm and dry to the touch (at room temperature, this may take several days), wrap it in plastic wrap or waxed paper and store it in a heavy-duty plastic bag in the refrigerator, where it should keep for several months.

APRICOT NECTAR

A S A CHILD, I loved everything about apricot nectar—except the taste of the metal can. Make your own nectar and you won't taste metal, just a smooth, sweet, delightful essence of summer.

For a refreshing drink, dilute your nectar with an equal measure of water or combine it with milk, cream, or half-and-half. Or use the nectar in sherbet or ice cream.

> 4 pounds ripe apricots, pitted (about 10 cups)
> 3 cups water
> About ⅔ cup sugar, to your taste
> About 6 tablespoons strained lemon or lime juice,
>   to your taste

1. In a preserving pan, combine the apricots and water. Cover the pan and simmer the apricots until they are soft, 10 to 15 minutes.

2. Puree the apricots with their liquid in batches in a blender. Pour the puree through a fine-mesh sieve back into the preserving pan.

3. Add the sugar and lemon or lime juice. Bring the nectar to a simmer over medium heat, stirring occasionally.

4. Pour the nectar into pint or quart mason jars. Add lids and rings, and process the jars in a boiling-water bath for 15 minutes.

BANANA

Banana Jam with Ginger,
   Raisins, and Rum   58

FAST-GROWING PERENNIALS in the genus *Musa*, bananas originated in the region encompassing Southeast Asia, Malaysia, and Indonesia. In the early fifteenth century, Portuguese sailors discovered the fruit in West Africa, where our word *banana* originated, and took it to the Canary Islands. A century later Spaniards planted bananas in Central America. There, in 1899, the United Fruit Company began exporting the big, sturdy, yellow Gros Michel variety to the United States and Europe.

Now bananas grow in humid tropical regions throughout the world and make up the fourth largest of all fruit crops. Because bananas can be picked green and ripened in storage, they are supermarket staples nearly everywhere. With their easy-to-remove jackets, starchy flesh, and lack of seeds, they are a perfect, potassium-rich snack—neat and quick to eat, and satisfying.

A banana stalk may look like a tree, but it grows from a rhizome and dies after fruiting once. Before it fruits, it produces a big purple bud, which in some varieties can be cooked and sliced for salad or curry, and then clusters of white flowers, whose ovaries develop parthenocarpically into clusters of fruits, called hands. To a banana grower, a "bunch" of bananas is made up from as many as 15 hands and can weigh 100 pounds or more.

People in the tropics enjoy many varieties of bananas, and nowadays American supermarket shoppers can try several of them. The shorter, thinner-skinned Cavendish has largely replaced the Gros Michel for the export trade. Also available in some supermarkets are the short, thick Manzano or apple banana, the aromatic Cuban Red, the little Lady Finger, and the big, thick-skinned plantains, which are eaten either green or ripe (when the skin has blackened) but are almost always cooked first.

You can probably grow your own bananas if you live in southern California or Florida. Planted from a sucker or piece of rhizome, a banana plant needs plenty of water and sun, protection from frost and wind, and mulch. Favored varieties in Florida and California include Dwarf Cavendish, Manzano, Lady Finger, and Orinoco. Even in USDA zone 7 you can grow hardy, non-fruiting bananas for their ornamental value.

For the recipe here you can use any banana meant for fresh eating, but most likely you'll use inexpensive yellow ones. Yellow bananas such as Cavendish are fully ripe when their skins have lost all trace of green and show some brown flecks.

If you have too many ripe bananas for jam or immediate eating, you might freeze them whole and peeled in a heavy-duty plastic bag, or mash them and freeze them in rigid containers. Later, you can use your frozen bananas in quick breads or smoothies.

BANANA JAM WITH GINGER, RAISINS, AND RUM

MAKES ABOUT 4 PINTS

 HEN BANANAS ARE CHEAP but your family is tired of them, this is a delightful way to preserve them.

1 cup golden raisins

1 cup boiling water

½ cup lime juice

Fine-cut zest of 2 limes

2 pounds (6 to 8) peeled just-ripe bananas

2½ cups sugar

½ cup coarsely chopped fresh ginger

2 tablespoons rum

1 Put the raisins into a small bowl and pour the boiling water over them. Let the raisins soak until the water is cool.

2 Put the lime juice and zest into a medium-size bowl. Slice the bananas into ¼-inch-thick crosswise slices. Toss the banana slices in the lime juice as you work. Add the raisins and their soaking water and toss again.

3 In a large bowl, layer the fruit mixture with the sugar, finishing with sugar. Cover the bowl and let it stand at room temperature for 8 to 12 hours.

4 Put the mixture into a preserving pan with the ginger. Heat the mixture over medium heat, stirring occasionally and gently, until the sugar is completely dissolved, and then raise the heat to medium-high. Cook the mixture, stirring often, for several minutes, until the jam mounds in a chilled dish. Stir in the rum.

5 Ladle the jam into hot sterile pint or half-pint mason jars. Add lids and rings, and process the jars for 10 minutes in a boiling-water bath.

BLACKBERRY

Blackberry Jelly   62

Blackberry Jam   63

Seedless Blackberry Jam   64

Small-Batch Blackberry Jam   65

Blackberry–Black Currant Jam   66

Raw Blackberry Jam   67

Blackberry-Quince Paste   68

Blackberry Paste   69

Blackberry-Apple Leather   70

Fermented Blackberry Syrup   72

Blackberry Vinegar   73

Blackberry Shrub   74

A T LEAST HERE ON THE WEST COAST, blackberries are the most democratic fruit. They grow everywhere and are generally free for the taking in parks, on roadsides, and in neglected places.

When we were seventeen my friend Marie and I took a two-week road trip up the West Coast, from Santa Rosa, California, into Canada. Because it was August and we had barely enough money for gas alone, we ate blackberries all along the way. When we stopped at Marie's aunt's house near Portland, Oregon, we cooked a blackberry pie that made up for all the proper meals we'd missed. This is how I learned that Oregon is Blackberry Heaven. In dry California, the berries are small and seedy, and in cool, wet Washington they are enormous and nearly tasteless. In Oregon, though, they are just right: medium-size and with just the right balance of sugar and acid. Goldilocks would approve.

The word *blackberry* can refer to any of hundreds, possibly thousands, of species in the caneberry genus, *Rubus*. Not all black-fruited caneberries are blackberries, though; some black caneberries are raspberries. And some blackberries, such as loganberries and tayberries, are, because of raspberry parentage, more red than black. You can tell a blackberry from a raspberry when you pick it: If the berry is hollow, with its solid center left hanging from the vine, you have a raspberry; if the center comes away with the berry, you have a blackberry.

Eighty-five percent of commercial blackberry production in the United States is in Blackberry Heaven, in the Willamette Valley and southernmost Washington. I suspect, however, that most of the blackberries people eat are wild ones that they have picked themselves. Spread by birds, blackberries grow over much of the world, wherever people don't grub them out. On the West Coast, the most common wild blackberries are *R. procerus*, the tasty-fruited but distressingly invasive Himalayan blackberry, with big, arching canes (this plant, misnamed by Luther Burbank, actually originated in Germany); *R. laciniatus*, the blander-fruited, thornier cutleaf evergreen blackberry, also a European transplant; and *R. ursinus*, the native, small-fruited but flavorful trailing blackberry, or dewberry.

Cultivated blackberries have been bred for characteristics such as large size and early fruiting as well as for distinctive flavor. These cultivars come in two main types, erect and trailing. Most of the trailing varieties grown in the United States were developed at Oregon State University. They include Olallieberries, which are grown mainly in California, and Marionberries, the Oregon favorite. Compared with the Himalayan, the Marion is big, long, and slightly bitter, but excellent for jam, pies, and wine. The University of Arkansas has developed more cold-hardy erect varieties, such as Navajo, Cherokee, and Apache, and new varieties that fruit on primocanes, the current year's growth. Semi-erect, thornless varieties have been developed in England and elsewhere.

If you want to plant blackberries, you'll need rich, well-drained soil. Set the plants against a fence or trellis them in a hedgerow to keep the planting neat and make picking easier. Even if you live in Blackberry Heaven, you should make sure your plants get water at least once a week. After the first year, you'll need to prune out the floricanes, the canes that have fruited, every winter.

Except for some of the hybrid berries with raspberry ancestry, blackberries turn from green to red to black as they ripen, and then they soften and begin to shrivel before falling to the ground. Don't bother picking mushy berries; they will have lost much flavor and pectin. If you're going to use your berries for jam or jelly, pick some that are still partially red for a higher pectin content.

If you must keep blackberries for a day or so before using them, store them in the refrigerator. For longer keeping, rinse and drain the berries, spread them in baking pans, and freeze them individually before packing them into bags or rigid containers.

BLACKBERRY JELLY

MAKES ABOUT 5 HALF-PINTS

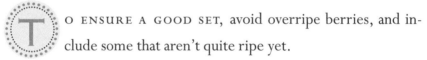O ENSURE A GOOD SET, avoid overripe berries, and include some that aren't quite ripe yet.

I prefer to render blackberry juice with a steam juicer (page 14), but you can certainly extract your juice the traditional way: Mash 4 pounds berries in a kettle, simmer them, covered, with ¾ cup water until they are soft (about 10 minutes), and then let the juice drip through a damp jelly bag for 8 to 12 hours. With either method, you'll need about 4 pounds blackberries to make 4 cups juice.

> 4 cups blackberry juice
> 3 cups sugar
> 2 tablespoons strained lemon juice

1 Heat the blackberry juice, sugar, and lemon juice together in a preserving pan over medium heat, stirring gently, until the sugar is completely dissolved. Raise the heat to medium-high, and boil

the mixture until it passes the spoon test (page 18), skimming the foam as needed.

2 Immediately remove the pan from the heat and ladle the jelly into half-pint mason jars. Add lids and rings, and process the jars in a boiling-water bath for 10 minutes.

BLACKBERRY JAM

MAKES ABOUT 4 PINTS

I F YOUR BLACKBERRIES ARE SMALL and seedy, do as my mother does. Put the berries through a food mill or chinois (conical sieve) as in the recipe for Seedless Blackberry Jam (page 64); you don't need to cook the berries first. Stir about half the seeds into the blackberry puree and discard the rest of the seeds.

4½ pounds blackberries
6¾ cups sugar
2 tablespoons lemon juice

1 In a preserving pan, mash the berries with a potato masher. Add the sugar and lemon juice, place the pan over medium heat, and cook, stirring gently, until the sugar is dissolved. Raise the heat to medium-high, and boil the mixture, stirring frequently, until a drop mounds in a chilled dish.

2 Ladle the jam into pint or half-pint mason jars, add lids and rings, and process the jars in a boiling-water bath for 10 minutes.

SEEDLESS
BLACKBERRY JAM

SOMETIMES MY CHILDREN ask me to make smooth black-berry jam, without any seeds. I like this version as much as they do.

> 2½ pounds blackberries
> 3 cups sugar
> 2 tablespoons lemon juice

1. Strain the blackberries through the fine screen of a food mill, the berry screen of a tomato strainer, or a chinois (conical sieve). Measure the puree; you should have 4 cups.

2. In a preserving pan, combine the berry puree, sugar, and lemon juice over medium heat. Heat the contents, stirring gently, until the sugar is completely dissolved. Raise the heat to medium-high and boil the mixture until a drop of it mounds in a chilled dish.

3. Ladle the jam into pint or half-pint mason jars. Add lids and rings, and process the jars for 10 minutes in a boiling-water bath.

SEEDLESS BLACKBERRY JAM WITH BRANDY

A little liquor gives blackberry jam a more complex flavor and slightly softer texture. Follow the recipe above, but stir in 2 tablespoons brandy just before ladling the jam into jars.

SEEDLESS BLACKBERRY JAM WITH GRAPPA AND JUNIPER BERRIES

I actually created this recipe not with grappa but with *aguardiente de hierbas*, homemade by a friend in Galicia, Spain. You will probably never find a commercial product like my friend Constantino's herbal grape liquor, but ordinary grappa or marc will do as a substitute. Try this jam in, or as, a sauce for roast meat.

Follow the recipe at left, but add 1 teaspoon lemon zest along with the berry puree, sugar, and lemon juice, and put 2 juniper berries in each ½-pint jar or 4 berries in each pint jar. When the mixture has reached the gelling point and the boiling has stopped, add 3 tablespoons grappa or marc, and then ladle the jam into the jars.

SMALL-BATCH BLACKBERRY JAM

MAKES ABOUT 1 PINT

 F YOU'VE PICKED or purchased a small quantity of berries and want to make jam to eat soon, try this low-sugar recipe.

1 pound blackberries
1¼ cups sugar

1   In a preserving pan, mash the blackberries with a potato masher. Add the sugar and heat the contents over medium heat, stirring gently, until the sugar is dissolved. Raise the heat to medium-high and boil the mixture until a drop mounds in a chilled dish.

2   Pour the jam into a jar and cap the jar tightly. Store it in the refrigerator, where the jam should keep for at least several weeks.

BLACKBERRY–BLACK CURRANT JAM

 LACK CURRANTS add a subtle but interesting note to blackberry jam.

2½ pounds blackberries
1 cup black currant juice (page 120)
4½ cups sugar

1 In a preserving pan, heat the berries, covered, over low heat until they are soft.

2 Remove the pan from the heat and mash the berries with a potato masher. Add the black currant juice and sugar, place the pan over medium heat, and cook, stirring gently, until the sugar is dissolved. Raise the heat to medium-high and boil the mixture, stirring frequently, until a drop of the jam forms a mound in a chilled dish.

3 Ladle the jam into pint or half-pint mason jars, add lids and rings, and process the jars in a boiling-water bath for 10 minutes.

RAW BLACKBERRY JAM

MAKES ABOUT 1 PINT

FOR A REALLY QUICK blackberry jam with all the fresh taste of the fruit, try this recipe, a variant of Cristina's Raw Raspberry Jam (page 314). This jam doesn't set, but it's thick enough for most purposes. Try it with pancakes or crêpes.

¾ pound blackberries
1½ cups sugar

1 In a bowl, mash the berries with a potato masher. Stir in the sugar until it has dissolved. Pour the jam into a jar and tightly cap it.

2 Store the jar in the refrigerator. Provided your berries were fresh-picked and free from mold, the jam should keep for a few weeks.

BLACKBERRIES THAT GROW ON TREES?

The black mulberry looks like a blackberry but grows on a tree. A cousin of the white mulberry, the kind whose leaves silkworms eat, *Morus nigra* is seldom grown commercially in the United States because the fruit is so highly perishable when ripe. If you have black mulberries in your garden, though, you can use them like blackberries and raspberries for preserving. In fact, some people think that black mulberries are among the best fruits for jelly.

Another mulberry species whose fruits can stand in for caneberries is *M. rubra*, a red-fruited native of the eastern United States.

BLACKBERRY-QUINCE PASTE

MAKES ABOUT 1½ POUNDS

BLACKBERRY SEASON passes before quinces ripen, but I always have plenty of blackberries in my freezer to combine with some of the quince crop. Cut this paste into small pieces and serve them as a snack, appetizer, or dessert, accompanied, if you like, by cheese or nuts.

1 pound quinces, quartered and cored (unpeeled)
¾ cup water
1 pound blackberries
2 cups sugar

1. Combine the quinces and water in a preserving pan over low heat. Simmer the quinces, covered, for 20 minutes.

2. Add the blackberries to the pan. Simmer the fruits together, covered, about 10 minutes, until the berries and quinces are both soft.

3. Pass the contents of the pan through the fine screen of a food mill, leaving the blackberry seeds behind.

4. Combine the pureed fruit and sugar in the preserving pan. Heat them over low heat, stirring gently, until the sugar is completely dissolved. Simmer the mixture, stirring constantly, for 25 minutes or more, until the mixture is thick and the spoon makes a clear trail across the bottom of the pan.

5. Spread the mixture about ¾ inch thick in lightly oiled dishes with vertical sides. Let the paste cool, and then turn it out of the

dishes to dry on a rack in a warm place, such as near a stove, in a food dehydrator, or, if your climate allows, in the sun.

6 When the paste is dry to the touch, cut it into smaller pieces, if you like, and wrap the pieces in plastic. Unless you'll be eating the paste soon or you're sure that it is thoroughly dry, store it in a heavy-duty plastic bag in the refrigerator. If it's sufficiently dry, it will keep for several months at room temperature.

BLACKBERRY PASTE

MAKES ABOUT 1½ POUNDS

I STRUGGLED FOR YEARS to find a way to make pastes from soft fruits without adding quinces or apples; whenever I tried, the pastes turned out too sticky or tasting caramelized or scorched. I was happy to finally develop this method, which produces something between a very thick jam and a very firm jelly.

2 pounds blackberries
1½ cups juice from cooked crabapples,
    other tart apples, or quinces (pages 13 to 15)
2 cups sugar
Extra-fine sugar

1 Put the blackberries into a pan set over low heat and simmer the berries, covered, until they are soft, about 10 minutes.

2 Strain out the blackberry juice through a damp jelly bag. Let the juice drip for 8 to 12 hours. Do not squeeze the bag.

3 In the preserving pan, combine the blackberry juice with the crabapple, apple, or quince juice. Over medium-high heat, reduce the combined juice by one-half, to 1½ cups total.

4 While the juice boils, pass the berries from the jelly bag through the fine screen of a food mill.

5 Stir the berry puree into the juice in the preserving pan and add the sugar. Heat the mixture over low heat, stirring, until the sugar is completely dissolved. Simmer the mixture, stirring often at first and almost constantly toward the end, for 40 minutes or more. When the paste is ready, your spoon will leave a clear path across the bottom.

6 Pour the paste about ¾ inch thick into lightly oiled dishes with vertical sides. Let the paste cool, and then cut it into bite-size pieces. Roll the pieces in extra-fine sugar and let them dry for a few days in a warm place, such as near a stove, in a food dehydrator, or, if your climate allows, in the sun. Store them in an airtight container at room temperature. They should keep for several weeks.

BLACKBERRY-APPLE LEATHER

A DISTINCTLY AMERICAN PRESERVE, fruit leather is beloved by hikers for its light weight, children for its sweet flavor and chewy texture, and parents for its lack of added sugar. Blackberries are a choice material for fruit leather because they are so abundant in much of North America. A little added applesauce improves the texture of the leather.

Exactly how you make your fruit leather will depend on your equipment and, perhaps, your climate. In hot, dry weather, you can dry fruit leather outdoors, on screens covered with cheesecloth to keep off insects. Most people, however, use electric dehydrators. The small, round ones come with plastic rings on which you spread the fruit puree. With a larger, box-shaped dehydrator, you tape plastic wrap over the racks and spread the fruit puree on the plastic wrap. Either sort of electric dehydrator should have a fan for circulating air and, preferably, a thermostat so you can use more heat at the beginning of the drying period and less toward the end.

5 pounds blackberries
1 pound applesauce

1. Pass the berries through the fine screen of a food mill, leaving the seeds behind. Stir the applesauce into the berry puree.

2. Secure plastic wrap over dehydrator screens, leaving an uncovered margin for air circulation, or use heavy-duty plastic sheets made to fit into your dehydrator. Spread the puree in a ¼-inch layer.

3. Dry the puree for approximately 1 day, rotating the screens for even drying and reducing the heat, if possible, after the first few hours.

4. When the leather is ready, it will no longer be wet or sticky, but it will still be pliable, not brittle. If it cracks or breaks when you try to roll it, mist it lightly with water from a spray bottle and dry it a little longer.

5. Roll each piece of leather with the plastic wrap on which it has dried. Store the rolls in a heavy-duty sealed plastic bag or tightly closed glass jar. It should keep well for a year or more.

FERMENTED BLACKBERRY SYRUP

MAKES ABOUT 3 PINTS

T HIS RECIPE produces a clear, slightly fermented syrup that serves as an appealing base for cold drinks. Try it with iced black or mint tea as well as plain or carbonated water.

2¼ pounds blackberries
About 3⅓ cups water
About 6⅔ cups sugar
About ⅔ cup strained lemon juice, to your taste

1 In two batches, whirl the blackberries briefly in a blender. Pour the puree into a 2-quart jar. Cap the jar loosely and let it stand at room temperature for 1 to 3 days, shaking or stirring the jar several times a day, until little bubbles rise in the jar and the aroma is a little winey. Strain the liquid through a damp jelly bag and measure the liquid.

2 In a kettle, combine the same volume of water as you have juice with twice that volume of sugar. Heat the contents over medium heat, stirring, until the sugar is dissolved. Raise the heat to high and boil the syrup until it reaches the soft-ball stage (page 19) or 235°F. Remove the kettle from the heat.

3 Stir the blackberry juice and lemon juice into the syrup. Bring the mixture to a boil and simmer it for 10 minutes.

4 Pour the hot syrup into pint or half-pint mason jars. Add lids and rings, and process the jars in a boiling-water bath for 10 minutes.

BLACKBERRY
VINEGAR

MAKES ABOUT 2½ CUPS

 SE THIS FLAVORED VINEGAR in salad dressings, marinades, and sauces, or turn it into Blackberry Shrub (page 74).

1 pound blackberries
2 cups red wine vinegar

1 Put the blackberries into a sterilized quart jar, and cover them with the vinegar. Let the jar stand, tightly covered with a plastic cap, for 3 to 4 weeks.

2 Strain the vinegar through a sieve and then through a damp jelly bag. Funnel the vinegar into sterilized bottles. Cap or cork the bottles and store them in a cool, dark place. The vinegar should keep for 4 to 6 months.

BLACKBERRY
SHRUB

MAKES ABOUT 2 QUARTS

T HE WORD *shrub*, which comes from the same Arabic root as *syrup*, refers to an acidulated fruit juice mixed with ice water. Shrubs were favorite drinks for hot summer days before the advent of commercial soft drinks.

To serve the shrub, mix 1 part syrup with about 3 parts combined water and ice. You can use soda water if you like, but try plain water first. The vinegar will provide a soda-like tingle on your tongue.

> 6 cups Blackberry Vinegar (page 73)
> 1½ cups sugar
> ¾ cup brandy (optional)

1. Combine the vinegar in a saucepan with the sugar. Stirring, bring the mixture to a boil over medium heat. Let the mixture boil for 10 minutes, and then let it cool. Stir in the brandy, if you are using it.

2. Funnel the shrub into sterilized bottles, and tightly cap or cork the bottles.

BLUEBERRY AND HUCKLEBERRY

Huckleberry Jam   77

Blueberry-Citrus Preserves   78

Huckleberries in Syrup   79

Blueberry Jelly   80

Fermented Blueberry or

　　Huckleberry Syrup   81

MY MOTHER ONCE TOLD of the first time she met Mr. Bones, my father's mysterious father, at his Oregon homestead. The old man made the three of them a supper of blueberries from his garden topped with cream from the neighbor's cow. It was a meal as eccentric as Mr. Bones, but just as wholesome, satisfying, and healthful as the blueberry itself.

Like the huckleberry, bilberry, and whortleberry, the blueberry is the fruit of a shrub in the *Ericaceae*, or heath, family. Sorting out these similar species is complicated. Most belong to the same genus, *Vaccinium*, although not all do; some berries called huckleberries belong to the closely related genus *Gaylussacia*. Some Easterners say that *all* huckleberries are *Gaylussacia*. Since no *Gaylussacia* species grow in the western United States, however, we Westerners have a different criterion for distinguishing between blueberries and huckleberries.

The genus *Vaccinium* has two taxonomic sections, Myrtillus and Cyanococcus. Cyanococcus species are native only to North America. They include highbush blueberries (*V. corymbosum*) and lowbush species such as *V. angustifolium*. Growing in natural abundance primarily around the Great Lakes and in New England, *V. corymbosum* and *V. angustifolium* are still commercially harvested in the wild. They are also the ancestors of most blueberry cultivars, whose fruits can grow up to an inch in diameter. Berries of these cultivars are important commercial crops in the Pacific Northwest and California as well as in Michigan, New Jersey, and North Carolina. To most Westerners, only Cyanococcus species are blueberries.

Western huckleberry species all belong to the Myrtillus section of the genus *Vaccinium*. Whereas Cyanococcus berries have many tiny, soft seeds, Myrtillus berries each have approximately ten larger, harder seeds. And whereas Cyanococcus berries are always dark, usually with a white bloom that makes them appear bluish, Myrtillus berries can be blue, purple, black, or red. Some Myrtillus species are native to Europe, where they came by the names bilberry and whortleberry. In the Northwest there are at least ten Myrtillus species, including one that is evergreen, one that has shiny black berries, some that have red berries, and one, the blue-berried and aptly named *V. deliciosum*, that is worth a long trip into the mountains to pick. Each of these species has berries much smaller than domesticated blueberries. Also, each of these species is adapted to special conditions, and none has been domesticated.

Blueberry cultivars are easier to grow in home gardens, but they, too, require special growing conditions: acid soil, plenty of mulch for their shallow roots, and frequent watering. If you're going to plant blueberries, choose varieties that have performed well for others in your area. For good pollination, it's best to plant more than one variety, and if you choose several varieties with different ripening periods you could have fresh blueberries nearly all summer long.

Blueberries are popular in muffins, pancakes, and cobblers, and they are best, I think, fresh off the bush or straight from the freezer (they don't stick together when they freeze). For syrups and other preserves, they benefit from the addition of lemon or other citrus juice and, sometimes, a little spice such as cinnamon.

Huckleberries vary greatly in appearance and taste, but because they tend to have a more tart and often a more intense or spicy flavor than blueberries, they generally need no added flavorings to make delicious jams and other preserves.

A 1998 study at Tufts University found that blueberries rank number one in antioxidant activity when compared with 40 other fresh fruits and vegetables. Eating blueberries may therefore reduce the likelihood of cancer, cardiovascular disease, and dementia. Huckleberries weren't tested in the study, but they are no doubt very good for you, too.

HUCKLEBERRY JAM

MAKES ABOUT 1½ PINTS

THE DELIGHTFUL, spicy flavor of huckleberries needs no adornment, and so I've kept this recipe simple. I've also kept the quantities small, because it's difficult not to eat every precious huckleberry you pick straight from the picking bucket, if not straight off the bush. If you manage to set some berries aside for preserving, though, this jam, on winter mornings, will bring back powerful memories of summer in the woods.

1½ pounds huckleberries
2¼ cups sugar

1. In a preserving pan, mash the huckleberries with a potato masher. Add the sugar and heat the mixture over medium heat, stirring gently, until the sugar is dissolved.

2. Raise the heat to medium-high and boil the mixture, stirring, until a drop of the jam mounds in a chilled dish.

3. Ladle the jam into pint or half-pint mason jars. Add lids and rings, and process the jars for 10 minutes in a boiling-water bath.

BLUEBERRY-CITRUS PRESERVES

MAKES ABOUT 3½ PINTS

ITRUS AND CINNAMON enliven the flavor of blueberries in this recipe.

2¾ pounds blueberries
⅓ cup strained orange juice
⅓ cup strained lemon juice
1 tablespoon grated orange zest
One 3-inch cinnamon stick
6 cups sugar

1 In a preserving pan, combine all of the ingredients. Heat them over medium heat, stirring gently, until the sugar has dissolved. Raise the heat to medium-high and bring the ingredients to a boil. Reduce the heat and simmer the mixture for 10 minutes, stirring frequently.

2 Remove the pan from the heat and cover it with a cloth. Let the pan stand at room temperature for 8 to 12 hours.

3 Return the pan to the heat and bring the contents to a boil. Continue to boil the mixture until the syrup has thickened a little. Test it by removing the pan from the heat, dropping a little of the preserves into a chilled dish and drawing your finger through the syrup. If the path remains clear, the syrup is thick enough. Remove the cinnamon stick from the pan.

4 Stir occasionally while allowing the preserves to cool for 5 minutes, and then ladle the preserves into pint or half-pint mason jars. Add lids and rings, and process the jars for 10 minutes in a boiling-water bath.

HUCKLEBERRIES IN SYRUP

MAKES ABOUT 3 PINTS

 F YOU CAN, preserve some of your huckleberry harvest in syrup to serve over ice cream or cake.

2 pounds huckleberries
1¾ cups water
1⅓ cups sugar
2 wide strips of lemon zest

1. Divide the berries among 3 pint or 6 half-pint mason jars.

2. In a saucepan, combine the water, sugar, and lemon zest. Stir the contents over medium heat until the sugar has dissolved. Raise the heat to medium-high and bring the syrup to a boil.

3. Immediately pour the syrup over the berries, straining out the lemon zest. Run a narrow spatula around the inside edge of each jar to release any air bubbles. Add lids and rings, and process the jars for 15 minutes in a boiling-water bath.

BLUEBERRY JELLY

MAKES 4 TO 5 HALF-PINTS

THE MANY TINY SEEDS in blueberries, I think, make these berries better for jelly than jam. This recipe actually started out as one for syrup, but I couldn't keep the syrup from gelling. Although blueberries are often described as being low in pectin and acid, I've seen blueberry juice gel before any sugar is added. Blueberry syrup therefore requires relatively more water and sugar, as in the syrup recipe that follows.

A steam juicer (page 14) is the best tool for extracting blueberry juice for jelly. If you don't have a steam juicer, simmer the berries, covered, with a little water until they are soft, and strain the juice first through a coarse-mesh strainer and then through a damp jelly bag. A cinnamon stick steamed or simmered along with the berries will add to the flavor of the jelly.

If your blueberries turn out to have too little pectin to make a firm jelly, relax! You will have a thick syrup for your pancakes and waffles.

> 3 cups blueberry juice
> 1 tablespoon strained lemon juice
> 3 cups sugar

1. In a saucepan, combine the blueberry juice, lemon juice, and sugar. Heat the mixture over medium heat, stirring gently, until the mixture comes to a boil. Raise the heat to medium-high and boil the mixture until it passes the spoon test (page 18).

2. Ladle the hot jelly into half-pint mason jars. Add lids and rings, and process the jars for 10 minutes in a boiling-water bath.

FERMENTED BLUEBERRY OR HUCKLEBERRY SYRUP

MAKES ABOUT 3 PINTS

L IKE THE RECIPE for Fermented Blackberry Syrup (page 72), this recipe produces a clear, dark red, slightly fermented syrup to mix with ice and plain water or soda water.

2¼ pounds blueberries or huckleberries
About 3 cups water
About 6 cups sugar
About ¾ cup strained lemon juice, to your taste

1 In two batches, whirl the blueberries or huckleberries briefly in a blender. Pour the puree into a 2-quart jar. Cap the jar loosely and let it stand at room temperature for 3 to 6 days, shaking or stirring the jar several times a day, until little bubbles rise in the jar and the aroma is a little winey. Strain the liquid through a damp jelly bag and measure the liquid.

2 In a kettle, combine the same volume of water as you have juice with twice that volume of sugar. Heat the contents over medium heat, stirring, until the sugar is dissolved. Raise the heat to high and boil the syrup to the soft-ball stage (page 19) or 235°F. Remove the kettle from the heat.

3 Stir the blackberry juice and lemon juice into the syrup. Bring the mixture to a boil and simmer it for 5 minutes.

4 Pour the hot syrup into pint or half-pint mason jars. Add lids and rings, and process the jars in a boiling-water bath for 10 minutes.

CANTALOUPE AND MUSKMELON

Cantaloupe Jam with Mint   84

Cantaloupe Jam with Vanilla   85

Cantaloupe Preserves with
    Cinnamon   86

T HE SPECIES *Cucumis melo*, or muskmelon, includes many kinds of melons, large and small, sweet and bland, and many of them might work in the recipes here. But I have tested these recipes with orange-fleshed fruits of what are perhaps the best-known *Cucumis* subspecies—*C. melo reticulatus* (also known as *C. melo melo* var. *reticulatus*) and *C. melo cantalupensis*.

C. melo reticulatus is sometimes called the "North American cantaloupe," sometimes "muskmelon" (as if it were the only muskmelon species), but most often in the United States simply "cantaloupe." This is the cantaloupe grown in California and Mexico and shipped to supermarkets all over the United States. The botanical name *reticulatus* refers to this melon's net-like—that is, reticulated—skin covering. Most of these melons are "sutured," with regular indentations from top to bottom. Gardeners can usually tell that North American cantaloupes are ripe when they slip from the vine with mild pressure from a thumb (if they separate on their own, they are usually over-ripe). Some of these melons are green-fleshed; others are orange inside. A favorite orange variety is Jenny Lind.

C. melo cantalupensis is also known as "European cantaloupe" or "true cantaloupe." European cantaloupe varieties have little or no netting; their skin is generally smooth, though some varieties are warty. Most varieties are round or even a little flattened at the poles rather than oval, with orange flesh rather than green. Most varieties also have prominent ribs. Sadly, these luscious, aromatic fruits are seldom seen in U.S. markets. Gardeners, however, can buy the seeds from catalogs. One ambrosial French variety, the gray-green-skinned Charentais, is popular among American home gardeners, who learn to judge its ripeness by scent and color (the gray-green turns to gold) rather than wait for the melons to slip from the vine.

Melons need a long, warm growing season; they take 80 to 100 days to reach maturity. Northern gardeners use various techniques to provide the right conditions: They lighten the soil with compost, plant in hills or on a south-facing slope, cover the soil with black plastic, and cover the vines with spun-polyester row covers. These techniques, combined with heavy irrigation and vigilant protection from cucumber beetles and other pests, usually result in a good crop of sweet, beautiful melons.

There is no better way to appreciate either European or North American cantaloupe than to eat it fresh, still warm from the sun or lightly chilled. Cantaloupes combine well with other fruits in fruit salads. Some Europeans fill the center of small, sweet melons with port. In Mexico and Central America, melons are blended with ice water and sugar into a refreshing hot-weather drink. I like to simply halve a melon around its equator, seed it, and eat it with a spoon.

But cantaloupes are good for preserving, too. I was amazed to find that such juicy fruits could make thick, though not firmly gelled, jams. More amazing to me still was how well the cantaloupe flavor, aroma, and bright orange color survived cooking, even long cooking. If you have more cantaloupes than you can eat, don't hesitate to try these recipes.

"It is easy to talk of melons, more difficult to grow them, but hardest of all to find the right moment to eat them."

—*Edward A. Bunyard,* The Anatomy of Dessert

CANTALOUPE JAM WITH MINT

MAKES ABOUT 2 PINTS

YOU COULD TRY OTHER HERBS—lemon mint, lemon basil, regular basil, scented geranium—in this smooth, soft jam.

2 pounds peeled, seeded, and coarsely chopped cantaloupe
3½ cups sugar
1 tablespoon lemon juice
1 small bunch spearmint

1 Cook the cantaloupe pieces over low heat in a covered preserving pan until they are tender, 20 to 30 minutes.

2 Puree the cantaloupe by putting it through the fine screen of a food mill. Combine the puree in the preserving pan with the sugar and lemon juice. Stirring, heat the contents over medium heat until the sugar is dissolved. Raise the heat to medium-high and boil the jam, stirring frequently, until a drop of it mounds slightly in a chilled dish.

3 Remove the pan from the heat. Swish the mint through the hot jam for about 30 seconds. Scrape the jam clinging to the mint back into the pan and discard the mint. Pick out any leaves that have come loose in the pan. Ladle the jam into pint or half-pint mason jars. Add lids and rings, and process the jars in a boiling-water bath for 10 minutes.

CANTALOUPE JAM WITH VANILLA

MAKES ABOUT 2 PINTS

T HIS RECIPE is a lumpier version of the preceding one, with vanilla instead of mint for flavoring. If you really like vanilla, use the full teaspoon; for subtler flavoring, use just ½ teaspoon. Or leave out the vanilla extract and use vanilla sugar in place of the plain sugar.

> 2 pounds peeled and seeded cantaloupe, cut into ½-inch cubes
> 3½ cups sugar
> 1 tablespoon lemon juice
> ½ to 1 teaspoon vanilla extract

1 Combine the cantaloupe, sugar, and lemon juice in a preserving pan. Heat the contents over medium heat, stirring, until the sugar is dissolved. Raise the heat to medium-high and boil the jam, stirring frequently, until a drop of it mounds slightly in a chilled dish.

2 Remove the pan from the heat, stir in the vanilla, and ladle the jam into pint or half-pint mason jars. Add lids and rings, and process the jars in a boiling-water bath for 10 minutes.

CANTALOUPE PRESERVES WITH CINNAMON

MAKES ABOUT 2 PINTS

I WASN'T SURE I WOULD LIKE the cinnamon in this recipe, but it brings out the flavor of the cantaloupe. Despite the long cooking, the cantaloupe keeps its lovely color and perfume. Try these preserves with pound cake or vanilla ice cream.

2 pounds peeled and seeded cantaloupe,
  cut into 1-inch-square pieces
3½ cups sugar
1 cinnamon stick
2 tablespoons strained lemon juice

1 In a preserving pan, layer the cantaloupe pieces and sugar. Bury the cinnamon stick in the mixture and pour the lemon juice over the top. Cover the pan and let it rest for 8 to 12 hours at room temperature, until most of the sugar has dissolved.

2 Over very low heat, dissolve the remaining sugar, stirring gently and occasionally. Simmer the contents until the cantaloupe pieces are partially translucent, about 1½ hours.

3 Remove the fruit with a slotted spoon. Bring the syrup to a boil and let it boil until it reaches the thread stage (page 18) or 230°F. Remove the pan from the heat, return the fruit to the syrup, and cover the pan with a towel. Let the preserves stand at room temperature for 8 to 12 hours.

4 Bring the preserves to a boil. Remove the cinnamon stick from the pan and let the preserves cool for 5 minutes. Give them a stir and then ladle them into pint or half-pint mason jars. Add lids and rings, and process the jars in a boiling-water bath for 10 minutes.

CARROT

Carrot-Apple Butter   88
Carrot Marmalade   89

EVERYONE KNOWS the humble carrot, sold cheap in every grocery store year-round and added to soups, stews, and salads like a boring cousin to a wedding list. On closer examination, though, the carrot becomes more interesting. It probably originated in or near Afghanistan and was introduced to Europe by the Arabs. It's a root vegetable that in its early use was grown for its aromatic leaves and seeds, like its relatives cilantro, dill, and fennel. (Today the carrot's weedy herbal form, Queen Anne's lace, seems loved only by gophers and rural flower arrangers.)

In past centuries, cooks loved carrots for their variety of colors—white, yellow, orange, red, and purple—and their sizes and shapes—round, finger-like, tapered, or cylindrical. Today's supermarkets usually stock only two kinds of carrots: pole-like orange ones, shorn of their fronds, and the same carrots lathed into short pegs and marketed as "baby carrots." But farmers' markets still sell classically tapered carrots with their fresh green tops, and home gardeners are again growing carrots in a wide range of colors, shapes, and sizes.

Whether they're orange or purple, long or short, carrots have outstanding virtues. They are rich in sugar and minerals as well as carotene, they keep well in a cool place for months, and they are as tasty raw as cooked. Try them in the recipes that follow.

CARROT-APPLE BUTTER

MAKES ABOUT 2½ PINTS

IKE REGULAR APPLE BUTTER, this thick, hearty sweet spread from eastern Europe has minimal added sugar. You might try adding sweet spices like cinnamon, allspice, and cloves in place of the vanilla extract. The butter is delightful on whole-wheat or raisin-bread toast or on bran or corn muffins.

> 2 pounds carrots, thinly sliced
> About 2 cups water
> 1¾ pounds peeled, cored, and thinly sliced tart apples
> 2 cups sugar
> ½ teaspoon vanilla extract

1 Put the sliced carrots into a kettle and barely cover them with water. Simmer the carrots, covered, until they are just tender. Add the apple slices and simmer them with the carrots until both are soft.

2 Puree the carrots and apples through the medium screen of a food mill. Return the puree to the kettle and add the sugar. Heat the mixture over medium-low heat, stirring until the sugar dissolves, and then continue to cook the mixture, stirring more and more frequently as the cooking continues, until the butter is darkened, glossy, and very thick. Remove the kettle from the heat and stir in the vanilla extract.

3 Pack the butter into pint or half-pint mason jars, leaving ¼ inch headspace. Give each jar a shake to settle the contents and then run a narrow spatula around the inside edge of the jar to remove any remaining air bubbles. Add lids and rings, and process the jars for 10 minutes in a boiling-water bath.

CARROT MARMALADE

MAKES ABOUT 2½ PINTS

R ECIPES LIKE THIS ONE appear in many old American cookbooks, and they make a beautiful, bright-orange preserve. Sometimes it's flavored with spices such as cinnamon, mace, and ginger, any of which you might add. Since I like the marmalade as an accompaniment to chicken or pork, I've included a little salt here.

2 pounds carrots, cut into ¼-inch rounds
1 large lemon
1 large orange
3 tablespoons lemon juice
4 cups sugar
1 teaspoon salt

1 Steam the carrots until they are tender, about 10 minutes.

2 Squeeze the juice from the lemon and orange. Discard the seeds and membranes and reserve the juice and rinds.

3 Coarsely grind the lemon and orange rinds and the carrots in a food grinder, or mince them with a knife. Combine the ground rinds and carrots in a preserving pan with the reserved juice, the additional lemon juice, the sugar, and the salt. Heat the mixture over low heat, stirring, until the sugar dissolves. Raise the heat and simmer the mixture for 20 to 30 minutes, until the syrup no longer separates from the pulp.

4 Pack the marmalade into pint or half-pint mason jars. Add lids and rings, and process the jars for 15 minutes in a boiling-water bath.

CHERRY

Cristina's Cherry *Compot*   91

Cherry-Flavored Brandy   93

Brandied Cherries   95

Cherry Preserves   96

Cherry-Currant Preserves   97

Cherry-Currant Jam   98

Candied Cherries   99

Cherry Syrup   101

Cherry Paste   102

Spiced Cherries   103

Maraschino Cherries   105

THERE ARE TWO basic types of cherries: sweet *(Prunus avium)* and sour *(P. cerasus)*. You are probably familiar with the most common sweet varieties—the dark, nearly black ones such as Bing and Lambert, and the yellow-fleshed ones such as Royal Anne and Rainier, whose skins have a red blush on one side. From late spring to midsummer, these types are widely available in markets. The fruits, which are mainly eaten fresh, tend to be large, and breeders are trying to make them larger still. The trees that bear sweet cherries tend to be big, too, although nurseries have begun using dwarfing rootstocks.

Sour cherries are preferred for pies and preserves. Today, unfortunately, they are generally sold in the United States only in cans and jars, although in some areas they are briefly available fresh in farmers' markets and even supermarkets. But sour cherry trees tend to be small and self-fertile, even when they're not on dwarfing rootstock, and so are quite suitable for gardens.

Don't be misled by the word *sour;* these cherries are delicious right off the tree. In my orchard I have two sour cherry trees, a Montmorency—the classic pie cherry, with bright red fruit—and a North Star, with darker red fruit, and I have come to like the fruits so well that I find Bings, Royal Annes, and their close relatives to be simply too bland even for eating raw.

In the Willamette Valley, where I live, cherries were once an important crop, but because our wet climate promotes both disease and pollination problems, and because people don't make nearly as many cherry pies as they used to, there are few cherry orchards remaining. The birds keep planting cherry trees for us, though, and the trees grow fast. The fruits are usually rather small and tart and sometimes a little bitter, but they are almost always delicious, and sometimes they taste better to me than any cherries I've ever bought.

You can grow your own cherries if you live in USDA zone 4, 5, 6, or 7 and have a sunny spot with well-drained soil. Choose varieties according to size and resistance to the major diseases in your area. Protect the fruit from birds; I use nylon netting for small trees and hang CDs to flash in the bigger trees. Pick the fruits when they are at their peak of color; their sugar content will be at its highest then.

In preserving cherries, keep in mind that the fruits are low in pectin. To get a firm jelly or jam, you must combine the cherries with high-pectin fruits such as currants or apples.

CRISTINA'S CHERRY COMPOT

MAKES 1 QUART

CRISTINA NICOARĂ, who lived for most of a year with my family as an exchange student, gave me a rough outline of this recipe over the phone from Moldova. She and her family had just picked cherries from a tree in their garden and made them into *compot*, the favorite Moldovan wintertime drink. When Cristina called, cherries were ripe in my garden, too, so I put up some in the same way.

You may think of compote as fruit in syrup, served in small cups. Moldovans use proportionately less sugar and more water, to produce a drink rather than a dessert. A few cherries are placed in each glass and eaten after the liquid is drunk.

In a Romanian cookbook that Cristina left at my house, I found a *compot* recipe in which the cherries were pitted. An advantage of making *compot*, however, is that pitting is unnecessary. This means you can use cherries too small to be pitted. I like to use deliciously bitter dark ones from a seedling tree in my yard.

Moldovan *compot* can be made with other fruits besides cherries. Plums, strawberries, apples, peaches, quinces, and pears are all used in Moldova, and sometimes two or more of these are mixed. Adjust the quantity of sugar to suit the fruit and your taste.

I like to serve cherry *compot* as a holiday treat for guests who don't drink alcoholic beverages.

¾ pound stemmed cherries
2½ cups water
⅓ cup sugar

1. Put the cherries into a quart mason jar. Bring the water to a boil in a saucepan and add the sugar; stir until it dissolves. Pour the syrup over the cherries in the jar. Release the bubbles in the jar and then add a little more boiling water, if necessary, to bring the level of the liquid to ½ inch from the top of the jar.

2. Add the lid and ring, and process the jar in a boiling-water bath for 25 minutes.

CHERRY-FLAVORED BRANDY

MAKES ABOUT 1½ QUARTS

THE TRADITIONAL CHERRY for this recipe is Morello, a small, dark red sour variety. I prefer to use the even smaller and darker, slightly bitter cherries that I use for Cristina's Cherry *Compot* (page 91). Tart and mildly bitter fruit best balances the sweetness of this warming drink.

Some writers advise poking each cherry several times with a needle, but I've found that if I stem my cherries they seem to release their flavor quite well through their stem holes. If you want to leave the stems on your cherries, do poke each cherry with a needle before putting it in the jar. Save time by poking the needle all the way through the fruit, bypassing the pit.

You can strain the cherries out after a few months to serve them at their best (assuming you don't want to use all of the liqueur at this point), or you can leave the cherries and brandy together for a year or more, although the cherries will shrivel and darken. Just strain out a little liqueur whenever you want it, for an apéritif or nightcap, and add a drunken cherry or two for interest.

About 2 pounds stemmed sour cherries
1 cup sugar
About 3 cups (one 750-milliliter bottle) brandy
3 to 4 drops almond extract (optional)

1. Layer the cherries and sugar in a 2-quart jar until they nearly reach the top. Cover the cherries with the brandy; add the almond extract, if you are using it. Tightly close the jar with a nonreactive cap and shake the jar to dissolve most of the sugar.

2. Store the jar for at least 3 months in a cool, dark place. Shake the jar occasionally during the first few days of storage so that all of the sugar dissolves.

3. If you would like to eat the cherries at their best, strain them out through a double layer of cheesecloth after 3 months or so (if you wait much longer, the cherries will have lost too much color and flavor). Put the brandy into a clean jar or bottle, and cap it tightly. Serve the cherries, if you like, with whipped cream.

4. The brandy will keep indefinitely.

HOW TO PIT CHERRIES

The best tool for pitting cherries depends on the variety you want to pit. In any case, don't buy a plastic pitter that screws onto a tabletop; the pressure on the plastic will, sooner or later, cause the contraption to break. Don't bother with flimsy sorts of hand-held cherry pitters, either. They simply don't work well, no matter the cherry variety.

For large cherries such as Bing, Van, and Royal Anne, a very good tool is a sturdy, stainless-steel handheld model; mine is German-made and about 5½ inches long.

Medium-size cherries can be pitted easily with a blunt-tipped needle (preferably one that is slightly curved and flattened near the tip) or simply with a gentle tug. When my North Star and Montmorency cherries are ripe and fresh off the tree (before they have been refrigerated), I can usually pit them by pulling the stems while gently holding and pressing the fruit with two or three fingers. This works particularly well with the Montmorency fruit.

Whether you pit your cherries with a handheld pitter, a needle, or just your fingers, work over a bowl so you save any juice that drips out.

BRANDIED CHERRIES

MAKES 2 PINTS

D ESPITE THE SIMILARITY in name and ingredients, this recipe is quite different from the preceding one. When brandy is just a flavoring for the cherries, you add just a little of it, and you heat-process your concoction if you plan to keep it long.

1½ pounds pitted cherries, with any
    juice from pitting (opposite page)
⅔ cup sugar
About ¼ cup brandy

1 Combine the cherries, their juice, and sugar in a preserving pan, cover the pan, and set it over very low heat.

2 When the sugar has completely dissolved, divide the fruit and syrup between 2 pint mason jars. Add enough brandy to fill the jars to ½ inch from the top. Add lids and rings, and process the jars for 10 minutes in a boiling-water bath.

"To eat cherries, preserved in spirits, is only an apology, and a very poor and mean one, for dram drinking; a practice which every man ought to avoid, and the very thought of giving way to which ought to make the cheek of a woman redden with shame."

—William Cobbett, The American Gardener, *1821*

CHERRY PRESERVES

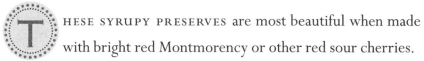

THESE SYRUPY PRESERVES are most beautiful when made with bright red Montmorency or other red sour cherries.

For a bitter-almond flavor, add a spice bag of blanched cherry kernels (page 104) before the first boiling and take it out before putting the preserves into jars. Or add a couple of drops of pure almond extract after the final boiling has stopped.

> 2½ pounds pitted sour cherries, with any juice
>   from pitting (page 94)
> 5 cups sugar
> 2 tablespoons strained lemon juice

1. Layer the pitted cherries with their juice and the sugar in a preserving pan. Let the pan stand for about 1 hour, until the sugar has drawn out some of the cherry juice.

2. Heat the mixture over medium heat, stirring occasionally and gently, until the sugar has completely dissolved. Raise the heat to medium-high and boil the mixture for 5 minutes, stirring occasionally. Remove the pan from the heat.

3. Cover the pan with a cloth and let the pan stand at room temperature for 8 to 12 hours.

4. Set the pan over medium heat and add the lemon juice. Bring the mixture to a boil and raise the heat to medium-high. Boil the mixture, stirring often and skimming off any foam, until the syrup thickens a little. Test it by removing the pan from the heat, dropping a little of the preserves into a chilled dish, and drawing your finger through the syrup. If the path remains clear, the syrup is thick enough.

5 Ladle the cherries and syrup into pint or half-pint mason jars. Add lids and rings, and process the jars in a boiling-water bath for 10 minutes.

CHERRY-CURRANT PRESERVES

CHERRIES AND RED CURRANTS ripen at about the same time and combine well to make firm preserves; currants provide the pectin that cherries lack and match the cherries' bright color. I like to use tart, red Montmorency cherries for this preserve.

1½ cups red currant juice (page 120)
4½ cups sugar
5 cups pitted red cherries (from about 2 pounds whole cherries), with any juice from pitting (page 94)

1 In a preserving pan, combine the currant juice and sugar. Dissolve the sugar over medium heat, stirring, and then add the cherries with their juice. Bring the mixture to a full boil and let it boil for 5 minutes. As it boils, skim off the foam.

2 Remove the pan from the heat. Let the mixture cool and then cover the pan. Let it stand at room temperature for 8 to 12 hours.

3 Bring the preserves to a boil over medium heat. Boil until the syrup passes the spoon test (page 18).

4 Skim off the foam and let the preserves cool for a few minutes before ladling them into pint or half-pint mason jars. Add lids and rings, and process the jars in a boiling-water bath for 10 minutes.

CHERRY-CURRANT JAM

THE INGREDIENTS HERE are the same as in Cherry-Currant Preserves (page 97), but the method is quicker and the result more homey, though just as tasty.

1½ cups red currant juice (page 120)
5 cups pitted red cherries, such as Montmorency (from about 2 pounds whole cherries), with any juice from pitting (page 94)
4½ cups sugar

1. Combine the currant juice, cherries, and any juice from the cherries in a preserving pan. Over medium heat, bring the mixture to a boil. Reduce the heat to low, cover the pan, and simmer the mixture until the cherries are quite tender, about 15 minutes. Remove the pan from the heat.

2. Add the sugar to the mixture and stir. Place the pan over medium heat and stir until the sugar is dissolved. Raise the heat to medium-high and boil the mixture, stirring often, until it passes the spoon test (page 18).

3. Skim off the foam and let the jam cool for a few minutes before ladling it into pint or half-pint mason jars. Add lids and rings, and process the jars in a boiling-water bath for 10 minutes.

CANDIED CHERRIES

MAKES ABOUT 1 CUP CANDIED CHERRIES

(AND ABOUT 1½ PINTS SYRUP)

WHEN YOU CANDY Montmorency cherries as described here, they turn from bright cherry red to brilliant scarlet. Although replacing most of the liquid in the cherries with sugar takes several days, the process takes very little effort, since if your cherries are properly ripe you can pit them as you pick them. With a gentle tug the fruit usually comes away whole, leaving the pit hanging from the stem.

To best preserve the cherries' fresh flavor, immerse them in the syrup as soon as you bring them into the kitchen.

Use candied cherries to decorate desserts, serve them as a confection, or package them attractively as a gift. Bottle the syrup to serve on pancakes, waffles, or crêpes or to mix with plain water or soda water as a hot-weather drink.

> 1¼ cups water
> 3¼ cups sugar
> ½ cup light corn syrup
> 1 pound pitted cherries (preferably a tart red variety such as
>   Montmorency), with any juice from pitting (page 94)

1 In a preserving pan, combine the water, ½ cup of the sugar, and the corn syrup. Stir the mixture over medium-low heat until the sugar dissolves, and then bring the syrup to a boil. Add the cherries and their juice. Heat the mixture to between 180° and 185°F, and then remove the pan from the heat. Cover the pan with a cloth and let the mixture stand for 18 to 24 hours.

2   With a wire skimmer, transfer the cherries to a bowl. Add ¾ cup of the sugar to the pan. Bring the syrup to a boil and skim off any foam. Remove the pan from the heat and return the cherries to the pan. Cover the pan with a cloth and let the mixture stand at room temperature for 18 to 24 hours.

3   With a wire skimmer, transfer the cherries to a bowl. This time, add 1⅓ cups of the sugar to the pan. Bring the syrup to a boil and skim off any foam. Remove the pan from the heat and return the cherries to the pan. Cover the pan with a cloth and let the mixture stand at room temperature for 18 to 24 hours.

4   Once more, use a skimmer to transfer the cherries to a bowl. Add the remaining ⅔ cup sugar to the pan. Bring the syrup to a boil and skim off any foam. Remove the pan from the heat and return the cherries to the pan. Cover the pan with a cloth and let the mixture stand at room temperature for 18 to 24 hours.

5   With a skimmer, transfer the cherries to a colander. Rinse them briefly with cold water and drain them well.

6   Bring the syrup to a boil and boil it until it is thick. Pour it into pint or half-pint mason jars. Add lids and rings, and process the jars in a boiling-water bath for 10 minutes.

7   Transfer the cherries to a rack or screen set over a dish to catch drips. Place the dish in a warm, dry place. Let the cherries dry until they are leathery; this may take a day or two. Store them in an airtight container in a cool, dry place. They will keep for at least several months.

CHERRY SYRUP

....

MAKES ABOUT 1½ PINTS

I F YOU WANT TO MAKE CHERRY SYRUP without taking the trouble to candy cherries, here is a simple way to do it. I use dark wild cherries in this recipe, but you can use any kind. If they are sweet cherries, you might add a little lemon or lime juice for a tarter flavor. Use the syrup in snow cones, granita, or sorbet, or serve it with cold sparkling water.

Make cherry juice either with a steam juicer (page 14) or by simmering the cherries with a little water until their juice runs and then straining the juice through a damp jelly bag.

2 cups cherry juice
2¾ cups sugar

1 In a large saucepan, combine the juice and sugar. Stir the mixture over medium heat until the sugar dissolves, and then bring the syrup to a boil. Boil it for 1 minute.

2 Funnel the syrup into a bottle, cap or cork it tightly, and store the bottle in the refrigerator. Or pour the syrup into pint or half-pint mason jars, add lids and rings, and process the jars in a boiling-water bath for 10 minutes.

CHERRY PASTE

T HE FIRST TIME OR TWO that I attempted to make fruit paste from cherries, the result was sticky and had a slightly burnt flavor. I had more luck when I added pectin-rich quince juice to the cherry puree. The juice of sour apples would work as well. Serve this as a dessert or snack, cut into small rectangles.

> 2½ pounds cherries, pitted (about 6 cups),
>   with any juice from pitting (page 94)
> 1 cup water
> 1 cup Homemade Quince Pectin (page 17)
> About 1½ cups sugar
> ¼ teaspoon almond extract (optional)

1 Combine the cherries, their juice, and the water in a preserving pan. Simmer the cherries, covered, for about 10 minutes, until they are tender. Put them through the medium disk of a food mill.

2 Put the puree into the pan. Stirring occasionally at first and frequently later, cook the mixture over medium heat until it is as thick as applesauce. Remove the pan from the heat.

3 Add the quince pectin, and then measure the volume of the mixture. Add 1 cup sugar for each 2 cups puree. Cook the mixture over medium heat, stirring almost constantly, until your spoon briefly makes a clear track on the bottom of the pan. Remove the pan from the heat and stir until the boiling stops. Stir in the almond extract, if you are using it.

4 Spread the mixture about ¾ inch thick in lightly oiled, vertical-sided dishes, and set the dishes in a warm place. When the top of

the paste is completely cool and firm, turn each piece out onto a rack to finish drying.

5 Wrap the pieces in plastic wrap and keep them in a heavy-duty plastic bag in the refrigerator. When they are adequately dried, they will keep for several months or longer. If you want to store them at room temperature, dry them very thoroughly first in a warm room, warm oven, or dehydrator.

SPICED CHERRIES

MAKES ABOUT 1 PINT

 HESE ARE A SPRIGHTLY accompaniment to roast goose, duck, chicken, or pork.

1 pint stemmed sweet cherries
1 cup white wine vinegar
½ cup sugar
⅓ cup white wine
Seeds from 1 cardamom pod
Small piece of a cinnamon stick
Pinch of ground mace
1 allspice berry

1 Put the cherries into a bowl or jar and cover them with the vinegar. Cover the bowl with a towel or cap the jar, and let the cherries stand for 8 to 12 hours.

2 Drain the vinegar into a saucepan. Add the sugar, wine, cardamom, cinnamon, mace, and allspice. Bring the liquid to a boil and then reduce the heat. Simmer the liquid for 15 minutes. Remove the pan from the heat and let the liquid cool.

3 Pour the liquid over the cherries, cover them, and let them stand at room temperature for 3 days.

4 Drain the liquid into a saucepan again and bring the liquid to a boil. Let it cool.

5 Put the cherries into a sterilized pint jar. Strain the cooled liquid over them, filling the jar to the brim, and cap the jar. An all-plastic cap is preferable; if you have only a metal cap (or metal lid and ring), line it with plastic wrap.

6 Store the jar in the refrigerator or another cool, dark place for at least 1 month before eating the cherries.

WHY CHERRIES LOVE BITTER ALMOND

Many older recipes for cherry preserves call for almond extract. The association between these two arose because in years past frugal householders didn't use just the fruit of the cherry; they used the nut, too. Inside every cherry pit is a little kernel that tastes like a bitter almond, the type of almond that gives true almond extract its aroma and flavor. The same flavor is in peach and apricot kernels. In fact, commercially packaged "pure" almond extract can be made from the pits of various fruits.

The use of cherry and other fruit kernels in home cooking may have lost favor partially because the kernels, like bitter almonds, contain small amounts of amygdalin, which breaks down into prussic acid, a poison. (Also known as laetrile, amygdalin is an unorthodox cancer treatment, often obtained in the form of ground apricot pits from Mexico.) Fortunately, prussic acid can be mostly eliminated through heating or soaking. In accordance with the findings of scientific studies in the 1990s, I advise blanching fruit kernels for 20 minutes before using them.

To crack cherry pits without a mess, put them into a plastic bag, hit them with a hammer, and remove the kernels. If you want to flavor your preserves with cherry kernels but leave them out of the finished product, you can crack and blanch them in a muslin spice bag and immerse the bag, shells and all, in your fruit mixture.

MARASCHINO CHERRIES

MAKES ABOUT 4 HALF-PINTS MARASCHINO CHERRIES
(AND ABOUT 2 CUPS SYRUP)

ORIGINALLY, MARASCHINO CHERRIES were Marasca cherries—a small Morello type that grow in Italy and Croatia—preserved in maraschino liqueur, a clear liqueur distilled from the same cherries and flavored with their crushed pits. What Americans now call maraschino cherries were developed in the 1920s by Ernest H. Wiegand of Oregon Agricultural College (now Oregon State University, or OSU) as a way of using locally grown Royal Anne cherries to make a similar preserve. Maraschino cherries couldn't be imported during Prohibition, and domestic cherries couldn't legally be preserved in alcohol. Besides, Oregon's big, fleshy Royal Annes got soft and shriveled in alcohol. So Wiegand put them into a brine solution, added red dye because Royal Annes are yellowish, and used almond extract instead of the cherries' own bitter-almond-flavored pits. (In 2000 the maraschino cherry was named the official fruit of OSU—to the chagrin, perhaps, of the many outstanding fruit breeders who have worked at the university.)

OSU researchers later developed this three-day method for a homemade version of factory-style maraschino cherries. The cherries turn out a little softer than their commercial counterparts (especially if you leave out the alum, a firming agent that is available in pharmacies), but the process is quicker than the commercial one. You might substitute other sweet cherries in this recipe, particularly if you'd like to leave out the food coloring, but they will likely turn out softer and darker.

2¼ pounds Royal Anne cherries, pitted (page 94)

2 tablespoons salt

1 teaspoon alum (optional)

1 quart plus 1½ cups water

4½ cups sugar

1 tablespoon red food coloring

2 tablespoons strained lemon juice

1 tablespoon almond extract

1. Put the cherries into a nonreactive bowl. Stir the salt and the alum, if you are using it, into 1 quart of the water, and pour the brine over the cherries. Let them stand for 8 to 12 hours.

2. Drain the cherries and thoroughly rinse them with cold water. Put them into a preserving pan. Add the sugar, the 1½ cups water, and the red food coloring. Heat the mixture over medium heat, stirring occasionally, until the sugar dissolves, and then raise the heat to medium-high and bring the mixture to a boil. Immediately remove the pan from the heat. Let it stand at room temperature for 24 hours.

3. Bring the mixture to a boil again. Remove the pan from the heat, and let it stand at room temperature for another 24 hours.

4. Add the lemon juice and almond extract to the pan. Bring the mixture to a boil and remove it from the heat.

5. Fill half-pint mason jars with the cherries and syrup to cover them. (You'll have leftover syrup; save it for cold drinks.) Add lids and rings, and process the jars for 10 minutes in a boiling-water bath.

COCONUT

Coconut-Caramel Jam   108

T HE COCONUT PALM is "the most useful tree in the world," according to Alan Davidson (*The Oxford Companion to Food*). "It provides not only food and drink, but also vessels to serve them in and fuel to cook them, as well as textile fibre, thatching and basket materials, timber, medicines, chemicals, and many other useful products."

The coconut palm thrives on sandy shorelines in humid tropical regions. It probably originated in the Malay Archipelago or South Pacific, and it may have spread from shore to shore partially on its own, since a coconut can float long distances and then germinate after being washed ashore. The tree came to the New World, though, on Spanish and Portuguese ships. Today many countries around the globe grow coconuts for processing and export. In Florida, coconuts are grown for their tropical appearance and for home use, although they have little commercial importance.

The coconut sold green or ripe in supermarkets is the stone of the fruit; the husk is removed before shipping. The green fruit, full of thirst-quenching, mildly sweet liquid, is often served as a drink and bowl in one, called *coco frío* in Spanish-speaking countries. The ripe fruit contains a little liquid along with its firm white flesh. Coconut milk is made from this flesh, by pouring boiling water over it and squeezing it. Commercially, the flesh is pulped and dried to make shredded or flaked coconut for cakes and confections. Fresh or dried coconut is also pressed to make cooking oil.

You'll need just one ripe coconut to make a heavenly jam with the recipe that follows.

COCONUT-CARAMEL JAM

MAKES ABOUT 1½ PINTS

I F YOU'RE NOT FROM THE TROPICS, extracting the meat from a fresh coconut can be intimidating. But the method described here makes the job safe and easy; heating the coconut in the oven both cracks its shell and makes the skin on the meat easy to remove with a vegetable peeler.

For anyone who likes coconut, a small scoop of this jam makes an irresistible dessert. The jam also makes a delightful filling for cakes and pastries.

> 1 medium-size coconut
> 2 cups sugar
> ¼ cup water
> 1 teaspoon vanilla extract

1 Preheat the oven to 375°F.

2 Pierce the "eyes" of the coconut with an ice pick, metal skewer, or similar sharp object. Drain the coconut liquid into a cup or bowl, and sniff or taste the liquid to be sure the coconut hasn't soured. If the liquid is sweet, strain it into a measuring cup. Add water, if necessary, to make 1 cup.

3 Place the coconut in the oven and leave it for about 25 minutes, or until the shell has cracked.

4 Take the coconut out of the oven and tap it all over with a hammer. Then give the coconut a hard whack. With a vegetable peeler, peel the brown skin off the meat. Cut the meat into small chunks. Combine them in a blender with the coconut liquid and blend until the coconut appears grated; you may need to do this in two or three batches. As an alternative, you can grate the coconut by hand and then combine it with the liquid.

5 Combine the coconut in a kettle with 1 cup of the sugar. Over medium heat, stirring, bring the mixture to a boil. Let it simmer for 10 minutes, stirring occasionally, and remove the kettle from the heat.

6 Make the caramel: Stir together the water and remaining 1 cup sugar in a pint measure. Heat the mixture in a microwave oven on high for 5 minutes, and then continue heating in 1-minute increments until the syrup turns golden. Heat it some more, in shorter increments, until it turns a deep amber. Immediately stir the caramel into the hot coconut mixture.

7 Return the kettle to the heat. Over medium-low heat, simmer the mixture, stirring frequently, for about 20 minutes, until it is quite thick and almost all of the liquid has evaporated. Remove the kettle from the heat, and stir in the vanilla extract.

8 Pack the jam firmly into one or more jars. Cap the jars tightly. When they have cooled, store them in the refrigerator.

CRANBERRY

Simple Cranberry Sauce   111

Cranberry-Quince Jelly   112

Cranberry Jam   113

Cranberry Marmalade   114

Cranberry-Quince Preserves   115

Brandied Cranberry Preserves   116

Candied Cranberries and
    Clear Cranberry Syrup   117

A S EVERY AMERICAN SCHOOLCHILD KNOWS, this low-growing evergreen shrub, *Vaccinium macrocarpon*, is native to North American bogs. Early European settlers apparently named it for cranes, either because the flowers resembled the birds or because cranes liked the fruit.

Commercially, cranberries are grown in wetlands in large beds, which are flooded to facilitate harvest. Cranberries are a major commercial crop in New England, New Jersey, the Pacific Northwest, the Great Lakes region, and several Canadian provinces. Because the berries ripen in the fall, they appear in stores just in time for Thanksgiving.

The cranberry has several special characteristics: It is high in acid (including ascorbic acid, or vitamin C), low in sugar, and high in a kind of pectin that gels with low levels of both sugar and heat. Its juice makes a good dye for fiber and food. Cranberries may be an effective remedy for urinary tract infections, and they contain a substance that inhibits the growth of *Streptococcus mutans*, the primary cause of dental plaque. Finally, cranberries keep extraordinarily well. You can refrigerate them for weeks or freeze them for months. Russian cooks sometimes preserve them in water alone.

Closely related to the cranberry is the lingonberry, or cowberry (the entire *Vaccinium* genus is named for the cow, *vacca* in Latin, presumably because cattle like these plants). This small dry-land berry, native to northern forests of Europe, Asia, and North America, is now commercially grown in the Pacific Northwest. To me lingonberries taste just like cranberries. You can use them in the same ways.

Before using cranberries, spread them out in a tray and pick out any that are soft or shriveled. Rinse and drain the good berries.

SIMPLE CRANBERRY SAUCE

MAKES ABOUT 2¼ CUPS

THIS IS THE SAUCE usually served with Thanksgiving turkey. If you have in the past bought canned cranberry sauce, you may not bother again once you know how easy it is to make your own.

> 1 cup water
> 12 ounces cranberries
> 1 cup sugar

1. In a saucepan, bring the water to a boil. Remove the pan from the heat and stir in the cranberries and sugar. Over medium-high heat, cook the mixture, uncovered, stirring occasionally, for about 10 minutes. You may notice a popping sound as the cranberries burst their skins. When the mixture has a jam-like consistency, remove the pan from the heat.

2. Serve the sauce hot, at room temperature, or chilled. It will keep in the refrigerator, tightly covered, for several weeks or longer.

CRANBERRY-QUINCE JELLY

MAKES ABOUT 3 HALF-PINTS

 ART CRANBERRIES AND TART QUINCES combine well in a jelly for the Thanksgiving table.

12 ounces cranberries
1 pound unpeeled, uncored quinces, finely chopped
2 cups water
About 2 cups sugar

1. Combine the cranberries, quinces, and water in a kettle or large saucepan. Bring the contents to a boil, cover the pan, and simmer the fruit for about 10 minutes. Mash the berries with a potato masher and simmer the fruit, covered, for about 5 minutes more, until it is quite tender. Drain the juice through a damp jelly bag for at least 6 hours.

2. Measure the juice and pour it into a preserving pan. For each cup of juice, add an equal volume of sugar. Stir the contents over medium heat until the sugar dissolves. Raise the heat to medium-high and boil the jelly until it passes the spoon test (page 18).

3. Pour the jelly into half-pint mason jars, and add lids and rings. Process the jars in a boiling-water bath for 10 minutes.

CRANBERRY JAM

MAKES ABOUT 1½ PINTS

T HIS JAM DIFFERS from Simple Cranberry Sauce (page 111) in that flavorings are added and the cranberries are seeded and pureed. With no graininess to guide them, your friends may not recognize the fruit in this jam, but they will love it anyway.

12 ounces cranberries

1½ cups water

4 thin crosswise slices tangerine or orange (unpeeled)

2 tablespoons chopped fresh ginger

1 cinnamon stick

2 cups sugar

1 Put the cranberries into a saucepan with the water, the tangerine or orange slices, and, in a spice bag, the ginger and cinnamon stick. Over medium-high heat, bring the contents to a boil. Reduce the heat, cover the pan, and simmer the contents for about 10 minutes, until the berries are soft. Remove the pan from the heat. Press the spice bag against the side of the pan, and remove the bag.

2 Put the berries through the fine screen of a food mill and then force the puree through a very-fine-mesh sieve to remove the cranberry seeds. You should end up with about 2⅓ cups puree.

3 Return the puree to the saucepan. Over medium heat, bring the puree to a boil. Remove the pan from the heat and stir in the sugar. Heat the mixture over medium heat, stirring, until the sugar is dissolved, and then raise the heat to medium-high. Boil the jam, stirring constantly, until a drop of the jam mounds in a chilled dish.

4 Ladle the jam into pint or half-pint mason jars, and add lids and rings. Process the jars for 10 minutes in a boiling-water bath.

CRANBERRY MARMALADE

 ERE ORANGE ZEST adds texture and a little bitterness to this lovely preserve.

12 ounces cranberries
Zest of 1 orange, in thin shreds
1½ cups water
1½ cups sugar

1. In a saucepan, combine the cranberries, orange zest, and water. Bring the mixture to a boil, and then reduce the heat. Simmer the mixture for 5 minutes. Remove the pan from the heat and stir in the sugar. Place the pan over medium heat and stir the contents until the sugar dissolves. Increase the heat to medium-high and boil the marmalade until a drop mounds in a chilled dish.

2. Ladle the marmalade into pint or half-pint mason jars, and add lids and rings. Process the jars for 10 minutes in a boiling-water bath.

HIGHBUSH CRANBERRIES

Unrelated to the true cranberry is the American highbush cranberry, *Viburnum trilobum*. This medium-large shrub, whose leaves turn a beautiful red in autumn, produces sour red berries high in pectin, although to me they don't look or taste much like cranberries. They are picked slightly underripe for sauce or jelly.

Another species of *Viburnum*, European highbush cranberry, looks much like American highbush cranberry but produces bitter, unpleasant-tasting fruit and less fall color.

CRANBERRY-QUINCE PRESERVES

Q UINCES RIPEN IN MID-AUTUMN, so it is natural to combine them with cranberries at the Thanksgiving table. This is a lovely alternative to Simple Cranberry Sauce (page 111).

1½ cups sugar

1½ cups water

½ pound (1 large) peeled and cored quince,
    cut into small cubes

12 ounces cranberries

1   In a preserving pan or large saucepan, combine the sugar and water. Bring the mixture to a boil, and then add the quince. Simmer for about 1 hour, until the syrup thickens and turns red.

2   Add the cranberries to the pan. Simmer the mixture, stirring occasionally and gently, until the berries are tender and the preserves have thickened to your liking.

3   Ladle the preserves into pint or half-pint mason jars, and add lids and rings. Process the jars for 10 minutes in a boiling-water bath.

BRANDIED CRANBERRY PRESERVES

WHEN MAKING PRESERVES, it's often easier to keep the temperature low and even—and thereby keep tender fruit intact—by using an oven, as in this recipe, rather than a stovetop. Brandied cranberries make treasured holiday gifts, and they are as delicious over ice cream or cake as they are with roast poultry or pork.

> 12 ounces cranberries
> 2 cinnamon sticks
> Zest of 1 orange, in thin shreds
> 1½ cups sugar
> ⅓ cup brandy or Grand Marnier

1 Spread the cranberries in an ovenproof 8 x 11-inch pan and nestle the cinnamon sticks among them. Sprinkle the orange zest and sugar over the cranberries and pour the brandy over all. Tightly cover the pan with aluminum foil and put the pan into an oven heated to 250°F (preheating isn't necessary).

2 After 30 minutes, gently stir the berries. Replace the foil and continue to cook the mixture for another 30 minutes, or until the berries are tender.

3 Store the cooled preserves in a covered container in the refrigerator, where they will keep, tightly covered, for at least several weeks. Or ladle them hot into pint or half-pint mason jars, add lids and rings, and process the jars for 10 minutes in a boiling-water bath.

CANDIED CRANBERRIES AND CLEAR CRANBERRY SYRUP

MAKES ABOUT 1½ CUPS CANDIED CRANBERRIES
(AND ABOUT 1 CUP SYRUP)

YOU CAN BUY CANDIED CRANBERRIES in any supermarket, but you probably won't find cranberry syrup on the shelves. Mix your homemade syrup with plain water or soda water for a refreshing drink, or serve it over ice cream or cake. This candying method is much simpler than others.

> 12 ounces cranberries
> 1 cup water
> 2 cups sugar

1. Combine the cranberries, water, and sugar in a flat-bottomed glass or ceramic heatproof dish that will fit into your steamer (I use a ceramic tart pan in a bamboo steamer set over a wok). Stir the berries gently and then steam them for 45 minutes.

2. Remove the dish from the steamer and let the berries cool. Stir them gently. Cover the dish with plastic wrap and let it stand at room temperature for 4 days, stirring occasionally.

3. With a slotted spoon, transfer the berries to a colander. Rinse the berries briefly in cold water and let them drain. Strain the syrup into a saucepan, bring the syrup to a boil, and pour it into a half-pint jar. Cap the jar tightly. When the jar cools, store it in the refrigerator.

4. Dry the berries on a rack in a food dehydrator or another warm place until they are no longer moist but still pliable. In a dehydrator, this will take no more than a day. Store the dried cranberries in an airtight container in a cool, dry place.

CURRANT

Red, White, or Black Currant Juice   120

Red Currant Jelly   121

Red or White Currant Preserves   123

Black Currant Jam   124

Black Currant Cordial   125

Raw Black Currant Jam   126

FRESH CURRANTS, small berries in the genus *Ribes*, are quite different from the little raisins that bear the same name. Both are named for tiny black grapes from Corinth, in ancient Greece. But fresh currants grow not on vines but on shrubs, and these shrubs are indigenous mainly to cooler climes. There are native species of currants in North America, Asia, Europe, and even Africa. Garden varieties are mainly European; they include *Ribes nigrum* (black currant) and *Ribes rubrum* (red currant). The white currant, botanically, is a red currant that has lost its pigmentation. Also popular among gardeners is the Jostaberry, a vigorous, disease-resistant black currant–gooseberry cross developed in 1977. Currants have been extensively bred in England, Scandinavia, Germany, the Netherlands, and elsewhere in Europe, and today many varieties are available that bear sweet, flavorful, and relatively large fruit.

Most Americans have never tasted a currant. This wasn't always so; until the early 1900s, currants were common garden plants in the United States. But then many states and the federal government outlawed the cultivation of all plants in the genus *Ribes*, on the grounds that they can serve as alternate hosts for a disease called white pine blister rust, which infects five-needled pine trees. Eventually, however, someone noticed that *Ribes* species grow wild in woodlands over much of the continent, and that these wild shrubs pose a greater threat to commercial foresters than plants on the farm or in the garden. So in 1966 the federal government removed its ban on currant and gooseberry growing, and since then most states have legalized the plants.

Sprightly flavored red and white currants hang in clusters like translucent beads. They ripen in midsummer, and for jelly they should be picked then, when their pectin content is high, although they will keep well on the bush for several weeks. Because of their high levels of pectin and acid, currants are often combined with other fruits in jams, jellies, and preserves. They are also valued for wine, sauces, and pie fillings.

As northern and eastern Europeans have long believed, black currants are a nutrient-rich food and powerful medicine. They have at least three times as much vitamin C, potassium, and magnesium as blueberries, four to six times as much calcium, and much more zinc, iron, folic acid, vitamin A, and flavenoids. Black currants have been shown to relieve vision problems and inflammation, stimulate the immune system, and fight fungal and viral infections. Even black currant seeds can be valuable in the diet; because of their high levels of essential fatty acids, minerals, and fiber, they have been crushed and incorporated into packaged breakfast cereal.

In preserving, black currants can be used in the same ways as red and white currants. They are especially appreciated in syrups and drinks as winter cold remedies and summer refreshments. In Burgundy, France, they are grown extensively to make crème de cassis.

Currants are very hardy and easy to grow. They aren't nearly as thirsty as blueberries, they apparently have no appeal for birds, and they do well in partial shade (I am growing some between rows in my orchard). Aphids love red currant leaves but seem to do little harm to the plant. Currant borers are a more serious pest, but they have failed to kill my plants. Currants are easily propagated from cuttings or by layering, so you can have many plants at little cost, provided you can resist buying new varieties every year.

For other recipes using currants, see Blackberry–Black Currant Jam (page 66), Cherry-Currant Preserves (page 97), Cherry-Currant Jam (page 98), and Raspberry–Red Currant Jam (page 313).

RED, WHITE, OR BLACK CURRANT JUICE

I FIND IT EASIEST to make currant juice with a steam juicer (page 14). If you don't have one, use this recipe as a first step in making currant jelly or cordial.

Some cooks say to stem currants before making them into juice; others say stemming is unnecessary. Perhaps the stems add a subtle flavor that some people don't like. I compromise by removing the large stems and leaving the tiny ones.

Red, white, or black currants, unstemmed
½ cup water for each pound of currants

1 Combine the currants and water in a kettle or large saucepan, cover the pan, and set it over low heat. Simmer the currants for 30 minutes, mashing them occasionally with a potato masher or the back of a wooden spoon. Drain the juice through a damp jelly bag for at least 6 hours. Do not squeeze the bag. If the juice isn't completely clear, empty the jelly bag, rinse the bag, and pour the juice through the bag again. For each pound of fruit, you should get about ¾ cup juice.

2 Store the juice in a covered container in the refrigerator if you'll be using it soon; otherwise, pour it into mason jars, add lids and rings, and process the jars for 10 minutes in a boiling-water bath.

FOR BLACK CURRANT CORDIAL (PAGE 125), a clear juice isn't necessary. In this case, you can squeeze the jelly bag both to speed its drainage and to extract as much juice as possible.

RED CURRANT JELLY

MAKES 2 TO 3 HALF-PINTS

THIS IS THE BRIGHT, clear red jelly that is melted and spread over fruit tarts or used for dipping whole large strawberries. Currant jelly is easy to make, since you don't need to remove the fruit from its delicate stems.

You can use the same recipe with white currants, although the jelly won't have the beautiful crimson color.

3 cups red currant juice (opposite page)
3 cups sugar

1 Combine the juice and sugar in a preserving pan. Heat the contents over medium heat until the sugar is completely dissolved.

CUMBERLAND SAUCE

The spicy flavor of red currants makes them a good match for savory foods. For 150 years, the English have been making their red currant jelly into Cumberland sauce, an accompaniment to meat and fried potatoes. To make Cumberland sauce, heat ¼ cup red currant jelly along with the thinly shredded zest of 2 oranges, 1 teaspoon Dijon mustard, a little salt and pepper, and, if you like, ground ginger. When the jelly melts, stir in ½ cup tawny port. Cook the sauce for 10 minutes more. Serve it cold.

Raise the heat to medium-high and boil the jelly until it passes the spoon test (page 18). Remove the pan from the heat.

2 Pour the jelly into half-pint mason jars. Add lids and rings, and process the jars for 10 minutes in a boiling-water bath.

BLACK CURRANT JELLY WITH PORT

To make black currant jelly, simply substitute black currants for the red ones. If you like, deepen the already rich flavor by adding 1 tablespoon tawny port for each cup of currant juice. Stir in the port when the setting point has been reached and the boiling has stopped.

BAR-LE-DUC PRESERVES

Bar-le-Duc is a town in Lorraine, France, that has been famous for its red and white currant preserves since the fourteenth century. The most costly of these preserves are seeded currants suspended like tiny jewels in syrup. How do you seed a currant? You cut the tip of a goose quill at a slant, and with this tool you very carefully incise the currant and extract, on average, seven seeds, without damaging the appearance of the fruit. According to the manufacturer, this work, a tradition passed from mother to daughter, requires the fingers of a fairy, the eyes of a lynx, and the patience of an angel.

RED OR WHITE CURRANT PRESERVES

MAKES ABOUT 2 PINTS

URRANT JAM OR PRESERVES can be more work to make than currant jelly, since for jam or preserves you must remove each tiny fruit from its stem. If the currants are all whole and unseeded, you may find you don't like the seedy texture anyway. I've compromised here by using some whole currants combined with currant juice.

2½ cups red or white currant juice (page 120)
1 pound stemmed red or white currants
3 cups sugar

1 Combine all of the ingredients in a preserving pan, and set the pan over medium heat. Heat the mixture, stirring no more than necessary, until the sugar is completely dissolved. Raise the heat to medium-high and boil the mixture until it passes the spoon test (page 18).

2 Let the preserves cool for a few minutes, give them a stir, and then ladle them into pint or half-pint mason jars. Add lids and rings, and process the jars for 10 minutes in a boiling-water bath.

BLACK CURRANT JAM

B LACK CURRANT JAM has a wonderfully strong, tart flavor, but the texture is unpleasant unless you remove the blossom ends of the currants. For an even smoother jam, remove some or all of the seeds by pressing the jam through the fine screen of a food mill.

2 pounds black currants
1 cup water
3 cups sugar

1 Stem the currants and snip off the blossom ends. Combine the currants with the water in a preserving pan. Cover the pan and simmer the currants for 20 minutes, or until they are quite tender.

2 Remove the pan from the heat and stir in the sugar. Heat the mixture over medium heat, stirring, until the sugar is completely dissolved. Raise the heat to medium-high and boil the mixture until a drop mounds in a chilled dish.

3 Ladle the jam into pint or half-pint mason jars, and add lids and rings. Process the jars for 10 minutes in a boiling-water bath.

BLACK CURRANT
CORDIAL

B LACK CURRANT JUICE is too strong-flavored to drink undiluted. For a refreshing hot-weather drink, mix one part of this concentrate with two parts chilled plain water or soda water. Try the concentrate also over cheese or ice cream.

As a remedy for winter colds, substitute honey for sugar in this recipe, and drink a little of the syrup, undiluted, to soothe a sore throat or relieve a cough.

Sugar
Strained lemon juice
Black currant juice (page 120)

1 Stir ½ cup sugar and 3 tablespoons lemon juice into each pint of black currant juice. Heat the mixture to a boil and boil it for 1 minute.

2 Pour the mixture into pint or quart mason jars. Add lids and rings, and process the jars for 10 minutes in a boiling-water bath.

RAW BLACK CURRANT JAM

T O RETAIN THE HIGH vitamin C content of black currants, preserve them raw, as Russians and other Eastern Europeans have long done.

¾ pound black currants, stemmed
1½ cups sugar

1 Blend the currants and sugar in a food processor or blender. Pack the jam into a jar and tightly cap it.

2 Store the jar in refrigerator. Provided your berries were fresh-picked and free from mold, the jam should keep for several weeks.

EGGPLANT

Eggplant Preserves   128

You wouldn't know it from shopping in a typical American supermarket, but eggplants come in a variety of sizes, from quail-egg to ostrich-egg size, and a variety of shapes, from a ball to a long, narrow cylinder. Eggplants vary in color, too, at least as much as do birds' eggs—from green to white to pink to purple to bicolored striped. The best eggplants, in my opinion, are the Japanese, Chinese, and Italian varieties. Usually more or less cylindrical, these tend to have the smallest seeds and the least bitterness.

If local markets don't offer good, fresh eggplants of the varieties you prefer, I hope you'll grow your own from seed. Start them when you start peppers or a little earlier, and set them out when the soil has warmed. They will grow about as tall and wide as pepper plants, but they will be more vulnerable to insects, especially flea beetles, so check your plants often to ensure a good harvest.

Whether or not you grow your own eggplants, and whatever their variety, be sure that you pick them or buy them when they are firm and shiny, and use them promptly. Dull-looking, soft, or spotted eggplants are past their prime.

EGGPLANT
PRESERVES

MAKES 3 TO 3½ PINTS

WHEN MY GARDEN PRODUCES too many eggplants to eat right away, I usually pickle the excess. But here is another good way to preserve the fruits, especially if members of your family don't like eggplant. Take the label off a jar of these preserves, and your family will happily eat eggplant without knowing it.

Many people dislike eggplant because some varieties are bitter, especially when they are overripe. The bitterness is usually removed or reduced either by salting and draining the eggplant or by piercing it and roasting it until it is very soft. This recipe uses a third technique, blanching and draining.

I've based this recipe loosely on one I found in a Spanish cookbook written by a Frenchman, but I suspect that the original version was from southeastern Europe or the Near East. The honey is added at the end of cooking to preserve its delicate flavor. The sesame seeds are a kind of culinary joke: They look like eggplant seeds but have their own rich, toasty flavor. Try these preserves on crisp bread or crackers with cultured butter, soft cheese, or cream cheese.

2¾ pounds eggplants, peeled and cut into ⅜-inch cubes

4½ cups sugar

Zest of 1 lemon

¼ cup strained lemon juice

1 teaspoon grated fresh ginger

2 tablespoons sesame seeds, toasted

2 tablespoons honey

1. In a big pot of boiling water, blanch the eggplant cubes in two batches for 3 minutes or until they are tender. Drain them in a colander and press them gently with a wooden spoon to remove much of their juice.

2. In a preserving pan, combine the drained eggplant cubes and the sugar. Stir gently. Let the mixture stand for about 2 hours, stirring once or twice, until the sugar is dissolved.

3. Stir the lemon zest, lemon juice, and ginger into the eggplant mixture. Cook the mixture over medium heat, stirring gently, until it is quite thick, about 15 minutes.

4. Stir in the sesame seeds and honey and remove the pan from the heat. Pack the preserves into pint or half-pint mason jars. Add lids and rings, and process the jars in a boiling-water bath for 10 minutes.

ELDERBERRY

Elderberry Jam   132

Elderberry Juice   133

Elderberry Jelly   134

Elderberry-Apple Jelly   135

Elderberry Rob   136

Raw Elderberry Syrup   137

A SHRUB NATIVE to both Europe and North America, the elder, *Sambucus*, is a once-treasured plant deserving renewed attention. The European legends and superstitions involving the elder are too numerous to summarize here, but they indicate that the plant provided powerful medicine in past centuries. Elder flowers have been used as an astringent, elder leaves in emollients and as an insect repellent. European elderberries have been used for treating colds, influenza, edema, insomnia, migraines, and rheumatism. The medicinal powers of the elder are mostly unproven, and in fact most parts of the plant are known to be somewhat toxic. But European elderberries are undoubtedly nutritious as well as tasty; like black currants, they are rich in vitamin C and other antioxidants. The plant has other benefits, too. Both European and American elders tend to form thickets and so make good hedgerows. They provide food and cover for wildlife and windbreaks for farms. Elder flowers are dipped in batter and fried and used to flavor preserves of other fruits. The berries make fine wine, pies, and candy as well as jam, jelly, and syrup. Last but not least, the tree is said to repel witches!

You may encounter any of four species of *Sambucus:*

S. nigra is the European black elder. North American nurseries are now stocking *S. nigra* cultivars with purple, gold, or variegated foliage as well as others developed for their large, tasty fruit.

Native to North America east of the Rockies is *S. canadensis*, the American black elder. The plant looks very much like its typical European counterpart, and the berries taste very similar and may have the same health-promoting properties. Through elderberry-breeding programs in New York, Pennsylvania, and Nova Scotia, cultivars such as York, Nova, Adams, Scotia, and Kent have been developed for flavor and large flower and fruit clusters. To me, my Nova elderberries taste much like black nightshade berries (page 161).

My favorite elder is *S. caerulea*, blue elder. Native to the western United States, it has blue berries with a whitish bloom. Although no garden cultivars are available, I think these are the tastiest elderberries. Blue elderberries look pale when raw, but when cooked into preserves they are nearly as dark as black elderberries.

Native to damp areas of the Pacific Northwest is *S. racemosa*, red elder. The flowers are very aromatic, and the small, seedy berries are a bright orange-red. Eaten raw, the berries are said to cause nausea, and some people consider them toxic in any form, yet they were once an important food for Native Americans. The berries are apparently harmless when cooked, and they are said to have antiviral powers. Today they are used for wine and jelly.

All elderberries are attractive to birds, so pick them as soon as they ripen.

A MYSTERIOUS NAME

The generic name *Sambucus* has nothing to do with the Italian liqueur Sambuca, which is flavored with anise, but may have something to do with the triangular stringed instrument that the ancient Romans called *sambuca* and that has since been called the *sackbut*. Perhaps sackbuts were once made of elder wood, although elder, with its hollow stems, has been more often made into wind instruments. Or maybe the *sambuca* was so named because it sounded as shrill as an elder whistle.

ELDERBERRY JAM

I FIRST MADE THIS JAM with blue elderberries, from a tree my daughter spotted in the parking lot of a Salvation Army store. The elder was growing through a crack in the asphalt beside a concrete ramp that led to nothing and only a few yards from a railroad track. But beautiful bunches of frosted blue berries hung from the branches.

If you don't have elderberries in your garden, go looking in late summer for a weed tree of either blue or black elder. Get the berries before the birds do!

> 2 pounds stemmed blue or black elderberries
> 3 cups sugar
> 3 tablespoons lemon juice

1 In a preserving pan, heat the elderberries over low heat, crushing them with the back of a wooden spoon or with a potato masher. When their juice begins to run, add 1 cup of the sugar. Stirring, bring the mixture to a simmer over medium-low heat.

2 Remove the pan from the heat and put the mixture through the fine screen of a food mill or a fine-mesh sieve to remove most of the seeds.

3 Put the berry puree back into the pan with the remaining 2 cups sugar and the lemon juice. Over medium-high heat, bring the mixture to a boil. Continue to boil it, stirring frequently, until a drop of the jam mounds in a chilled dish.

4 Ladle the jam into pint or half-pint mason jars. Add lids and rings, and process the jars for 10 minutes in a boiling-water bath.

ELDERBERRY JUICE

I T'S ESPECIALLY EASY to make elderberry juice with a steam juicer (page 14). If you don't have one, you can use this recipe as a first step in making elderberry jelly or syrup. Each pound of berries will make about ¾ cup juice.

Blue, black, or red elderberries, stemmed

1 Put the elderberries into a kettle or large saucepan, mash them with the back of a wooden spoon or with a potato masher, and cover the pan. Set it over low heat. Simmer the berries for about 15 minutes, until their juice runs.

2 Drain the juice through a damp jelly bag. If you're making syrup, squeeze the jelly bag both to speed its drainage and to extract as much juice as possible. If you're making jelly, don't squeeze the bag.

ELDERBERRY JELLY

I HAD TROUBLE GETTING elderberry jelly to gel when I used old recipes, which call for adding water. But the jelly gels beautifully when I use undiluted juice from just-ripe berries. I love the rich, wine-like flavor of this jelly.

3 cups Elderberry Juice (page 133)
2 tablespoons strained lemon juice
2¼ cups sugar

1 Combine all of the ingredients in a preserving pan. Over medium heat, heat the contents until the sugar is completely dissolved. Raise the heat to medium-high, and boil the jelly until it passes the spoon test (page 18).

2 Ladle the jelly into hot sterilized half-pint mason jars. Add lids and rings, and process the jars for 10 minutes in a boiling-water bath.

QUICK ELDERBERRY-APPLE JELLY

If you have Homemade Apple Pectin (page 17) on hand, you can make Elderberry-Apple Jelly by combining one part elderberry juice with one part Homemade Apple Pectin. Use 3 tablespoons strained lemon juice and 3 cups sugar for 4 cups combined juice.

ELDERBERRY-APPLE JELLY

ELDERBERRIES COMBINE WELL with other fruits that ripen at the same time. Instead of the apples called for here, you might use crabapples, red or black currants, or damson plums.

2 pounds tart apples, thinly sliced (unpeeled and uncored)
1½ pounds stemmed blue, black, or red elderberries, crushed
1 cup water
3 tablespoons strained lemon juice
About 3 cups sugar

1   Combine the apples, elderberries, and water in a preserving pan over medium heat. Cover the pan, bring the contents to a boil, and then simmer them until the apples are very soft.

2   Strain the mixture first through a colander and then through a damp jelly bag. Measure the juice. Return it to the pan with the lemon juice and 3 cups sugar for each 4 cups juice. Heat the mixture over medium heat until the sugar is completely dissolved, and then raise the heat to medium-high. Boil the mixture until it passes the spoon test (page 18). Remove the pan from the heat.

3   Immediately pour the jelly into hot sterilized half-pint mason jars. Add lids and rings, and process the jars for 10 minutes in a boiling-water bath.

ELDERBERRY
ROB

ROB IS AN OLD ENGLISH WORD, derived from Arabic, for a boiled-down fruit syrup, sometimes with honey or sugar added. Elderberry rob is believed to keep cold and flu viruses from replicating. Take a tablespoon or two in a cup of hot water.

Black elderberry juice
Sugar or honey

1. In a saucepan, combine equal volumes of elderberry juice and sugar or honey. Heat the contents over medium heat, stirring, until the sugar dissolves. Raise the heat to medium-high, and boil the mixture to a thick syrup.

2. Pour the rob into sterilized bottles, and cap or cork them tightly. Store the bottles in a cool, dark, dry place, where the rob should keep for at least a year.

RAW ELDERBERRY SYRUP

MAKES ABOUT 2 CUPS

THIS IS MY OWN VERSION of elderberry rob, although since the juice isn't cooked the syrup isn't rob at all, properly speaking. And because there is no cooking, the berries' nutrients are better preserved. Using honey instead of sugar also makes the syrup more healthful.

1 pound stemmed black elderberries
1 pound honey

1. Crush the berries lightly with a potato masher. Mix the berries and honey in a quart jar. Cover the jar tightly and let it stand for 2 weeks at room temperature. Shake the jar at least once a day.

2. Strain the syrup through cheesecloth or a fine-mesh sieve. Funnel the syrup into a sterilized bottle. Tightly cap or cork the bottle and store it in the refrigerator, where the syrup should keep well for several months. Use the berries, if you like, in pancakes or quick breads.

FEIJOA
(PINEAPPLE GUAVA)

Feijoa Jam   139

THIS SOUTH AMERICAN NATIVE thrives in coastal California, in New Zealand, and in other places with moderate summers and cool winters (but no cooler than about 15°F). The feijoa, or pineapple guava, is a slow-growing evergreen shrub that can reach 15 feet high and wide. With its leathery, silver-green foliage, the shrub makes a lovely hedge or windbreak, and when trained as a tree a feijoa can grow to 25 feet. The fruit varies considerably in size and shape but is generally comparable to a fuzzy kiwi or guava. The sweet, highly perfumed flesh reminds people of pineapple, guava, strawberry, or a combination of these. The skin is edible, and the seeds are barely noticeable.

I hope that in the future feijoa fruit will be available in markets. Until then, any fruit lover with the right growing conditions should consider planting this shrub.

FEIJOA JAM

AMONG ALL THE SHRUBS I've planted here in the Willamette Valley, feijoa is one of my favorites. In 13 years, however, my feijoa plants have produced ripe fruit only once; usually, heavy fall frosts destroy the fruit. So I've relied on my daughter, who forages for fruit on the campus of Mills College, to experiment with feijoa jam. This is her recipe.

This jam has a low sugar content, so you'll want to keep the jar in the refrigerator.

> 1 pound (about 3 cups) chopped feijoas
> 1 cup sugar

1. Put the fruit into a preserving pan or nonreactive skillet. Cover the pan and cook the fruit over medium-low heat until it is tender.

2. Remove the pan from the heat and stir in the sugar. Place the pan over medium heat and heat the mixture, stirring, until the sugar is dissolved. Raise the heat to medium-high and boil the jam, stirring often, until a drop of it mounds in a chilled dish.

3. Pour the jam into one or more jars and cap the jars tightly. When the jam has cooled, store the jars in the refrigerator, where the jam should keep well for a few months.

FIG

Fig Jam   142

Smooth Fig Jam   143

Low-Sugar Fig-Ginger Jam   144

Fig Preserves   146

Fig Preserves with Fennel and Bay   147

Whole Figs in Vanilla-Flavored Syrup   148

Fig-Almond Cake   148

AN OFTEN ENORMOUS TREE or shrub with big, tropical-looking leaves and a milky sap that irritates the skin, the fig was one of the earliest food plants cultivated by humans. In the eastern Mediterranean region and western Asia, archaeologists maintain, people have been growing figs for over 11,000 years. The trees are still an important food source throughout the Mediterranean region, and they are also popular in other regions of the world with mild winters and dry summers, such as Chile, Australia, South Africa, and California.

The fig is actually not a fruit at all but a *synconium*, a sort of hollow pod lined with hundreds of tiny flowers. If these flowers are to be pollinated, an insect must enter a tiny opening at the end of the synconium. The caprifig is pollinated by a tiny wasp, and the Smyrna fig needs cross-pollination by the caprifig. The San Pedro fig needs pollination for its second crop but not its first. Most garden varieties of fig need no pollination.

Depending on the cultivar, a fig tree can produce as many as three crops of synconia per year. Most produce two, when growing conditions are right: the breba, which grows on the preceding year's wood, and the main crop, which grows on the current year's wood (*breba* is a Spanish word from the Latin *bifera*, "twice-producing"). Ripening in midsummer, brebas tend to be larger and sweeter but far less numerous than the main-crop figs. Depending on the variety of fig tree and where it grows, the gardener may be able to harvest a breba crop, a main crop, or both.

For Californians, the most familiar fig cultivar is the Black Mission. Said to be native to the Balearic Islands, it was first planted in California by padres at Mission San Diego in the late 1700s and from there carried northward to the other Spanish missions. With purple-black fruits that are pink on the inside, these big, spreading trees grow well throughout much of the state and have prolific breba crops.

Best adapted to cooler areas such as the Pacific Northwest is the Desert King, a green-skinned, pink-fleshed, San Pedro–type fig that originated in Madera, California, around 1920. From my two Desert King trees I generally get a good breba crop, but the frost always hits long before the second crop ripens. One tree grows vigorously against the south side of the house, but because it is subject to spring frost damage there I grow it as a shrub, with three or four trunks. The other tree grows quite slowly but handsomely north of the house.

Other fig cultivars popular in the United States include Brown

SHOWING THE FIGS

An odd word in the English language is *sycophant*. Derived from Greek, the word refers to a defamer, toady, deceiver, or self-serving flatterer. In Greek, though, *sykophantēs* literally means "fig revealer." Plutarch said the term was applied by ancient Greeks to someone who informed against another for exporting figs illegally or stealing the fruit of sacred fig trees. Others have said that ancient Greek tax collectors were called sycophants because they publicly handed in the figs, wine, and oil that others paid in taxes. The *Oxford English Dictionary* suggests the term may refer to an obscene gesture but doesn't attempt to describe the gesture or its meaning. Others suggest that Greek informers may have waved a fig leaf.

FIG   141

Turkey, with purplish brown skin and pinkish flesh; Blanche (or Italian Honey or Lattarula), with yellow-green skin and very sweet white flesh; and Adriatic, with green skin and strawberry-colored flesh.

Figs do not ripen after harvest; they should be picked only when they have softened. If you won't be using picked figs immediately, refrigerate them for no longer than about two days.

Fresh figs generally require very little preparation. To make them into jam or preserves, cut away any remaining stem, and then simply chop or slice the rest of each fruit. Some varieties, I'm told, are best peeled, but these varieties aren't commonly grown in the United States. In my research I found numerous recipes that call for blanching whole figs before proceeding, but the only purpose I can guess for this step is to wash out any ants that may have crawled into the end of the fig. In my experience, ants usually enter only split or very ripe figs. If I suspect there may be ants in some of my figs, I halve these fruits before using them.

For other recipes using figs, see *Cogna* (page 175) and Peach-Fig Jam (page 233).

FIG JAM

MAKES ABOUT 2½ PINTS

WITHOUT EVEN LEMON as an added ingredient, this simple, chunky jam has a pure fig flavor. If you prefer a more complex flavor, add ½ teaspoon ground anise seed or cinnamon.

2 pounds chopped ripe figs
½ cup water
3 cups sugar

1. In a preserving pan, combine all of the ingredients. Stir over medium heat until the sugar is dissolved, and then raise the heat to medium-high. Boil the jam for about 10 minutes, stirring, until it has thickened.

2. Ladle the jam into pint or half-pint mason jars. Add lids and rings, and process the jars for 10 minutes in a boiling-water bath.

SMOOTH FIG JAM

MAKES ABOUT 2½ PINTS

YOU'LL WANT A SMOOTH JAM if you'll be using it to fill cookies or pastries.

2 pounds chopped ripe figs
½ cup water
3 cups sugar

1. Combine the figs and water in a preserving pan and set the pan over medium heat. Cook the figs, uncovered, until they are tender. Put them through the medium screen of a food mill.

2. Return the fig puree to the preserving pan and add the sugar. Stir the mixture over medium heat until the sugar dissolves. Raise the heat to medium-high and cook, stirring, until the jam has thickened and a drop mounds in a chilled dish.

3. Ladle the jam into pint or half-pint mason jars. Add lids and rings, and process them for 10 minutes in a boiling-water bath.

FIG   143

LOW-SUGAR FIG-GINGER JAM

G INGER PAIRS WELL with figs in this low-sugar, chunky jam. The recipe makes only one pint, so you can easily store the whole batch in the refrigerator. If you'd like to make enough to store in the pantry, you can double the recipe.

1 pound chopped ripe figs

1 cup sugar

3 tablespoons lemon juice

¼ cup chopped crystallized ginger, store-bought or
    homemade (page 165)

1 Combine all of the ingredients in a preserving pan and set the pan over medium heat. Stir until the sugar is dissolved, and then raise the heat to medium-high. Cook the mixture, stirring, until the jam has thickened and a drop mounds in a chilled dish.

2 Ladle the jam into 1 pint jar or 2 half-pint jars, and cap the jars tightly. After the jars have cooled, store them in the refrigerator, where the jam will keep well for months. For pantry storage, use mason jars, add lids and rings, and process the jars in a boiling-water bath for 10 minutes.

NO-SUGAR-ADDED FIG JAM

For the most wholesome filling for Fig Bars (opposite page), you can substitute pureed figs for the Smooth Fig Jam: Place 1 pint pureed figs in an 8-inch square pan and heat in a 250°F convection oven for about 3 hours, stirring at least once per hour.

FIG BARS

Makes about 2 dozen bars

If you like Fig Newtons, you'll love this homemade version. You can substitute whole-wheat pastry flour for all or part of the white flour, and another thick jam, such as Golden Quince Marmalade (page 302), for the fig jam.

¾ cup (1½ sticks) unsalted butter, softened

¾ cup light brown sugar

1 egg, separated

⅓ cup milk

1 teaspoon vanilla extract

2¾ cups unbleached all-purpose flour, plus more as needed

½ teaspoon salt

About 1 cup Smooth Fig Jam (page 143)

1. Preheat the oven to 350°F.

2. In a large bowl, cream the butter and sugar. Beat in the egg yolk. Beat the milk and vanilla into the butter-sugar-egg mixture, and then stir in the flour and salt. Add a bit more flour if the dough is sticky.

3. On a well-floured board, roll the dough into a 12 × 16-inch rectangle ⅛ inch thick and cut it into 4-inch-wide strips. Spoon jam down the length of each strip, 1 inch from one long and two short sides. Rub a little egg white along the short edges and the long edge farthest from the jam. Roll each strip from the jam side, press the ends together, and lay each strip seam-side down on an ungreased baking sheet.

4. Bake the strips for about 15 minutes, until they begin to brown at the ends. Cut them into 2-inch pieces while they are still hot. The bars will keep for a week at room temperature.

FIG   145

FIG PRESERVES

THESE PRESERVES turn out much like a jam but with larger pieces. For spicier preserves, heat 4 thin slices of fresh ginger or ½ teaspoon cloves in a spice bag, along with the fig mixture.

2 pounds just-ripe figs, quartered

2 cups sugar

⅓ cup strained lemon juice

1 In a preserving pan, layer the figs with the sugar and pour the lemon juice over. Let the pan stand for 8 to 12 hours at room temperature, until most of the sugar is dissolved.

2 Place the pan over medium-low heat. Cook the preserves, stirring only very occasionally and gently, until the figs are partially translucent and the syrup is slightly thickened, 30 to 40 minutes.

3 Ladle the preserves into pint or half-pint mason jars. Add lids and rings, and process the jars for 10 minutes in a boiling-water bath.

FIG CONSERVE

This is a slightly more complex version of Fig Preserves. Follow the directions above, but add the grated zest of 1 orange and ½ cup coarsely chopped toasted walnuts after 30 to 40 minutes of cooking, when the figs are partially translucent. Bring the preserves to a boil, and simmer them for 3 minutes more before ladling them into jars.

FIG PRESERVES WITH FENNEL AND BAY

MAKES ABOUT 3 PINTS

I'VE BASED THIS RECIPE on an Italian one that uses small, wild, whole peeled figs. Although my figs are large and need no peeling, the unusual seasonings complement their flavor well. I recently combined these preserves with some leftover pastry dough to make a delightful little tart.

2½ pounds just-ripe figs, halved
5 cups sugar
2 Mediterranean bay leaves
¼ teaspoon fennel seeds
Zest of 1 lemon, in thin shreds
3 tablespoons strained lemon juice

1. In a preserving pan, layer the fig halves with the sugar. Let the mixture stand for 12 to 24 hours at room temperature.

2. Place the pan over medium heat and add the remaining ingredients. Stir gently and occasionally until the sugar is completely dissolved. Raise the heat to medium-high and boil the preserves for about 5 minutes, until the syrup reaches the thread stage (page 18) or 230°F. Remove the pan from the heat and let the preserves cool for a few minutes.

3. Ladle the preserves into pint or half-pint mason jars, tearing the bay leaves to divide among the jars. Add lids and rings, and process the jars for 10 minutes in a boiling-water bath.

FIG   147

WHOLE FIGS IN VANILLA-FLAVORED SYRUP

MAKES ABOUT 2½ PINTS

 HESE ARE LOVELY served topped with fresh cream or sour cream or over ice cream, gelato, or rice pudding.

3 cups sugar
1½ cups water
½ vanilla bean
3 tablespoons strained lemon juice
2¼ pounds just-ripe figs
3 tablespoons rum (optional)

1. In a preserving pan, combine the sugar and water. Stirring occasionally, dissolve the sugar over low heat. Add the vanilla bean half, lemon juice, and figs. Cook the figs at a bare simmer for about 2 hours, occasionally turning them gently, until they look glossy and almost translucent.

2. Remove the pan from the heat, remove the vanilla bean, and let the figs cool 5 minutes. Add the rum, if you like. Ladle the figs into pint or half-pint mason jars and cover them with the syrup. Add lids and rings, and process the jars in a boiling-water bath for 10 minutes.

FIG-ALMOND CAKE

MAKES ABOUT 2 POUNDS

 CREATED THIS RECIPE in imitation of a similar preserve I encountered in Spain, although that was probably made with dried figs. I call this preserve a cake because of the grainy texture the nuts provide, but it can be used in the same ways as pastes made from quince and other fruits. On hikes and camping trips, the cake is a gourmet's energy bar.

You can leave out the honey if you prefer.

3 pounds figs, halved
3 tablespoons water
Pinch of fennel seeds
Grated zest of 1 lemon
1 cup honey
1 cup shelled almonds, finely chopped or ground
1 teaspoon ground cinnamon

1. If the figs are quite tender, skip to step 2. Otherwise, combine the figs and the water in a nonreactive kettle. Simmer the figs over low heat, covered, for about 10 minutes, until they are tender.

2. Puree the figs through the medium screen of a food mill. Return them to the kettle and add the fennel seeds and lemon zest. Cook the mixture over medium-low heat, stirring almost constantly to avoid splatters, until the mixture is very thick. This will take at least 40 minutes.

3. Stir in the honey, almonds, and cinnamon. Pour the mixture about ¾ inch thick into lightly oiled small, straight-sided dishes. Dry the cakes in the sun, in a food dehydrator, or in another warm place until their tops are no longer sticky, and then turn them out of the dishes and continue drying the cakes until none of their surfaces are sticky. This may take a week or longer.

4. Wrap the cakes in plastic and store them in a heavy-duty plastic bag in the refrigerator, where they should keep for several months.

FIG   149

FLOWERS

Rose Petal Jelly   152

Rose Petal Preserves   153

Rose Petal Syrup   155

Rose Hip Butter   156

Rose Hip Syrup   158

Violet Syrup   159

MANY FRAGRANT FLOWERS have been used for food and medicine. *Martha Washington's Booke of Cookery* has recipes for the blossoms of rose, violet, borage, rosemary, chicory, and gillyflower (clove-scented carnation). Jasmine and orange-flower blossoms are used in Chinese kitchens, and elder flowers sometimes flavor English gooseberry jam. But two flowers are enduring favorites for use in sweet preserves: roses and violets. These two are represented here along with the fruit of the rose.

The cultivation of roses, like that of so many fruits, began in western Asia. Mesopotamians developed the distillation of rose water in the third and fourth centuries, and the Arabs were the first to use rose water for flavoring food. The Ottoman Turks introduced culinary uses for roses to Bulgaria (where the Valley of the Roses is still famed for its rose water, rose oil, and rose-petal preserves), and the Crusaders did the same for much of medieval Europe. Roses were believed to be strengthening to the heart, refreshing to the spirit, and cooling to the body.

In Europe, the culinary use of roses declined with the introduction of vanilla, and in the United States roses have never been a popular flavoring. (The recipes in Martha Washington's book were passed on to her from English ancestors. I haven't found any flower recipes in nineteenth-century American cookbooks.) But Italians love rose gelato; many pastry cooks in Europe and the United States candy rose petals; and rose-petal preserves are still prized in parts of Europe.

In the Middle East and India roses have never lost favor as a flavoring. Rose water often scents such foods as Turkish delight, baklava, halva, and lassi, and rose syrup is diluted to make a refreshing drink. On an Indian blog I found a recipe for diced watermelon flavored with rose syrup, combined with ice, and served in a glass.

Petals of the most fragrant rose varieties are collected for culinary uses. In Europe and western Asia, these varieties include *Rosa gallica*, which was cultivated as early as 1200 B.C. in Persia; *R. x damascena*, the hybrid damask rose; the climbing, musky scented *R. moschata*, the musk rose; and *R. centifolia*, the cabbage rose, a French hybrid developed for making rose oil. North Americans might also use *R. rugosa*, from Asia, as well as native roses such as *R. nutkana*, the nootka rose of the western United States, and *R. woodsii*.

Roses are also valued for their fruits, or hips, which are rich in vitamin C. According to Alan Davidson (*The Oxford Companion to Food*), English schoolchildren during World War II were sent to gather rose hips to make syrup, which was issued as a dietary supplement for small children and is still sold for feeding to babies. The rose varieties traditionally used for hips in Europe are the briar rose or dog rose, *R. canina*, which is native to Europe and parts of Africa and Asia and now grows wild over much of the United States, and the eglantine or sweetbriar rose, *R. eglanteria*, a native of Europe and western Asia that is now an invasive species in New Zealand and Australia. For rose butter or jam, I prefer *R. rugosa*, with its bigger hips.

Sweet violets, *Viola odorata*, were once believed effective for treating hoarseness, fever, and inflammation of all kinds. Violets are still valued in Europe for making aromatic blue syrup, violet water, and violet candies. A few French companies make violet syrup for sale internationally, but you can make your own if violets grow wild in your lawn or garden. One of the French syrup makers, Monin, suggests making iced violet tea (add a teaspoon or two of the syrup and a tablespoon of sugar to a glass of tea over ice) and stirring a little violet syrup into champagne. For best effect, garnish the champagne glass with a violet blossom.

Whether you collect rose blossoms, rose hips, or violet blossoms for preserving, do be sure the plants haven't been sprayed with pesticides.

For other recipes using rose petals, see Strawberry-Rose Preserves (page 331) and Rhubarb-Rose Preserves (page 323).

ROSE PETAL JELLY

....

MAKES ABOUT 4 HALF-PINTS

FOR THIS CLEAR RED, fragrant jelly I like to use pink rugosa roses or the heady-scented wild roses that grow along the roadsides here in western Oregon. Thankfully, the wild roses bloom before the county herbicide truck comes along, but I have planted some in my garden so they won't be contaminated by road dust. The pink moss roses in my garden also work well for jelly, but, unlike the wild roses and the rugosas, the moss roses lose their color with cooking, so I heat some barely scented red roses along with them. Even fragrant white roses work well when I add some red roses for color.

To pick rose petals, grasp the flower by the calyx with one hand and, with the other hand, pull out all the petals at once.

Try this jelly as a filling for almond or pistachio thumbprint cookies or sandwiched between shortbread cookies.

4 ounces (about 5 cups) fragrant pink or red rose petals

3 cups water

2 cups condensed apple juice (page 15)

3 cups sugar

¼ cup strained lemon juice

1. Combine the rose petals and water in a large saucepan. Simmer the rose petals, uncovered, for 15 minutes, stirring when the water gets hot to submerge all of the petals. Strain the liquid through a damp jelly bag. You should get about 3 cups.

2. In a preserving pan, combine the condensed apple juice and the rose water with the sugar and lemon juice. Bring the mixture to a boil over medium heat, stirring. Raise the heat to medium-high and boil the liquid until it passes the spoon test (page 18).

3. Pour the jelly into half-pint mason jars, and add lids and rings. Process the jars for 10 minutes in a boiling-water bath.

ROSE PETAL PRESERVES

MAKES ABOUT 3 HALF-PINTS

FOR THIS RECIPE your rose petals should be tender as well as fragrant and clean. If the rose variety you are using has petals that are thick and pale at the base, pull the petals from the calyx all at once, and hold their outer ends as you snip off the bases with scissors held in your other hand. Check for insects as you drop the blossoms into a bowl. (On my handwritten recipe is an old note in my daughter's childish script: "Stinkbugs don't add to the flavor.") If necessary, wash and dry the rose petals in a salad spinner.

The best roses for preserves, I've found, are wild ones, such as nootkas. It takes time to pick enough of their petals, in single whorls, to make preserves. Since you'll need about 10 cups, you might want to pick the blossoms over two or three days. They will keep this long in a plastic bag in the refrigerator. Rose Petal Preserves make a lovely topping for yogurt or vanilla ice cream as well as buttered toast.

8 ounces (about 10 cups) tender, fragrant pink or
   red rose petals
2 cups water
2 cups sugar
¼ cup strained lemon juice (seeds and pulp reserved)

1. Combine the rose petals and water in a kettle. Heat the contents over very low heat, covered, for 30 minutes.

2. Strain off the liquid, pressing the mass of petals with a large spoon to extract all of the liquid. You should end up with about 1 cup of liquid and 1 packed cup of rose petals.

3. Put the liquid into a preserving pan with the sugar and lemon juice. Heat the contents over medium heat, stirring, until all of the sugar has dissolved.

4. Raise the heat to medium-high. Put the lemon seeds and pulp into a spice bag. Stir the rose petals into the liquid in the pan, and add the spice bag. Boil the mixture rapidly until a drop mounds on a cold dish. Remove the pan from the heat.

5. Press the spice bag against the side of the pan, and remove the bag. Ladle the hot preserves into half-pint mason jars. Add lids and rings, and process the jars for 10 minutes in a boiling-water bath.

ROSE PETAL
SYRUP

A s with rose petal jelly (page 152) and Rose Petal Preserves (page 153), you'll want to use very fragrant, unsprayed roses to make this beautiful, clear red syrup. Then pour it over a cake or peeled peaches, dilute it with cold water to make a refreshing drink, or dribble it over vanilla ice cream and top with chopped nuts.

> 5 ounces (about 6 cups) fragrant pink or red rose petals
> 3½ cups water
> About 2¾ cups sugar

1 Combine the rose petals and water in a large saucepan set over medium heat. When the water gets hot, stir to submerge all of the petals. Bring the contents to a boil, and then reduce the heat and simmer the rose petals for 15 minutes.

2 Strain the rose water through a damp jelly bag and measure the volume of the liquid. Measure out an equal amount of sugar, and combine the rose water and sugar in the saucepan. Heat the mixture over medium heat until the sugar is completely dissolved, and then bring the syrup to a full boil.

3 Remove the pan from the heat. Let the syrup cool, and then store it in a tightly capped bottle in the refrigerator.

ROSE HIP
BUTTER

R OSE HIPS ARE OF COURSE FRUITS, not flowers, but I include them here because people generally grow roses for their blossoms. And I call this pretty red preserve butter rather than jam because, although it is cooked very quickly, it is thick and smooth like apple butter.

The best rose varieties for this recipe bear big, red fruits. Especially recommended are varieties of *Rosa rugosa*, a hardy native of Asian coasts whose fruits have been known in the Puget Sound region as "sea tomatoes" or "beach tomatoes" and in New England as "beach plums." Rugosa varieties, such as Rubra (red), Alba (white), and Frau Dagmar Hastrup (crimson) thrive without spraying in diverse growing conditions and so are ideal for organic gardens.

Many recipes for rose hip jam (or butter) advise picking the hips after the first frost. Frost may help convert starch to sugar in the fruit and thereby result in a clearer jelly or syrup. But for rose hip butter, at least, I recommend collecting your hips as they ripen instead of waiting until after a frost, when many of the fruits may have rotted away. Pick fruits that are bright red but still firm, because it's too hard to scoop the seeds from mushy hips.

If you want to make a lot of rose hip butter at once, you might pick the hips as they ripen during the summer, seed and freeze them until you're ready to use them, and then double or triple the quantities in this recipe. If you do this, of course, you'll probably want to process the jars in a boiling-water bath.

When you prepare your rose hips, don't worry about a few stray seeds; your main goal is to get out the many tiny hairs that grow around the seeds. Use a small spoon to scrape out the seeds and hairs together.

½ pound trimmed, halved, and seeded ripe rose hips
¾ cup water
About 1½ cups sugar

1. In a saucepan, combine the hips and water. Cover the pan, bring the contents to a boil, and simmer the hips until they are tender, 10 to 12 minutes.

2. Put the hips with their cooking liquid through the fine screen of a food mill. Measure the pulp; you should have about ¾ pound (or about 1½ cups).

3. For each ¼ pound (or ½ cup) of pulp, use ½ cup sugar. Stir the pulp and the sugar together in the saucepan. Heat them over low heat until the sugar is dissolved, stirring constantly, and then raise the heat to medium-high. Bring the mixture to a boil, still stirring constantly.

4. Remove the pan from the heat, and transfer the rose hip butter to a jar. Cap the jar tightly.

5. When the jar is cool, store it in the refrigerator, where it should keep well for several months.

ROSE HIP SYRUP

MAKES ABOUT 1¾ CUPS

THIS SYRUP IS MUCH EASIER to make than Rose Hip Butter (page 156), because you don't need to seed the hips. The syrup has been popular in the past as a health food, because rose hips are rich in vitamin C—many times richer in vitamin C than oranges. To make the syrup as healthful as possible, I use honey instead of sugar and minimize the amount of heating.

Rose hips picked after the first fall frost are likely to be sweeter and lower in starch, which could make syrup cloudy.

Use rose hip syrup to sweeten tea, fruit salad, or poached fruits, or to pour over sponge cake or pancakes.

1¼ cups water
½ pound trimmed ripe rose hips, minced in a food
    processor or blender
About 1 cup honey

1 Bring the water to a boil in a covered saucepan. Add the rose hips, cover the pan, and bring the contents back to a boil. Immediately remove the pan from the heat and let it stand for 15 minutes.

2 Strain the juice through a damp jelly bag. This will take at least several hours. For a clear syrup, do not squeeze the bag.

3 Measure the volume of the syrup and combine it in a saucepan with an equal amount of honey. Bring the mixture slowly to a boil, and then boil it rapidly for 3 minutes.

4 Pour the syrup into a jar and cap it tightly. When the syrup is cool, store it in the refrigerator.

VIOLET SYRUP

MAKES ABOUT 1 CUP

I N MY GARDEN, violets are the first flowers to perfume the air in spring. With their low, spreading habit and pretty green leaves, they make a lovely ground cover, and they are a welcome invader in my lawn and flower beds. Violet blossoms make a brilliant blue syrup with a fascinating floral flavor. It's wonderful for pouring over ground ice, mixing with soda water, or making a flavored ice.

Picking enough violets to make syrup takes time, so I've kept the quantities small here. You can multiply the quantities, of course.

Do make sure that you pick your violets from a pesticide-free lawn or garden bed.

> 2 ounces (about 2½ cups) stemmed violets
> 1⅓ cups water
> About ⅔ cup sugar

1 Combine the flowers and water in a saucepan. Simmer the contents, uncovered, for 15 minutes. (For an even more intense flavor, reheat the violet water with a fresh batch of petals.)

2 Strain the mixture through a damp jelly bag. Measure the volume of the liquid and combine it in a preserving pan with an equal volume of sugar. Heat the mixture over medium heat, stirring, until the sugar is completely dissolved. Raise the heat to high and bring the syrup to a full boil.

3 Remove the pan from the heat. Let the syrup cool, and then store it in a tightly capped bottle in the refrigerator.

FLORAL ICE

Make a special snow cone simply by pouring floral syrup over shaved ice, or try this flower-flavored granita.

1 cup Rose Petal Syrup (page 155) or Violet Syrup (page 159)
2 tablespoons lemon juice
1½ cups water

Combine all of the ingredients in an 8- or 9-inch square glass or metal pan, preferably one with a cover. Put the pan into the freezer for about 45 minutes, until ice forms around the edges. Rake the mixture with the tines of a fork to break up the crystals and distribute them evenly. Return the pan to the freezer. Repeat the raking after about 40 minutes, and again every 35 minutes or so thereafter for a total freezing time of 3½ to 4 hours. When you're finished, you should have a uniform mixture of coarse, dry crystals. I like to serve this in parfait glasses.

GARDEN HUCKLEBERRY

Garden Huckleberry Jam   162

ALTHOUGH YOU may never have heard of this plant, you probably know it or one of its variants by sight, since they grow as weeds throughout much of the world. Luther Burbank called one variant Sunberry and claimed to have created it by cross-breeding; it was later shown to be an African species, *Solanum retroflexum*. The name garden huckleberry has been most often applied to the large-fruited *S. scabrum*, whose seeds are sold in garden catalogs. The most widespread of similar species, *S. americanum*, is hard to distinguish from *S. nigrum*, an Old World species that grows as a weed in North America. All of these species, and others like them, are commonly known as black or garden nightshade.

Like its cousins the tomato and the potato before it, black nightshade is widely considered poisonous. From ancient Greece to colonial Africa to the American Midwest, however, people have recognized it as a valuable food plant. The leaves truly can be poisonous, as can the berries of some species, when eaten raw or green. Cooked and sweetened, however, ripe garden huckleberries or sunberries make fine pies and jams. The small black berries that grow wild in my garden look and taste remarkably like black elderberries.

To avoid risking a belly ache, collect only fully ripe berries without bitterness or astringency, and be sure to cook them.

GARDEN HUCKLEBERRY JAM

MAKES ABOUT 1½ PINTS

AKE SURE YOU KNOW what kind of nightshade berries you're picking, and avoid the green ones.

2 pounds stemmed garden huckleberries
3 cups sugar

1 In a preserving pan, slowly heat the berries, crushing them with the back of a wooden spoon or with a potato masher. When they are soft, add the sugar. Over medium heat, stir until the sugar is dissolved. Raise the heat to medium-high, and boil the mixture until it has thickened and a drop mounds in a chilled dish.

2 Ladle the jam into pint or half-pint mason jars. Add lids and rings, and process the jars for 10 minutes in a boiling-water bath.

BLACK NIGHTSHADE AS MEDICINE

The glycoalkaloids that can make black nightshade species bitter and toxic also make these plants powerful medicine. Scientists have discovered that one of their glycoalkaloids, solanine, kills *Giardia* parasites. In East Africa raw *S. nigrum* berries are eaten to ease chronic stomach pain and ulcers. The Hmong, who eat black night-shade leaves as a vegetable, say that they are a tonic for elderly hearts. *A Barefoot Doctor's Manual* recommends the plant for fever, swelling, and abscesses. In many places black nightshade is used to treat eye inflammations, and in Japan and China the plant has been shown effective against some cancers.

The glycoalkaloid content of black nightshade—and therefore its medicinal value and toxicity—may depend not only on the species but also on the age of the plant and its growing conditions.

GINGER

Ginger Preserved in Syrup   164

I WON'T SUGGEST that you should grow your own ginger, because it is a tropical plant—in the United States, only Hawaii grows ginger commercially—and because today the rhizomes are available in nearly every American supermarket (this wasn't true before the 1970s). If you want to preserve your own ginger, though, you won't want to use the dry, brown rhizomes from the grocery store. For fresh, young ginger—pale and fat, with thin skin and pink stem stumps—you must visit a good Asian market.

Ginger is a proven remedy for nausea, and it has also been used for centuries to treat colds, infections, arthritis, indigestion, and loss of appetite.

GINGER PRESERVED
IN SYRUP

R ECIPES FOR GINGER PRESERVES vary greatly, and most seem more complicated than necessary. I've settled on a simple method here. The cream of tartar is added to keep the syrup from crystallizing.

If you prefer, you can cut the ginger crosswise into thin rounds instead of dicing it into cubes.

Preserved ginger is heavenly over poached or canned pears or pound cake. Also try it as a finishing glaze for grilled pork or chicken.

> 1 pound young ginger
> 2½ cups water
> 2 cups sugar
> ½ teaspoon cream of tartar

1. With a sharp stainless-steel knife held perpendicular to the root, scrape the thin skin off the ginger. Cut the ginger into small cubes, approximately ⅜ inch square. Put the ginger into a saucepan, cover the ginger well with the water, and bring the contents to a boil. Cover the pan and simmer the ginger for at least 30 minutes, until it is tender. Remove the ginger with a slotted spoon.

2. Add the sugar and cream of tartar to the pan—or, for a less fiery syrup, discard the cooking water and combine the sugar and the cream of tartar in the saucepan with 2 cups fresh water. Stir the mixture over medium heat until the sugar is dissolved. Raise the heat to medium-high, and boil the syrup until it is reduced to about 1½ cups. Add the ginger and bring the contents to a boil.

Remove the pan from the heat, cover it with a cloth, and let it stand at room temperature for 8 to 12 hours.

3 Return the pan to the heat and simmer the ginger, uncovered, until the syrup reaches the thread stage (page 18) or 230°F, about 30 minutes.

4 Pour the ginger and syrup into a sterilized pint jar and cap it tightly. The ginger should keep in a cool, dark place for as long as a year.

CRYSTALLIZED GINGER

Make Ginger Preserved in Syrup. When the cooking is complete, remove the ginger with a slotted spoon to a rack set over a tray. Let the ginger dry in a warm place until it is no longer moist. Roll the dried pieces in granulated sugar and store them in an air-tight container (you'll have about 1 cup). Use the syrup for flavoring hot or cold drinks or sauces, add it to a stir-fry or a glazing sauce for grilled pork or chicken, or put it into a dipping sauce for pot stickers or spring rolls. Crystallized ginger is an excellent remedy for a queasy stomach.

For recipes using crystallized ginger, see Low-Sugar Fig-Ginger Jam (page 144), Rhubarb-Ginger Preserves (page 322), Preserved Pears with Ginger (page 242), Quince Preserves with Grated Quince (page 304), Lemon-Ginger Marmalade (page 192), Peach and Ginger Jam (page 232), and Mango-Orange-Ginger Jam (page 198).

GOOSEBERRY

Gooseberry Jam   167

LIKE CURRANTS, gooseberry bushes belong to the genus *Ribes* and so for many years were outlawed in the United States (page 118). As a result, American cooks and gardeners are just beginning to rediscover gooseberries. The berries are grown commercially in both Oregon and Washington but aren't yet widely available in markets. American gooseberry cultivars have long been available from nurseries, however, and European cultivars are becoming popular as well for home gardeners.

The English name for this plant may have originally been *gorseberry*, because the shrub is quite thorny. It is deciduous, about 3 feet tall and as much as 6 feet wide, with thin stems and deeply lobed leaves. It tolerates cold winters and prefers moderate summers (don't try to grow it in a hot, dry climate). Prune the plant by removing stems after four to five years to make way for new ones.

Instead of *gorseberry*, the original English name might have been *grossberry*, because the berries—colored green, white, golden, pink, or purple—are much larger than currants, from ½ to 1 inch long. European cultivars, such as Careless, Clark, and Fredonia, typically have bigger berries, and many people think these berries taste better, too.

Ripening in midsummer, tart gooseberries are delicious raw, but they are especially valued for pies, jams, and preserving whole in syrup. They keep well in the refrigerator for a week or more after picking. Before making them into jam, you'll want to pluck off the dry remains of each blossom as well as the stem at the opposite end.

GOOSEBERRY JAM

FOR THIS JAM I USE Oregon Champion gooseberries. During the relatively slow cooking, the jam turns a rich brown.

4 pounds gooseberries, stems and blossom ends removed
½ cup water
About 5 cups sugar

1 Combine the gooseberries and water in a kettle. Simmer the berries, covered, until they are very soft, about 40 minutes.

2 Put the gooseberries through the medium screen of a food mill to remove most of the seeds. Measure the volume of the puree and return it to the kettle. For each 2 cups puree, add 1½ cups sugar. Over medium-low heat, stir the mixture until the sugar dissolves. Simmer the mixture until it is as thick as a thin jam (it will thicken more on cooling), 30 to 40 minutes.

3 Ladle the jam into pint or half-pint mason jars. Add lids and rings, and process the jars for 10 minutes in a boiling-water bath.

GOOSEBERRY AND ELDER FLOWER JAM

In England, aromatic elder flowers are a traditional flavoring for gooseberry jam. If an elderberry bush grows in your garden, it will probably be in flower when you harvest your gooseberries. Follow the recipe for Gooseberry Jam, but put 12 elder-flower umbels (umbrella-shaped clusters) into a spice bag and add the bag to the pan when the sugar dissolves. Remove the bag before ladling the jam into jars.

GRAPE

Concord Grape Jam   170
Concord Grape Jelly   172

Grape Molasses   173
Cogna   175

LTHOUGH MANY SPECIES OF GRAPES are native to Europe, Asia, or North America, most grape breeding and cultivation have involved just two species: *Vitis vinifera*, the favored wine grape, with many cultivars used for table grapes and raisins, and *V. labrusca*, the slip-skin native of northeastern North America, which includes Concord, Niagara, and Catawba.

Native to western Asia from Turkey to Afghanistan, *V. vinifera* came to Greece with the Phoenicians about 1000 B.C. and quickly spread around the Mediterranean. By the mid-nineteenth century, wine industries based on *V. vinifera* were established in North and South America, South Africa, and Australia. Today California supplies the United States and other countries not only with wine but with *V. vinifera* table grapes (Thompson Seedless, Flame Seedless, and Black Monukka), seedless raisins made from Thompson grapes, and tiny Zante raisins, called currants because this *V. vinifera* species was first grown at Corinth, in Greece. Zante grapes are sometimes sold fresh as "champagne grapes."

All seedless grapes have some *V. vinifera* ancestry. These include not only the supermarket varieties but many others that will grow in cooler climates. Some of them, including Einset, Vanessa, Himrod, Interlaken, and my favorite, the very prolific pink-fruited Canadice, thrive here in western Oregon. These grapes all make good raisins.

Gardeners in cold regions have to rely on *V. labrusca*, the fox grape. Valiant and Beta are Concord-type cultivars that are hardy to –50°F. They are among the hardy grapes grown in such places as North Dakota, Minnesota, Ontario, and even Manitoba.

V. labrusca isn't just for the cold north, though. Some cultivars, at least, do well in California and other warmer regions. *V. labrusca* grapes all have seeds, but they can be fine table grapes; slipping off the skin with one's tongue can add to the pleasure of eating them raw. They are rich in pectin, and they are preferred over any *V. vinifera* for making jelly, jam, and heat-extracted juice. *V. labrusca* vines are also used as rootstock for *V. vinifera*, because they resist the infamous plant louse phylloxera.

A third grape species, the muscadine (*Muscadinia rotundifolia* or *V. rotundifolia*), is of culinary if not commercial importance in the United States. Because of a difference in number of chromosomes, the muscadine is often considered to be in a genus separate from that of other grapes. This grape is native to the hot, humid southeastern United States and is the only grape species widely grown there. White or bronze muscadines used to be called scuppernongs, after a local Native American tribe, but now the whole species—black, purple, white, or bronze—is called muscadine, and only one variety is called scuppernong. Like *V. labrusca*, the large, highly aromatic muscadines are valued for juice and jelly. Some people eat them raw, although the skins are so tough that they are often spat out.

VERSATILE VINIFERA

Vitis vinifera has other uses, too. Ripe grapes are used for vinegar, and half-ripe grapes for verjuice (or *verjus*, French for "green juice"), which is used in place of lemon juice or vinegar for souring. The leaves are used as edible wrappings for meat, rice, and vegetable mixtures, and a light-flavored oil, rich in polyunsaturated fats, is commercially extracted from the seeds. Some cooks like to use grapeseed oil for mayonnaise because the oil emulsifies so easily.

CONCORD GRAPE JAM

T HIS OLD RECIPE was developed for *Vitis labrusca* grapes, the native American "foxy" varieties and their hybrids, such as Concord. These grapes are too tart and strongly flavored to make good wine, but they make delicious juice, jelly, and jam, with a flavor you may remember from your childhood in association with the trade name Welch's. The quality I like best about these grapes is that the fruits slip easily out of their skins, in your fingers or on your tongue, so you can enjoy the luscious texture of a naked grape without any laborious peeling. To make jam, you mash a bowlful of the grapes together and then pick out the skins, so you can cook the skins together with the pulp, for their texture and pectin, after straining out the seeds.

2 pounds Concord or other slip-skin grapes
2½ cups sugar

1 In a preserving pan, mash the grapes with a potato masher, a few handfuls at a time. Pick out the skins, and put them into a small bowl.

2 Over medium heat, bring the pulp to a boil. Reduce the heat, cover the pan, and simmer the pulp for 15 minutes.

3 Press the pulp through a sieve to remove the seeds. Combine the strained pulp with the skins and measure the volume; you should have 3 cups. Put the pulp and the sugar into the preserving pan and heat the contents over medium heat, stirring, until the sugar has completely dissolved. Raise the heat to medium-high and

Vitis labrusca, the native American slip-skin grape of which Concord is the best-known variety, is often called the fox grape. In his book *The Grape Grower*, Lon Rombough maintains that this isn't because the fruit smells like foxes, or because people who drank too much *V. labrusca* wine were once said to be "foxed." As we know from Aesop, foxes like grapes. *V. labrusca*, according to Rombough, makes particularly fine fox fare, and this grape may actually *need* the fox. The ripe fruits tend to fall off the clusters to the ground, where four-footed animals, aided by the grapes' strong odor, can easily find them. The large seeds, which might be damaged by a bird's gizzard, survive the trip through a fox's digestive track, and the fox disperses them around the woodlands that are the grape's natural habitat, thereby sowing new vines.

boil, stirring often, until the jam has turned a glossy dark purple (if you're using dark grapes) and thickly coats the spoon.

4 Remove the pan from the heat, ladle the jam into pint or half-pint mason jars, and add lids and rings. Process the jars in a boiling-water bath for 10 minutes.

SPICED CONCORD GRAPE JAM

If the flavor of Concord grape jam is too frank for you, add a little spice. Follow the directions given, but put 4 cardamom pods, lightly crushed, and one 3-inch cinnamon stick in a spice bag, and keep the bag in the pan both when you cook the grape pulp and when you cook the pulp and sugar together. Squeeze the bag against the side of the pan before giving the jam a final stir and packing it into jars.

CONCORD GRAPE JELLY

MAKES ABOUT 4 HALF-PINTS

WITH MANY VARIETIES OF GRAPES, jelly made from the juice just doesn't set without the addition of other fruit juices or packaged pectin. I have repeatedly found that juice from my Canadice grapes, boiled with sugar, "sheets" well (page 18) but never forms a gel (the resulting syrup is an unattractive brown, anyway). My neighbor's Concord grapes, however, make a clear, beautiful dark purple jelly every time. Other dark *Vitis labrusca* grapes, the native grapes of northeastern America, should work as well for jelly, as should other species of wild American grapes, such as muscadines. The grapes should be just ripe or slightly underripe for a high pectin content. To help ensure that your jelly doesn't turn out too soft for your taste, I've added an apple to this recipe.

To avoid finding crunchy bits in your grape jelly, you need to let the juice rest overnight so that tartrate crystals will form and can be strained out. Save the crystals for your family to admire. They are cream of tartar, the acidic substance sometimes used with baking soda in baked goods or added to egg whites before beating.

USING A STEAM JUICER

A steam juicer (page 14) works well as an alternative method for making grape juice for jelly. Because grapes have a high water content, you may need to draw off the juice during steaming to keep the juice section from overflowing into the water below.

3 pounds Concord or other dark fox grapes

1 just-ripe apple, thinly sliced (unpeeled and uncored)

3 cups sugar

1. Put the grapes into a kettle, a few handfuls at a time, and crush them with a potato masher. Add the apple slices. Over medium heat, bring the fruit to a boil. Reduce the heat, cover the pan, and simmer the fruit for 15 minutes.

2. Pour the contents of the pan through a strainer into a bowl. Cover the bowl and refrigerate it for 12 to 24 hours.

3. Pour the juice through a damp jelly bag and measure the volume of the juice; you should have 4 cups. Pour the juice into a pre-serving pan and add the sugar. Heat the mixture over medium heat, stirring, until the sugar is completely dissolved, and then raise the heat to medium-high. Boil the mixture, skimming off the foam, until the liquid "sheets" from a cold spoon (page 18).

4. Pour the liquid into half-pint mason jars, and add lids and rings. Process the jars in a boiling-water bath for 10 minutes.

GRAPE MOLASSES

GRAPE MOLASSES is simply boiled-down grape must, or the juice derived from pressing, cooked slowly to a rich brown syrup. This ancient preserve goes by many names, including *arrope* (from an Arabic word meaning "protected") and *mostillo* in Spain, *mostarda* and *saba* in Italy, and *pekmez* in Turkey.

Sometimes these names are applied to molasses made from other fruits, such as figs or pomegranate. In South America, where *arrope* refers to any gelled fruit preserve made without added sugar, the best known type is made of *tunas*, cactus pears.

Sometimes other fruits, such as pumpkin, quince, or melon, are preserved in grape molasses. In parts of Italy, any jar of whole fruits or large pieces of fruit in syrup may be labeled *mostarda*.

In Spain, *arrope* is used to fortify wines, to make them into liqueurs with rounded flavor and enhanced sweetness. In Turkey, *pekmez* is used in the preparation of many desserts. Grape molasses is also dribbled on toast, salads, steak, yogurt, ice cream, and sheep's milk cheese, and used as a marinade for duck and other meats.

At least 2 quarts grape must

1 If you make your own wine, save some of the must to simmer down to a syrup. If you don't have a fruit press, pull at least 5 pounds of grapes from their stems and rinse them in a broad, flat-bottomed colander (so you can pick out any insects, spiders, or moldy fruits). Put the grapes through a tomato strainer—a device for separating skins and seeds from fruit—or heat them briefly in a covered kettle and then press them through a strainer fine enough to catch the seeds.

2 Pour the juice into a kettle. Simmer it until it is thick, but stop before it begins to caramelize. The simmering will take at least 1½ hours, longer if you're using more juice.

3 Pour the syrup into one or more half-pint mason jars, add lids and rings, and process the jars for 10 minutes in a boiling-water bath. Or, if you're using just one jar, cap it tightly and, when it has cooled, store it in the refrigerator, where the grape molasses should keep well for at least 6 months.

COGNA
(MIXED FRUIT-AND-NUT
CONSERVE FROM PIEMONTE)

MAKES ABOUT 2 PINTS

FROM THE FOOT OF THE ITALIAN ALPS comes this spiced harvest-time treat. *Cogna* is like old-fashioned apple butter but with a mix of fruits and ample quantities of nuts. You start with fresh-pressed grape must (which is why this preserve is also known as *mostarda dulce d'uva*), but if you don't make your own wine you can put table grapes through a food mill or even use heat-extracted grape juice. To have figs at the appropriate time you must have access to a tree that ripens its second crop, or you could use some breba (first crop) figs from your freezer. Serve *cogna* on bread or with soft cheese.

> 2 cups shelled hazelnuts
> Four 3-inch cinnamon sticks
> 16 cloves
> 6 cups fresh-pressed red grape juice, preferably of a wine
>   variety, strained of seeds
> 1 pound peeled and cored apples, sliced thick
> 1 pound peeled and cored pears, sliced thick
> 1 pound stemmed and halved fresh figs
> 2 cups shelled walnut pieces

1. Spread a single layer of hazelnuts in a baking pan, and roast them at 275° to 300°F until their skins have cracked and the meat under the skin has darkened a bit, about 20 minutes. Cover the nuts with a towel, and leave them to cool.

2. Put the cinnamon sticks and cloves into a spice bag. Put the juice, apples, pears, and figs into a preserving pan and add the spice bag. Bring the mixture to a boil and simmer it until it becomes thick, dark, and glossy, like apple butter. This will take at least 1 hour, and probably 2 hours or more.

3. While the fruits cook, rub the hazelnuts with the towel and remove as much of their skins as you can.

4. When the *cogna* is ready, stir in the hazelnuts and walnuts. Spoon the conserve into jars and cap them tightly. Store the jars in the refrigerator, where the *cogna* will keep for several weeks, at least.

GRAPEFRUIT

Red Grapefruit Marmalade   178

A CROSS BETWEEN the pommelo and the orange, this favorite breakfast fruit developed by chance in Barbados in the eighteenth century. The tree was apparently named for its tendency to bear fruit in clusters.

Grapefruit was slow to catch on, probably because it's hard to peel cleanly and because the membranes and pith as well as the outer rind are quite bitter. But sectioning the fruit with a knife, or simply cutting the fruit in half and spooning the flesh out of the membranes, lets you enjoy all the grapefruit's sweetness with little of its bitterness.

Until the early twentieth century, all grapefruits had "white," or pale yellow, flesh. Like the grapefruit itself, the first red varieties developed as chance seedlings. Red varieties have since grown so much in popularity that white grapefruits can be hard to find. Many people think red grapefruits are sweeter, although scientists say this isn't generally true.

The United States is by far the world's largest producer of grapefruits, which are grown in Florida, Texas, California, and Arizona. Mexico has recently become a big grapefruit producer too, and is now exporting the fruits to the United States.

RED GRAPEFRUIT
MARMALADE

MAKES ABOUT 2 PINTS

ECTIN-RICH RED GRAPEFRUIT makes excellent pink-orange marmalade. It can be as bitter as bitter orange marmalade, but it doesn't have to be. Changing the cooking water repeatedly, as directed in this recipe, makes the flavor much milder.

2 red grapefruits (about 1¼ pounds)
4 cups water
About 3½ cups sugar
3 tablespoons lemon juice

1. If the fruits aren't home-picked or labeled organic, put them in a colander in the sink and pour boiling water over them to remove any wax. Scrub them well.

2. Cut the grapefruit peels into quarters without cutting through the flesh of the grapefruits. Remove the peels and reserve the peeled grapefruits. Put the peels into a large nonreactive saucepan and cover them with water. Bring the contents to a boil, reduce the heat, cover the pan, and simmer the peels for 5 minutes.

3. Drain the peels and add fresh water. Simmer them as before for 5 minutes, drain them, and again simmer them for 5 minutes in fresh water. Drain the peels and let them cool. Slice the peels very thinly.

4. Remove any pith from the peeled grapefruits. Cut them crosswise into thin slices, discarding any seeds and the "rag" in the center of the fruit. Cut the slices into small pieces, saving all juice. Put the flesh and peel into a preserving pan or nonreactive kettle along with the 4 cups water. Bring the contents to a boil, reduce

the heat, and simmer the mixture, uncovered, for 45 minutes or until the peels are quite tender.

5 Measure the volume of the mixture and return it to the pan with an equal volume of sugar and the lemon juice. Stir the mixture over medium heat until the sugar is dissolved, and then raise the heat to medium-high. Boil the mixture, skimming off any foam, until it mounds in a chilled dish or reaches 220°F.

6 Remove the pan from the heat and let the marmalade cool for 5 minutes. Ladle it into pint or half-pint mason jars, add lids and rings, and process the jars for 10 minutes in a boiling-water bath.

KIWI

Kiwi Jam   181

Kiwi Preserves   182

Strawberry-Kiwi Jam   183

WHEN KIWIFRUIT first became widely available in North American markets, in the 1970s, many people scorned the fruit. It was too tart for them, I guess, or too fuzzy. (To foodies, writes David Kamp in *The United States of Arugula*, the kiwi "became a symbol of culinary tackiness, the mark of a clueless chef or restaurateur trying too hard to be chic.") But those of us who love tart fruit and don't mind peeling it had no such complaints. Ripening late in the year, kiwis keep well into the winter, look gorgeous when sliced to show their bright green flesh with a ring of tiny black seeds, and taste smooth and moist, with a contrasting little crunch from the seeds. Pound for pound, kiwis have more than twice the level of vitamin C in oranges, and they have high levels of potassium and magnesium as well. They also make beautiful jams and preserves.

Native to southeast Asia, *Actinidia deliciosa*, fuzzy kiwi, has long grown wild on the margins of Chinese forests. The fruit was unknown in the West until the turn of the twentieth century, when a New Zealander brought seeds home from China. Vines that grew from the seeds first fruited in 1910, and the propagation of these vines led to commercial plantings. "Chinese gooseberry," as it was then known, was introduced to California in the 1930s, but neither farmers nor shoppers showed much interest until the early 1970s. Today kiwis are commercially grown in Australia, Chile, Europe, and Japan as well as in California and New Zealand. In the winter, you'll find them in nearly every supermarket. Golden-fleshed as well as green-fleshed kiwis are sometimes available.

Although *A. deliciosa* is considered marginal here in Oregon's Willamette Valley, the vine thrives and produces abundant fruit in every local garden in which I've seen it. Gardeners in colder regions might have to settle for one of the other *Actinidia* species, all of which are native to Asia. *A. arguta*, hardy kiwi (or, in Canada, grape kiwi), produces 1-inch oblong fruits with smooth, edible skins; Mark Hurst of Sheridan, Oregon, markets them nationally as "baby kiwis." *A. kolomikta*, Arctic Beauty kiwi, has very small fruits, but they have twenty times the level of vitamin C of citrus fruits. Many *A. kolomikta* cultivars, mainly developed in Russia, are now available from One Green World, a nursery in Molalla, Oregon, as are *A. arguta* cultivars from the United States and other countries.

Kiwi species and cultivars differ in hardiness and trellising needs, and most require planting a male vine along with the female for pollination. Be sure you know what you're getting before ordering vines.

KIWI JAM

MAKES 1½ TO 2 PINTS

FUZZY KIWIS make a very tart, golden-green jam with tiny black spots. You can peel the kiwis with a paring knife or halve the fruits and spoon out the flesh.

2 pounds fuzzy kiwis, peeled and coarsely chopped
2 cups sugar

1. Put the chopped kiwis into a preserving pan, and crush them with a potato masher. Add the sugar. Heat the mixture over medium heat until the sugar dissolves. Raise the heat to medium-high and boil the mixture, stirring, until a drop mounds in a chilled dish.

2. Ladle the jam into pint or half-pint mason jars. Add lids and rings, and process the jars in a boiling-water bath for 5 minutes.

KIWI
PRESERVES

MAKES ABOUT 1½ PINTS

UZZY KIWIS MAKE BEAUTIFUL, clear green preserves. This simple recipe brings out the tropical flavor of the fruit.

1½ pounds fuzzy kiwis, peeled and cut into ⅜-inch cubes
3 cups sugar

1. In a preserving pan, layer the diced kiwi with the sugar. Cover the pan with a cloth and let it stand at room temperature for 8 to 12 hours.

2. Heat the mixture over medium heat until the sugar dissolves. Raise the heat to medium-high and boil the preserves until the syrup falls from the spoon in large, slow drops. Remove the pan from the heat and let the preserves cool for about 5 minutes.

3. Ladle the preserves into pint or half-pint mason jars. Add lids and rings, and process the jars for 10 minutes in a boiling-water bath.

STRAWBERRY-KIWI
JAM

YOU MIGHT EXPECT the red and green of these fruits to mix into the color of mud, but this jam turns out red and perfumed like strawberries. The kiwis provide acid for balanced flavor and a good gel, as well as pretty, crunchy little black seeds and an exotic flavor that may keep your breakfast guests guessing.

1 pound hulled strawberries
1 pound peeled fuzzy kiwis
3 cups sugar

1 Combine the fruits in a preserving pan and mash them with a potato masher. Stir in the sugar. Heat the mixture over medium heat, stirring, until the sugar dissolves. Raise the heat to medium-high and boil the jam until a drop mounds in a chilled dish.

2 Ladle the jam into pint or half-pint mason jars. Add lids and rings, and process the jars for 10 minutes in a boiling-water bath.

KUMQUAT

Kumquat Preserves with Honey   185

Kumquat Marmalade   187

I NEVER APPRECIATED KUMQUATS until the day I watched two little boys climb over piles of oranges and grapefruits to reach the high-priced little orange fruits in a basket at the center of a Safeway produce counter. I bought some, too, and found that my children also bore the slight bitterness of the kumquat's rind for the wondrous experience of eating the fruit whole. Kumquats are sweet, tart, tenderly chewy, and amazingly fragrant, with a bitterness that just balances the other sensations.

Looking like tiny oranges, kumquats are closely related to citrus fruits, but botanists have put them into their own genus, *Fortunella* (after Robert Fortune, the explorer and plant collector who intro-

DRIED KUMQUAT PEELS

I discovered how astonishingly aromatic kumquat peels are after I noticed that my daughter was peeling kumquats instead of eating them whole. I placed the thin, pith-free skins in a dish in a warm place, and when the skins were dry I packed them into a jar. Kumquat peels preserved this way keep their color and fragrance for a year or more and made an appealing substitute for citrus zest.

duced them to London in 1846). Native to southeast China, the little trees are hardier than citrus trees and so have long been cultivated in cooler parts of China and Japan. Today they are commercially grown in California, Texas, and Florida as well as Asia and elsewhere.

Two main types of kumquats are grown in the United States. *F. margarita*, or Nagami kumquat, is an inch or two long and oval. Widely sold in the United States, Nagami is quite tart and preferred for marmalade. *F. crassifolia*, or Miewa kumquat, is round, less tart, nearly seedless, and preferred for eating raw. It is much harder to find in stores.

Like citrus fruits, kumquats ripen mainly in the winter, although they can produce several crops each year. The fruits are readily available in markets and likely to be quite fresh from December through February.

You can grow your own kumquats outdoors if your winter temperatures stay above 20°F. In a colder climate, you can plant the trees in pots and bring them into a well-lit room in the winter.

KUMQUAT PRESERVES WITH HONEY

MAKES 1 PINT

I T'S SAID THAT THE CHINESE have for centuries preserved kumquats in honey, although nowadays they more often use sugar. In this recipe I combine the two sweeteners to produce a gloriously pretty and tasty spoon sweet.

1 pound stemmed kumquats

1½ cups water

¾ cup sugar

½ cup honey

1 Put the kumquats into a bowl and pour enough boiling water over to cover them. Let them stand for 10 minutes and then rinse them well with cold water.

2 Cut a slit through the skin of each kumquat at the stem end; this will keep the fruit from bursting. Put the kumquats into a saucepan and cover them with cold water. Bring the water to a boil and boil the kumquats for 10 minutes. Drain and rinse them.

3 In a saucepan, slowly bring to a boil the 1½ cups water, sugar, and honey. Skim off the foam and add the kumquats. Simmer them for about 25 minutes, until they are partially translucent. Remove the pan from the heat, cover the pan with a cloth, and let the mixture stand at room temperature for 8 to 12 hours.

4 Over medium heat, bring the mixture back to a boil. Remove the pan from the heat and, using a slotted spoon, transfer the kumquats to 1 pint or 2 half-pint mason jars. Boil the syrup briefly to thicken it a bit, and then pour it over the kumquats. Add lids and rings, and process the jars for 15 minutes in a boiling-water bath.

KUMQUAT MARMALADE

MAKES ABOUT 2 PINTS

K UMQUATS MAKE A LOVELY ORANGE, barely bitter marmalade, and with less than a pound of the precious fruits
you can make a generous supply.

12 ounces stemmed kumquats

5 cups water

4 cups sugar

1 Slice the kumquats crosswise into thin rings, removing the seeds
with the tip of your knife. Put the seeds into a spice bag, put the
bag and the kumquats into a saucepan, and add the water. Bring
the contents to a boil, and boil them, uncovered, for 15 minutes,
skimming off the foam. Remove the pan from the heat, cover it
with a cloth, and let the pan stand at room temperature for 8 to
12 hours.

2 Add the sugar to the pan and place the pan over medium heat.
Stir until the sugar is dissolved, and then raise the heat to
medium-high. Bring the mixture to a boil and let it boil for 1
minute. Remove the pan from the heat, cover it with a cloth, and
let it stand at room temperature for 8 to 12 hours.

3 Bring the kumquat mixture slowly to a boil. Raise the heat to
medium-high and boil the mixture until it passes the spoon test
(page 18) or a jelly thermometer reads 220°F.

4 Remove the pan from the heat and skim off the foam. Press the
spice bag against the side of the pan, and remove the bag. Let the
marmalade cool for 5 minutes, and then ladle it into pint or half-
pint mason jars. Add lids and rings, and process the jars for
10 minutes in a boiling-water bath.

LEMON AND LIME

Lemon Jelly   190

Lemon-Ginger Marmalade   192

Lemon Curd   193

Lime Syrup   194

T HESE TWO FRUITS, one subtropical and one tropical, are together valued throughout most of the world as acidifiers, flavor enhancers, and pectin sources.

Lemons probably originated in India, and the Romans may have brought them to the Mediterranean region as early as the first century A.D. The Arabs established orchards in the same region by the fourth century, but until the sixteenth century the lemon's primary use in Europe was probably medicinal (as you might guess from its botanical name, *Citrus medica*). Columbus brought lemons on his second voyage to the New World, and the Spanish planted them at their California missions in the 1730s. After the Gold Rush in 1849, commercial orchards were planted, and today California produces more lemons than all of Europe combined.

Most commercially grown California lemons belong to one of two similar varieties—Eureka, originally from Italy, and Lisbon, originally from Portugal. Lisbon produces a large crop in late winter and a small crop in early summer; Eureka produces throughout the year.

Home gardeners in California have long favored the Meyer lemon, which thrives at the northern end of the citrus belt, where temperatures stay above 20°F. Introduced from China by Frank N. Meyer in 1908, the Meyer is actually a cross between a lemon and a mandarin or orange. The juicy, tender-skinned Meyer is less acidic than true lemons. Following the lead of Alice Waters and her colleagues at Chez Panisse, chefs and food writers all over the United States have lately been praising and demanding this fruit. It can, however, be very difficult to find in markets.

True limes, the little round kind, probably originated in Malaysia and from there made their way to India. Arabs brought them to Spain and Italy, but, in the relatively cool Mediterranean climate, lime cultivation didn't last long. Instead the Spanish and Portuguese planted limes in Mexico, Central and South America, and the West Indies. These limes, *C. aurantifolia*, are sometimes called Key limes because they grow wild in the Florida Keys and were briefly grown commercially there; they are also called bartender limes, because for most of the twentieth century, in the United States north of Florida, they could be found only in bars. But the huge wave of Mexican immigrants in the 1990s made these limes a standard item in supermarkets. Since the limes, too, come from Mexico, it makes sense to call them Mexican limes. With their strong fragrance and mild bitterness, Mexican limes are essential for margaritas and Key lime pies and preferred in Mexican cooking.

The larger, thicker-skinned limes with which you may be more familiar are *C. latifolia*, the Tahiti, Persian, or Bearss lime. Actually not a lime at all but a likely cross between a true lime and a citron, the Tahiti lime was introduced to California via Tahiti in 1875. Commercial production of Tahiti limes in the United States is now limited mainly to Florida; large quantities are imported from Mexico. Tahiti limes are less bitter and less fragrant than Mexican limes and can be substituted for lemons for most purposes.

All limes and lemons start out green and ripen to yellow. Limes are sold green partially to distinguish them from lemons.

Whatever their color, make sure the lemons and limes you buy are firm if you want to use their zest. If your zester won't work on a too-soft lemon or lime, a vegetable peeler probably will, but it will remove more of the bitter white pith.

Supermarket lemons and limes are treated with fungicide and wax, so scrub them with a brush before using them for preserves or zest.

Because of their high ascorbic acid (vitamin C) levels, lemons and limes can prevent oxidation of other fruits. To keep cut pears, apples, quinces, or other fruits from browning, sprinkle them with lemon and lime juice and toss them. When making jam, adding lemon or lime juice to fruits low in ascorbic acid can also help prevent darkening at the top of the jar.

Adding lemon or lime juice to less tart fruits can provide the acid needed to produce gelling. And adding lemon or lime flesh or rind—or seeds, in a spice bag—provides pectin for low-pectin fruits.

For other lemon recipes, see Candied Lemon Peel (page 224) and Sweet Orange–Lemon Marmalade (page 217). For other lime recipes, see Hot Green Pepper–Lime Jelly (page 257), Mango-Lime Jam (page 197), and Tomatillo-Lime Marmalade (page 340).

LEMON JELLY

MAKES ABOUT 4 HALF-PINTS

EMONS MAKE A JELLY that is clear, golden, and at once sweet, tart, and bitter, like marmalade without the peel.

1 pound lemons
7 cups water
About 4½ cups sugar

1 If the fruits aren't home-picked or labeled organic, put them in a colander in the sink and pour boiling water over them to remove any wax. Scrub them well.

2 Cut the lemons crosswise into thin slices. Put the slices into a nonreactive kettle and cover them with the water. Cover the ket-

tle with cloth or plastic wrap and let the kettle stand at room temperature for 24 hours.

3 Over medium-high heat, bring the contents of the kettle to a boil. Reduce the heat and simmer them for 40 minutes.

4 Pour the mixture into a damp jelly bag set over a bowl, and let the liquid drip for several hours.

5 Measure the liquid; you should have about 5 cups. Pour half of the liquid into a preserving pan. For 2½ cups liquid, add 2¼ cups sugar. Stir the mixture over medium heat until the sugar has dissolved, and then raise the heat to medium-high. Boil the mixture until it passes the spoon test (page 18) or reaches 220°F on a jelly thermometer.

6 Immediately pour the jelly into half-pint mason jars and add lids and rings. Cook the remaining lemon liquid and sugar in the same way, and fill more jars with the jelly. Process the jars for 10 minutes in a boiling-water bath.

LIME JELLY

Make this in the same way as Lemon Jelly, substituting limes for the lemons.

LEMON AND ROSEMARY JELLY

The strong flavors of lemon and rosemary complement each other well. To make a fine spread for a lamb sandwich, rinse and dry a bunch of rosemary and clip off four sprigs about as long as your jelly jars are high. Lightly bruise the rest of the bunch with a rolling pin or your fist. Put one rosemary sprig in each jar, and make Lemon Jelly according to the directions. As soon as the jelly reaches the gel point, remove the preserving pan from the heat, grasp one end of the bunch of rosemary, and gently swish it through the jelly for 30 seconds or so. Pour the hot jelly into the jars. Add lids and rings, and process the jars as described for Lemon Jelly.

LEMON-GINGER MARMALADE

EMONS AND GINGER COMBINE to make a marmalade with a refreshing double bite.

1½ pounds lemons

6 cups water

½ cup minced fresh ginger

½ cup minced crystallized ginger, store-bought or
   homemade (page 165)

4½ cups sugar

1 If the fruits aren't home-picked or labeled organic, put them in a colander in the sink and pour boiling water over them to remove any wax. Scrub them well.

2 Remove the zest of the lemons in thin shreds. Put the shreds into a saucepan with 1 cup of the water. Simmer the zest, covered, for 1 hour or until it is soft.

3 While the zest begins simmering, chop the rest of the fruit, reserving all juice. Put the fruit, with seeds, pith, and juice, into a nonreactive kettle. Add the remaining 5 cups water and the fresh ginger. Bring the mixture to a boil, lower the heat, and simmer the mixture, uncovered, for 1 hour.

TIPS FOR JUICING

To make juicing easier, roll lemons and limes firmly on a countertop before cutting them. Or try one of these tricks: Zap them in a microwave oven for 10 seconds per lemon or lime, or put them in a bowl of hot tap water for 10 minutes.

4. Drain the zest, reserving both the zest and its cooking liquid.

5. Pour the mixture of lemon pulp and ginger into a colander set over a bowl, and then strain both the juice and the cooking liquid from the zest through a damp jelly bag. In a preserving pan, combine the strained liquid with the zest, the crystallized ginger, and the sugar. Over medium heat, stir the mixture until the sugar dissolves. Raise the heat to medium-high and boil the marmalade until it passes the spoon test (page 18) or reaches 220°F on a jelly thermometer.

6. Remove the pan from the heat and immediately ladle the marmalade into half-pint mason jars. Add lids and rings, and process the jars in a boiling-water bath for 10 minutes.

LEMON CURD

MAKES ABOUT 1 PINT

A FAVORITE TREAT IN ENGLAND, lemon curd is an extra-rich, tangy custard that makes an excellent filling for cakes, tarts, cream puffs, and the like. The English also use it as a topping on shortbread, scones, and other breads.

Lemon curd must not boil. You can make it in a saucepan set on a burner, but for even cooking I prefer a double boiler.

2 large eggs
2 large egg yolks
2/3 cup strained lemon juice
6 tablespoons unsalted butter, softened
1 cup sugar
Grated zest of 1 lemon (optional)

1 In a bowl, beat the eggs and yolks until they are smooth. Beat in the lemon juice.

2 Melt the butter in the top of a double boiler over medium-low heat. Stir in the sugar and then the egg–lemon juice mixture. Continue stirring until the curd thickens, about 5 minutes. When the curd is ready, you should be able to draw a path on the back of the spoon with your finger (a thermometer inserted into the curd will read 160°F). Stir in the zest, if you are using it.

3 Pour the hot curd into one or more jars, and cap them tightly. Store them in the refrigerator or freezer. Lemon curd will keep in the refrigerator for at least 1 week, or in the freezer for at least 2 months.

LIME CURD

Make this in the same way as Lemon Curd, substituting limes for the lemons.

LIME SYRUP

MAKES 1 TO 1½ PINTS

USE THIS RECIPE to make excellent limeade (2 to 3 tablespoons syrup to 1 cup water over ice) with a hint of the bitterness and fragrance of the lime peel, or add the syrup instead of Rose's Lime Juice or sweet-and-sour mix to alcoholic mixed drinks. For the strongest flavor, use Mexican limes.

2 cups sugar
1 cup water
Zest of 2 limes
1 cup lime juice

1. Combine the sugar, water, and lime zest in a saucepan. Heat the mixture over very low heat, stirring occasionally, until the sugar is dissolved. Bring the syrup to a boil and boil it until it reaches the soft-ball stage (page 19) or 235°F on a jelly thermometer.

2. Add the lime juice to the saucepan and bring the syrup to a boil. Pour it through a tea strainer into pint or half-pint mason jars. Add lids and rings, and process the jars in a boiling-water bath for 10 minutes. Or strain the syrup into any bottle or jar, cap it tightly, and store the cooled container in the refrigerator, where the syrup should keep well for months.

LEMON SYRUP

Follow the recipe for Lime Syrup, substituting lemons for the limes.

LIME-GINGER (OR LEMON-GINGER) SYRUP

Citrus and ginger combine well for refreshing cold drinks in summer and for flu and cold remedies in winter. Follow the recipe for Lime Syrup (substituting lemon, if you prefer), but heat a few slices of fresh ginger along with the sugar, water, and zest.

MANGO

Mango-Lime Jam   197
Mango-Orange-Ginger Jam   198

A GREAT BLESSING to the people of the tropics, the mango tree is a typically large, spreading evergreen that provides ample shade and an annual crop of fruits that, depending on the variety, can weigh as much as 3 pounds each. India produces the most mangoes in the world, but the tree thrives and has naturalized in many countries. When I visited West Africa shortly after the height of mango season, the dirt streets seemed to be paved with mango pits.

In the United States, mangoes grow only in southern Florida and the extreme south of California. California has little or no commercial production, but Florida farmers have been growing and exporting mangoes since 1910 (many of the Florida orchards were lost, unfortunately, to Hurricane Andrew in 1992). Selected to withstand long shipping and rough handling, the Florida varieties are unpleasantly fibrous; you must avoid eating the flesh close to the pit if you have no dental floss handy.

But there are hundreds of mango varieties, and most are far superior to the commercial Florida varieties. Mango cultivars fall into two broad categories: the Indian types, which produce brightcolored fruits that resist rough handling but that don't grow true from seed, and the Southeast Asian or Philippine types, which produce larger crops of more perishable, pale green– or yellow-skinned fruit and seedlings very much like the parents.

Today supermarkets carry Mexican mangoes of the second type as well as the Florida varieties. The Philippine or Manila mango and the closely related Ataulfo or champagne mango are small, flat, and yellow, with flesh that is tart, soft, creamy, and nearly fiber-free.

For residents of southern Florida, at least one nursery carries dozens of mango cultivars. These include such selections as the aptly named Lemon Meringue mango from Burma; the highly aromatic, honey-flavored Mallika; the Brahm Kai Meu, crunchy as an apple; the enormous Beverly; and several "condo mangoes"—trees with a maximum height as low as 6 feet.

Whichever mango variety you choose, you should avoid eating the skin of the fruit, since it can cause an allergic reaction in some people.

To dice a mango, cut along either side of the broad pit to separate the two halves. Cut the flesh in a checkerboard pattern without cutting through the skin. Turn each half inside out by pushing up the center on the skin side, and then slice the mango cubes away from the skin.

MANGO-LIME JAM

MAKES ABOUT 2 PINTS

MANGO JAM can almost be mistaken for peach jam and, if the mangoes are well-ripened and aromatic, can be just as luscious. Try it in a glaze for shrimp or scallops.

2 pounds peeled and diced mango
½ cup lime juice
2¾ cups sugar

1 Put the mango cubes and lime juice into a preserving pan. Stirring often, simmer until the mango is tender. Remove the pan from the heat and mash the mango lightly with a potato masher.

2 Add the sugar to the pan. Over medium heat, stir until the sugar is dissolved. Raise the heat to medium-high and boil the jam until a drop mounds in a chilled dish.

3 Ladle the jam into pint or half-pint mason jars. Add lids and rings, and process the jars in a boiling-water bath for 10 minutes.

MANGO-ORANGE-GINGER JAM

MAKES 2½ TO 3 PINTS

F YOU DON'T LIKE GINGER, you can leave it out of this jam.

2 pounds peeled and diced mango
⅔ cup orange juice
3 cups sugar
½ cup crystallized ginger, store-bought or homemade (page 165)

1 Put the mango cubes and orange juice into a preserving pan. Stirring often, simmer until the mango is tender. Remove the pan from the heat and mash the mango lightly with a potato masher.

2 Add the sugar and ginger to the pan. Over medium heat, stir until the sugar is dissolved. Raise the heat to medium-high and boil the jam until a drop mounds in a chilled dish.

3 Ladle the jam into hot sterilized pint or half-pint mason jars. Add lids and rings, and process the jars in a boiling-water bath for 10 minutes.

MEDLAR

Medlar Jelly   200
Medlar Butter   202

HAVE YOU BLETTED YOUR MEDLARS?" read a button I saw many years ago at a fruit lovers' convention. A medlar, I learned, was a strange fruit that had to be ripened—or actually *over*ripened—in storage. To find out more, I had to order a medlar tree for my orchard.

The medlar is not to be confused with the so-called Japanese medlar—the tart, orange-fleshed loquat, which is delightful eaten straight off the tree (I don't preserve loquats because, sadly, the lovely evergreen trees produce no fruit here in the Willamette Valley). The medlar tree, a deciduous member of the family Rosaceae, is small and handsomely spreading with a lovely spring floral display. Its fruit looks much like a large greenish-brown rose hip, with an open five-pointed calyx end. Because of its appearance, Shakespeare and his contemporaries called the medlar the open-arse.

The medlar probably originated in Persia or thereabouts, and in the Near East and southern Europe the fruit no doubt ripens reliably on the tree. But in wetter, colder regions it tends to get moldy. So, traditionally, you pick the fruit on a dry day in November, pack it in straw-filled boxes, and bring the boxes indoors. After several weeks, the fruit should be "bletted," or softened (the word *blet* comes from the French *devenir blet*, "to get sleepy").

I have found that it's best to do without the straw, which tends to

"This remarkable fruit, which, though wild in Britain, has been cultivated for many centuries, has apparently little justification for its existence."

—*May Byron*, May Byron's Jam Book, 1917

hide rotting fruit. I simply spread my medlars in cardboard boxes and check for moldy ones about once a week. The fruits are ready when they feel soft and the pale yellow flesh has turned brown; the calyx ends may even be swollen with the start of fermentation. Slightly fermented medlars are fine to eat; moldy ones are not. Often the mold is on the inside only, so the fruit looks fine until you cut it. For this reason I cut my medlars approximately into quarters—the knife tends to slip around the big seeds, so the fruit ends up more crushed than quartered—and dispose of any fruits with blackened parts before weighing the medlars for preserving.

The aroma of cooking medlars might best be described as earthy. Don't worry about this; the flavor of the bletted fruit combined with sugar has a unique but true appeal.

MEDLAR JELLY

MAKES 3 TO 4 HALF-PINTS

I FOUND SEVERAL RECIPES for medlar jelly in British cookbooks. Most called for seeding the medlars, but I found this to be a lot of unnecessary trouble. And even when I combined bletted and unbletted fruit, the juice was apparently too low in pectin to gel. Some recipes I found included lemon, which contributes necessary acid as well as pectin. But I didn't get a true jelly until I added crabapple juice.

Medlar jelly has a pretty, dark pink color and a curious, spicy flavor that reminds me of autumn leaves.

3 pounds bletted medlars, quartered

3½ cups water

Zest of 3 lemons, in wide strips

2 cups Homemade Crabapple or Apple Pectin (page 17)

½ cup strained lemon juice

3 cups sugar

1 Put the medlars into a kettle, cover them with the water, and cover the kettle. Bring the contents to a simmer and simmer the medlars for 2 to 3 hours, until the liquid is well colored. Strain the liquid first through a colander and then through a damp jelly bag.

2 Measure the juice. Boil it, if necessary, until you have just 2 cups. Add the crabapple or apple pectin, the lemon juice, and the sugar. Heat the contents over medium heat until the sugar is completely dissolved, and then raise the heat to medium-high. Boil the mixture until the drops are heavy and slow (this jelly may not pass the spoon test). Ladle the jelly into half-pint mason jars, add lids and rings, and process the jars for 10 minutes in a boiling-water bath.

MEDLAR BUTTER

T HIS BUTTER REQUIRES only brief cooking and no spices, but it turns out like thick, dark, spiced applesauce. You can make the butter with the pulp left over from making medlar jelly, but I prefer to skip the jelly making in favor of full-flavored butter.

> 3½ pounds bletted medlars, quartered
> 2½ cups water
> 4 cups sugar
> ⅔ cup strained lemon juice

1. Combine the medlars and water in a kettle. Simmer the medlars, covered, for 1 hour. Press the medlars through a strainer to remove the skins and seeds. You should end up with about 3½ cups pulp.

2. In a kettle, combine the medlar pulp, sugar, and lemon juice. Heat the mixture over low heat, stirring constantly to prevent spattering, until the butter is thick and chocolate colored. If it becomes too thick, add a little water.

3. Pack the butter into pint or half-pint mason jars. Add lids and rings, and process the jars for 10 minutes in a boiling-water bath.

NUTS

Green Walnut Preserves 207

Chestnuts in Syrup 208

Chestnut Cream 210

Rebecca's Hazelnut-Chocolate
Spread 211

ERE I CONSIDER THREE NUTS: the chestnut, the walnut, and the hazelnut.

Among the nuts familiar to our tables, chestnuts stand out as starchy and sweet rather than fatty. They are eaten raw, boiled, steamed, and roasted, and in soups, soufflés, purees, rice dishes, and many desserts. Dried and ground into flour, as they are in Italy, chestnuts have many more uses still.

One chestnut species, *Castanea dentata*, once dominated the forest canopy of the eastern United States and was greatly valued for its timber as well as its nuts. In the early twentieth century, though, the trees were almost entirely wiped out by an airborne fungal blight from Asia. Researchers are trying to revive the native tree, and a few farmers are growing hybrid nuts. But many Americans today have never even seen a chestnut.

New Yorkers continued to enjoy warm, fresh-roasted chestnuts until at least the mid-1980s, because immigrants from southern Europe sold them on the street corners of Manhattan every November and December. In the mountains of southern Europe, where a species native to western Asia thrived, chestnuts had been the chief dietary staple for thousands of years. European chestnut production declined steeply in the 1980s, however, partially because of an imported disease, and has continued to decline since.

China and Japan each have their own blight-resistant native species of chestnut, and today Asia dominates world production. South Korea produces even more chestnuts than China; Italy and Turkey are third and fourth, respectively, among the world's producers of chestnuts.

Usually imported from Asia, chestnuts are occasionally available in supermarkets, but you are more likely to find good, fresh ones at an Asian or Italian market in November or December. Buy only plump, firm nuts that are heavy for their size and that have shiny, undamaged shells. You can also order U.S.-grown nuts through the Internet from small farms in Oregon, Washington, and elsewhere. Don't expect to find fresh chestnuts anywhere, though, before late fall or after early winter. The highly perishable nuts are sold as quickly as possible.

To roast chestnuts, make a ½-inch slit through each shell at the base, and cook them in a 400°F oven for 15 to 20 minutes. Or heat them in a pan over a low fire for 30 to 35 minutes. Then wrap them in a clean kitchen towel so they stay soft while they cool.

If you have more nuts than you can eat right away, shell them and store them in airtight containers in the refrigerator or freezer. Chestnuts will keep for up to six months in the refrigerator and up to a year in the freezer.

If you are lucky enough to have your own chestnut tree, harvest the nuts at least every other day so they don't have a chance to dry

HAZELNUTS OR FILBERTS?

Until the 1980s, Oregonians tended to reserve the word *hazelnut* for the native nut, *C. cornuta*; farmed hazelnuts were called *filberts*, an old name that may have arisen because hazelnuts begin to ripen around August 20, the saint's day of the seventh-century monk Philibert. Marketing people scrapped *filbert* for *hazelnut* because they thought the latter sounded better. Most Oregonians now use the words *filbert* and *hazelnut* interchangeably.

out or get moldy. To develop their best flavor, according to Oregon State University Extension, you should spread out the unpeeled nuts to cure at room temperature for three to five days, and then put them into a can with two small nail holes on opposite sides an inch from the top. Put the lid on the can, and set the can in the refrigerator for two weeks. By changing starches to sugar, this process develops a fine flavor in the nuts. If the rounded side of the nut feels springy when pressed, the nut is ready to use or to shell and freeze.

The Persian walnut, *Juglans regia*, is a Eurasian cousin of the American pecan, hickory, butternut, and black walnut. From southeastern Europe to China, the Persian walnut has been valued since ancient times for its oil and for the brown dye made from its husks. You may know this nut as the English walnut, because the English once dominated the world walnut trade, but the nut actually didn't reach England until the fifteenth century, only slightly earlier than it reached North America.

Although the walnut thrives over much of the temperate world, commercial production in the United States is almost entirely limited to California. Only China, which developed very thin-shelled walnuts, produces more; Iran and Turkey are third and fourth among the world's producers.

Persian walnuts fall to the ground as they ripen, when the nuts naturally come free of their husks (this isn't true of black walnuts, which may retain their husks through the winter). Before rain can start the growth of mold, pick up the nuts and spread them to dry, or hang them in sacks, under cover. Wear gloves when you harvest the nuts, or the husks will stain your fingers black. Ideal temperatures for drying are 95° to 105°F. After a few days of drying, store the nuts at 55°F or lower, or shell them and refrigerate or freeze them in airtight containers.

An easy way to shell a walnut is to hit it on the end with a hammer.

The genus *Corylus* includes nine trees or shrubs in the birch family with small, rich nuts. North America has two species: *C. americana*, native to the eastern states and provinces, and *C. cornuta*, the beaked hazelnut, named for the long, curved end of the nut's husk; the latter species grows from coast to coast. Both produce small, hard-shelled nuts. For commercial and domestic production, Americans have long preferred *C. maxima*, from southern Europe, whose nut in its husk looked like a helmeted head (*Corylus* comes from a Greek word for "helmet," and the English sometimes call hazelnuts *cobnuts*, from the Old English *cop*, "head"). *C. maxima* has relatively big nuts with thin shells, as does *C. colurna*, the Turkish hazelnut.

Eastern hazelnut orchards long ago succumbed to eastern filbert blight, a fungal disease spread from the resistant *C. americana*. In western Oregon, where *C. maxima* has been cultivated since 1858, the blight didn't appear until the 1970s. Relying on vigilance and spraying while breeders develop resistant varieties, Willamette Valley farmers today produce at least 98 percent of the hazelnuts grown on North American farms, and about 3 percent of the world's hazelnuts (most of which come from Turkey). Typically a hedgerow shrub in Europe, *C. maxima* is grown in Oregon as a single-stemmed orchard tree.

Hazelnuts are mature when they pop from the husk and fall to the ground. They should be gathered quickly, especially if the weather has been wet, and dried and stored like walnuts.

Hazelnuts may be most nutritious raw, but they are tastiest roasted, as described on page 212. Store the roasted nuts in airtight containers in the refrigerator or freezer. Use them in desserts, grind them into butter, or eat them just as they are. They combine especially well with chocolate.

For other recipes using walnuts, see Fig Conserve (page 146) and Prune Plum Conserve (page 277). For a recipe using both walnuts and hazelnuts, see *Cogna* (page 175).

GREEN WALNUT PRESERVES

MAKES 2 PINTS

FIRST DISCOVERED these preserves in a little Portland market run by a man from Sarajevo; the jar came from Armenia. I was familiar with pickled green walnuts, which are popular in England, but these related preserves were new to me. I soon learned that they are well known in Greece, Romania, Moldova, and other countries of southern and eastern Europe, as they were also in England in the seventeenth century. Recipes vary a good deal—for example, sometimes the nuts are peeled, and sometimes they are not—but they are always picked young, from late June to mid-July, and soaked in cold water for a time to remove bitterness. I developed these preserves to taste as much as possible like the delicious ones I bought from the man from Sarajevo.

Serve one to three nuts per person on tiny plates, or chop the nuts and serve them with a little of the syrup over ice cream.

> 2¼ pounds green English walnuts, picked between late
>   June and mid-July
> 4½ cups sugar
> 3 cups water
> 2 tablespoons strained lemon juice
> 16 cloves
> 6 allspice berries
> One 2-inch cinnamon stick

1 Thinly peel the developing walnut husk with a vegetable peeler or paring knife. (Wear gloves for this task, or else your fingers will be stained black for a week.) Immediately drop each peeled

nut into a bowl of cold water. When all the nuts are in the bowl, set a plate on top and weight it to keep the walnuts from floating.

2 Soak the walnuts at room temperature in water to cover them for 5 to 6 days, changing the water twice each day.

3 In a preserving pan, combine the sugar, the 3 cups water, and the lemon juice. Stir the mixture over low heat until the sugar is dissolved, and then raise the heat to medium-high and bring the mixture to a boil. Let it boil for about 15 minutes, until it becomes a heavy syrup (it should drip in slow, heavy drops from a spoon after cooling for a minute).

4 Drain the nuts well and add them to the syrup. Put the cloves, allspice, and cinnamon into a spice bag and add it to the pan. Bring the mixture to a boil and simmer it for 30 minutes. Remove the pan from the heat, cover it with a cloth, and let it stand at room temperature for 8 to 12 hours.

5 Again bring the mixture to a boil and let it simmer for 30 minutes. Remove the pan from the heat. Press the spice bag against the side of the pan before removing the bag.

6 Divide the walnuts and syrup between 2 pint mason jars. Add lids and rings, and process the jars in a boiling-water bath for 10 minutes.

CHESTNUTS IN SYRUP

MAKES 2 PINTS

Y OU MAY HAVE SEEN this preserve at a fancy-foods store among other expensive little bottled treats from Europe. Especially when homemade, chestnuts in syrup make a beautiful and delectable gift.

1½ pounds chestnuts in their shells

1¼ cups sugar

¼ cup light corn syrup

3 cups water

½ vanilla bean, split lengthwise

1. With a knife, slit each shell on its flat side without piercing the nut meat. Put the nuts into a pan and cover them completely with water. Bring the water to a boil, reduce the heat, and simmer the nuts for 20 minutes.

2. Drain off the water and let the chestnuts dry in the pan over very low heat, shaking the pan a few times; this will help keep the nuts from falling apart when you peel them. Remove the pan from the heat and leave the chestnuts in the pan just until they are cool enough to handle.

3. Peel the chestnuts and remove the skins, if they adhere to the flesh, with a paring knife. Throw away any nuts with a black area or an unpleasant smell.

4. In a pan, combine the sugar, the corn syrup, the 3 cups water, and the vanilla bean. Heat gently, stirring, until the sugar dissolves, and then raise the heat and bring the liquid to a boil. Add the chestnuts and simmer them, uncovered, for 30 minutes. Remove the pan from the heat, cover it with a towel, and let the mixture stand at room temperature for 12 to 24 hours.

5. Bring the mixture to a boil over medium heat and simmer the nuts, uncovered, for 5 minutes. Remove the vanilla bean and divide the nuts and syrup between 2 pint mason jars. Add lids and rings, and process the jars in a boiling-water bath for 10 minutes.

CHESTNUT CREAM

....

MAKES ABOUT 2½ CUPS

O ME CHESTNUTS TASTE LIKE dry, mealy sweet potatoes—not the very sweet orange ones called yams, but the
pale yellow ones. If you like sweet potatoes, you will probably love
this treat.

Chestnut cream makes a wonderful filling for a chocolate cake. You
can also use chestnut cream in ice cream, mousses, and soufflés.

1 pound chestnuts in their shells
½ vanilla bean
About 1½ cups sugar
2 teaspoons dark rum (optional)

1. With a knife, slit each chestnut shell on its flat side without piercing the nut meat. Put the nuts into a saucepan and cover them
completely with water. Bring the water to a boil, reduce the heat,
and simmer the nuts for 20 minutes.

2. Drain off the water from the pan and let the chestnuts cool until
you can handle them. Then peel the chestnuts and remove the
skins, if they come off easily (leaving some attached won't do any
harm). Throw away any nuts with a black area or an unpleasant
smell.

3. Return the nuts to the saucepan and add the vanilla bean half and
just enough water to cover the nuts. Cover the pan, bring the
mixture to a boil, and reduce the heat. Simmer the chestnuts for
about 30 minutes, until the nuts are tender. Drain off and reserve
the liquid, and remove and reserve the vanilla bean. Weigh the
nuts; you should have about 1 pound.

④ Chop the nuts coarsely, and then grind them in a blender or food processor with about 3 tablespoons of the cooking liquid (discard the remainder). Put the puree into the saucepan. Add three-quarters as much sugar, by weight, as you have nuts, or 1½ cups sugar for 1 pound of cooked chestnuts. Split the vanilla bean half lengthwise, scrape the seeds into the pan, and add the pod to the pan. Heat the mixture over low heat, stirring, until the sugar dissolves, and then continue heating and stirring until the mixture thickens a bit and pulls away from the bottom of the pot. Remove the vanilla pod and stir in the rum, if you are using it.

⑤ Pack the hot chestnut cream into small wide-mouth jars and cap the jars. When the jars are cool, store them in the refrigerator, where the chestnut cream should keep for at least several weeks.

REBECCA'S HAZELNUT-CHOCOLATE SPREAD

MAKES ABOUT 1½ CUPS

I LOVE BOTH HAZELNUTS AND CHOCOLATE and like to combine them in cakes and other desserts, so I've always thought I should like Nutella, the commercial hazelnut-chocolate spread so popular with European children. But I don't, not at all. So one day when my daughter was making hazelnut butter, I asked her to develop a better hazelnut-chocolate spread. She did, and it had a full, rich chocolate-and-hazelnut flavor with no unpleasant overtones. You can spread it between cake or cookie layers or on bread or simply eat it with a spoon.

To make hazelnut butter, crack and remove the nut shells and spread the nuts on a baking pan. Roast the nuts at 275° to 300°F until the skins crack and the nut meats under the skins begin to color, about 20 minutes. Remove the pan from the oven, cover the nuts with a towel, and let them cool. Rub them with a towel to remove most of the skins. Grind the nuts in a powerful blender (I use a Vita-Mix) or juicer (my mother uses a Champion), a small quantity at a time, adding a little hazelnut or walnut oil, if necessary.

1 cup high-quality extra-dark chocolate chips
2 tablespoons milk
3 tablespoons unsalted butter
1 cup hazelnut butter

1. Combine the chocolate chips, milk, and butter in the top half of a double boiler and heat them gently until the chocolate and butter melt. Stir, add the hazelnut butter, and stir again until all of the ingredients are well combined.

2. Pack the mixture into one or more jars or plastic containers and store the containers in the refrigerator, where the spread will keep for several weeks, at least.

ORANGE

Orange Honey   215

Orange Slices in Honey Syrup   216

Sweet Orange–Lemon Marmalade   217

Blood Orange Marmalade   219

Orange Jelly   221

Orange Curd   222

Candied Orange Peel   223

F THE TWO MAIN TYPES OF ORANGES, bitter and sweet, I've only ever seen the latter in the United States. But, because this book is about preserving, and because English marmalade—properly made from bitter oranges, never sweet—is such an important part of the history of fruit preserves, I'll discuss both types here. Besides, I hear that bitter oranges are beginning to show up in some stores, especially in cities with large Latino populations. If you find bitter oranges in the market, try them!

Native to southeast Asia, the bitter, sour, or Seville orange, *Citrus aurantium*, was brought by the Arabs to southern Spain by the end of the twelfth century. It was the only orange known in Europe for over 500 years, and when it was brought to the Americas it naturalized in many areas. It is said to be very seedy and too sour to eat out of hand, but it has important virtues: It is much richer in pectin and more aromatic than other oranges, and it is richer in vitamin C than lemons. This is the orange that flavors the liqueurs triple sec, Grand Marnier, and curaçao. Its peel provides an essential oil for perfumes and flavorings. And all parts of the fruit are used in traditional English and Scottish marmalades.

Sweet oranges, locally grown, were mentioned in an Italian manuscript in 1541, but they probably weren't planted extensively in Europe until after Vasco da Gama returned from India in 1498 with a superior variety. Because they were said to come from China, sweet oranges came to be known as China oranges or *C. sinensis* (they are still called *chinas* in Puerto Rico). Columbus brought both sweet and sour oranges to the New World, and they thrived in the West Indies. By 1565 the Spanish had planted sweet oranges in Florida, and a century later they introduced the fruit to California, thus sowing the seeds for two great rival industries.

There are many varieties of sweet oranges, but I'll mention only the two most familiar in the United States and a third that's unusual but hard to miss when it appears in markets.

Navel oranges, grown extensively in the Mediterranean region as well as in California, are seedless, easy to peel, and outstandingly flavorful. A navel orange is easy to recognize by the "baby" fruit embedded in the blossom end. Navels came to California from Brazil and, before that, to Brazil from Portugal, but they probably originated in China.

Valencia oranges, grown in both California and Florida, have a thinner rind, a few seeds, and ample juice. Although these oranges got their name when a Spanish citrus expert visiting California thought them similar to a variety grown near Valencia, Spain, they are probably actually of Portuguese origin.

Blood oranges, with their red and orange mottled skin and flesh, probably arose from a mutation in Sicily in the seventeenth century. Although they have long been popular in Italy and other Mediterranean countries, commercial production has only recently begun in the United States. The most popular variety, Moro, thrives in California's interior valleys. Its aromatic flesh, like its peel, varies greatly in color, from one orange to another and within a single orange. You might cut one orange to find it uniformly ruby red inside, and then cut another whose flesh is orange mottled with red.

If you can't pick your oranges directly off the tree, try to find some labeled organic if you're planning to use the peels. Most oranges and other citrus fruits are treated with fungicide, dye, and wax before shipping.

Oranges and other citrus fruits contain in their pith and seeds a large proportion of proto-pectin, or pectose. For this reason, long, slow simmering is needed to extract the pectin required for gelling.

For other recipes using oranges, see Pear-Apricot-Orange Preserves (page 245) and Strawberry-Orange Jam (page 329).

ORANGE HONEY

MAKES ABOUT 2 PINTS

 THIS OLD RECIPE produces a fragrant orange-flavored honey. Orange Honey is not meant to gel.

4 cups strained fresh orange juice
⅓ cup grated orange zest
3 cups light honey (such as clover or blackberry)

Combine all of the ingredients in a preserving pan or large saucepan. Boil them gently to a thick syrup or to 220°F on a jelly thermometer. This should take about 40 minutes. Strain the syrup into sterilized jars and cap the jars tightly. The honey will keep well for at least a year in a cool, dry place.

ORANGE SLICES
IN HONEY SYRUP

MAKES 3 HALF-PINTS

RRANGED to look like whole sliced oranges in rounded half-pint jars, this preserve makes a handsome gift.

3 large oranges (about 2 pounds)
1 cup sugar
¾ cup light honey (such as clover or blackberry)
3 tablespoons strained lemon juice
1 cinnamon stick
6 cloves
6 allspice berries

1 If the fruits were store-bought and not labeled organic, put them in a colander in the sink and pour boiling water over them to remove any wax. Scrub them well.

2 Cut a thin slice from either end of each orange, so that you can see the flesh and membranes. With a sharp knife, cut out the orange sections along the membranes, from one end of the orange to the other, through both flesh and peel. Put the orange sections into a nonreactive saucepan and cover them with water. Bring the contents to a boil. Reduce the heat and simmer the oranges for 40 minutes, until they are slightly tender. Drain them.

3 In a nonreactive saucepan, combine the sugar, honey, and lemon juice. Put the cinnamon, cloves, and allspice into a spice bag and add it to the pot. Over medium heat, stirring, bring the mixture to a simmer. Add the oranges and simmer them for about 1 hour, until they are quite tender.

4 Press the spice bag against the side of the saucepan before removing the bag. Pack the orange slices vertically, peels out, in

3 rounded half-pint mason jars. Add a slice in the center and cover the oranges with the hot syrup. Add lids and rings, and process the jars for 10 minutes in a boiling-water bath.

SWEET ORANGE–LEMON MARMALADE

MAKES 2½ TO 3 PINTS

THE ENGLISH BEGAN IMPORTING oranges in the late fifteenth century, and by the seventeenth century they were making bitter orange marmalade. Early orange marmalades were made in the style of their quince ancestors: The peels and pulp, along with some apples, were boiled and beaten into a paste. Early in the eighteenth century, marmalade makers started leaving out the apples and sometimes shredding the orange peels and cooking them in a clear jelly, though the jelly was still solid enough to slice. It was the Scots, through their confectionery industry in Glasgow, who turned orange marmalade into a dense and sticky but spreadable breakfast treat, to eat with tea and toast.

Although in the eighteenth century sweet oranges became common in Britain, they were scorned by marmalade connoisseurs, who said that sweet orange marmalades turned out cloudy (I haven't found this to be so). To add to the acid and pectin of sweet oranges, marmalade makers combined them with lemons, as in this recipe.

This marmalade uses the whole peel of the orange, not just the zest, but omits the pulp. Lemons are combined with oranges to match the pectin and acidity of bitter oranges.

1 ¾ pounds oranges, halved

½ pound lemons

9 cups water

9 cups sugar

1 If the fruits were store-bought and not labeled organic, put them in a colander in the sink and pour boiling water over them to remove any wax. Scrub them well.

2 Juice the oranges and lemons, using an electric juicer if you have one, and running it long enough to clean most or all of the pulp out of the peel. Strain the juice into a nonreactive kettle.

3 Gather the strained seeds and pulp in a piece of cheesecloth. Scrape out any membrane remaining in the peels, and add it to the cheesecloth. Cut each peel half in half. Cut out any navels, and add them to the cheesecloth. Tie up the cheesecloth, and add it to the kettle. Slice the peel quarters very thinly crosswise and put them into the kettle. Add the water. Bring the mixture to a boil and simmer it, stirring occasionally, for 2 hours or until the peel is quite soft.

4 Remove the cheesecloth bag, pressing it firmly against the side of the kettle to extract the liquid. Add the sugar to the kettle. Over medium heat, stir the mixture until the sugar is dissolved. Raise the heat to medium-high and boil the mixture until a drop mounds in a chilled dish. Skim off any foam and let the marmalade cool for 10 minutes.

5 Give the marmalade a stir and ladle it into pint or half-pint mason jars. Add lids and rings, and process the jars for 10 minutes in a boiling-water bath.

DARK MARMALADE

In the late eighteenth century, sugar prices rose in Britain. Since brown sugar was a little cheaper than white, thrifty cooks began using the darker sugar for marmalade. To make Dark Marmalade, follow the directions above, but substitute brown sugar for the white.

CHUNKY MARMALADE

According to C. Anne Wilson (*The Book of Marmalade*, 1986), Frank Cooper's late-nineteenth-century marmalade, dark and loaded with big pieces of peel, was the favorite of dons and under-graduates at Oxford University. Male marmalade-eaters in England, Wilson says, still tend to prefer thick-cut marmalade.

To make Chunky Marmalade, follow the directions above, but coarsely chop the peel instead of thinly slicing it. To make it dark like Oxford marmalade, substitute brown sugar for the white.

BLOOD ORANGE MARMALADE

MAKES ABOUT 4 HALF-PINTS

T HE FLESH OF MORO ORANGES seems to me less tart than that of other oranges, but it is more aromatic, almost like blackberries. The special flavor comes through in this orange-red jelly with fine strips of paler peel.

2¼ pounds blood oranges
7 cups water
3 tablespoons lemon juice
2½ to 3 cups sugar

1 If the fruits aren't home-picked or labeled organic, put them in a colander in the sink and pour boiling water over them to remove any wax. Scrub them well.

2 Using a vegetable peeler, remove the zest of the oranges in large strips, leaving behind as much of the white pith as possible. Slice the strips crosswise into very thin shreds. Put the shredded zest into a saucepan with 2½ cups of the water.

3 Cut the oranges into chunks without removing their pith. Put the orange chunks into a nonreactive kettle with the remaining 4½ cups water.

4 Bring the contents of both pans to a boil. Reduce the heat and crush the orange chunks with a potato masher. Gently boil the contents of both pans, uncovered, for 1 hour, stirring occasionally.

5 Drain the liquid from the saucepan of orange zest into the kettle of oranges, reserving the zest. Pour the contents of the kettle into a damp jelly bag set over a bowl. Let the juice drip for several hours and then measure it. You should have 2½ to 3 cups of juice. Discard the contents of the jelly bag.

6 Combine the juice in a preserving pan with the zest, the lemon juice, and 1 cup of sugar for each cup of juice. Over medium heat, stir the mixture until the sugar dissolves. Raise the heat to medium-high and boil the mixture until it reaches 220°F on a jelly thermometer or mounds in a chilled dish. Remove the pan from the heat and let the marmalade cool for 5 minutes.

7 Give the marmalade a stir and ladle it into half-pint mason jars. Add lids and rings, and process the jars for 10 minutes in a boiling-water bath.

ORANGE JELLY

N O LAW SAYS THAT ORANGE JELLY has to have rind float-ing in it, yet recipes for plain orange jelly are hard to find. This one uses Homemade Orange Pectin.

> 1 cup strained fresh orange juice, preferably Valencia
> 1 cup Homemade Orange Pectin (page 17)
> 2 tablespoons strained lemon juice
> 1½ cups sugar

1 Combine all of the ingredients in a preserving pan. Stir the con-tents over medium heat until the sugar dissolves, then raise the heat to medium-high. Boil the jelly, skimming off the foam, until the jelly passes the spoon test (page 18) or the temperature reaches 220°F on a jelly thermometer. Remove the pan from the heat.

2 Ladle the jelly into half-pint mason jars. Add lids and rings, and process the jars for 10 minutes in a boiling-water bath. After re-moving the jars from the bath, leave them undisturbed for 2 days, since the jelly may take this long to set.

CINNAMON-ORANGE JELLY

Cinnamon and orange make an irresistible flavor combination. Follow the directions for Orange Jelly, but add a cinnamon stick to the ingredients before heating them, and remove it just before ladling the jelly into jars.

VANILLA-ORANGE JELLY

This combination of flavors reminds me of ice cream I had as a child. The half-gallon box was packed half with vanilla ice cream, half with orange sherbet, in alternating cubes. Follow the directions for Orange Jelly, but add a vanilla bean along with the sugar to the preserving pan. Remove the vanilla bean before putting the jelly into jars.

ORANGE CURD

MAKES ABOUT 1 PINT

LIKE LEMON CURD, orange curd is used to fill tarts and spread on toast. You might also use it as a topping for cheesecake.

2 large eggs
2 large egg yolks
½ cup strained fresh orange juice
3 tablespoons strained lemon juice
6 tablespoons unsalted butter, softened
1 cup sugar
Grated zest of 1 orange (optional)

1 In a bowl, beat the eggs and yolks until they are smooth. Beat in the orange juice and lemon juice.

2 Melt the butter in the top of a double boiler over medium-low heat. Stir in the sugar, and then stir in the egg–lemon juice mixture. Continue stirring until the curd thickens, about 5 minutes. When the curd is ready, you should be able to draw a path on the back of the spoon with your finger (a thermometer inserted into the curd will read 160°F). Stir in the zest, if you are using it.

3 Pour the hot curd into one or more jars and cap them tightly. Store them in the refrigerator or freezer. Orange curd will keep in the refrigerator for at least 1 week, in the freezer for at least 2 months.

CANDIED
ORANGE PEEL

MAKES ABOUT 2 CUPS

T HIS RECIPE PRODUCES pretty strips of tender, sugared rind that are only mildly bitter. Eat them as candy, or chop them and add them to breads and cakes.

4 medium-size oranges
1 ¾ cups sugar
⅔ cup water

1. If the fruits aren't home-picked or labeled organic, put them in a colander in the sink and pour boiling water over them to remove any wax. Scrub them well.

2. Cut the orange peels into quarters without cutting through the flesh. Remove the peels (save the peeled oranges for another use). Put the peels into a large nonreactive saucepan and cover them with water. Bring the contents to a boil, reduce the heat, and simmer the peels until they are tender, about 30 minutes. Drain the peels and let them cool.

3. Using a grapefruit spoon, carefully scrape most of the pith off the peels. Cut them into thin strips.

4. In the saucepan, combine 1¼ cups of the sugar and the water. Over medium heat, gently stir the contents until the sugar dissolves. Add the peel. Cook the peel in the syrup over low heat until the peel is partially translucent, 45 minutes to 1 hour. Raise the heat and boil the contents, stirring, until the syrup reaches the thread stage (page 18) or 230°F on a jelly thermometer. Remove the pan from the heat and let the peels cool in the syrup for 30 minutes.

5 Spread the remaining ½ cup sugar on a dinner plate. Pour the contents of the pan into a strainer held over a bowl. Drop the drained peels onto the sugared plate. With a fork, toss the peels in the sugar. Let them cool.

6 Store the peels in an airtight tin or jar in a cool, dark, dry place. The peels will keep well for at least a year.

CANDIED LEMON PEEL

Make this just like Candied Orange Peel (page 223), but substitute 6 lemons for the 4 oranges.

OREGON GRAPE

Oregon Grape Jelly   226

A S A CHILD, my daughter thought of the world as the Garden of Eden and ignored all my warnings about strange and forbidden fruits. Only once did she have regrets, when she was nearly two and still unable to speak. She ran to me in a panic, pulled me across the garden to a little hedge of Oregon grape, and frantically pantomimed that she had eaten one of the dark little berries and been poisoned by it.

If you ate an Oregon grape raw, you too might guess that the little fruits are poisonous, for they are very tart, a little bitter, and not at all sweet. But they are rich in pectin and make a fine jelly. Nearly black in color, the jelly has a grape-like but much spicier flavor.

In either its tall form (*Mahonia aquifolium*) or its short form (*M. nervosa*), Oregon grape is unrelated to true grapes. The plant is an evergreen shrub with prickly, holly-like leaves and bright yellow blooms. Indigenous only to the western part of the Pacific Northwest, from northern California to the southern coastal region of British Columbia, Oregon grape is widely grown elsewhere as a drought-resistant landscaping plant.

Although Native Americans never ate the berries in large quantity as a food, instead using them medicinally (for liver, gallbladder, and eye problems and as a remedy for shellfish poisoning), Oregon grape berries are today used for wine as well as jelly. For jelly, they are sometimes combined with the berries of salal, a shrub indigenous to the same region.

OREGON GRAPE JELLY

RECOMMEND MAKING Oregon grape juice with a steam juicer (page 14). If you don't have one, combine the berries with half their volume of water in a nonreactive kettle and boil them gently, uncovered, for 15 minutes, mashing them after the first 10 minutes. Then drain the juice through a damp jelly bag and boil the juice for 10 minutes to reduce it before proceeding.

3 cups Oregon grape juice
2¼ cups sugar

1 Combine the juice and sugar in a preserving pan. Over medium heat, stir the contents until the sugar is dissolved. Raise the heat to medium-high and boil the mixture until it passes the spoon test (page 18) or the temperature reaches 220°F on a jelly thermometer.

2 Remove the pan from the heat and skim off any foam. Immediately pour the jelly into half-pint mason jars. Add lids and rings, and process the jars for 10 minutes in a boiling-water bath.

PAPAYA

Papaya Preserves   228
Papaya Jam   229

THIS OVERSIZED, TREE-LIKE woody herb is native to southern Mexico and Central America but now grows all over the tropics and subtropics. Although it can live for as long as 20 years, it is commercially productive for only about three and a half. It cannot withstand freezing temperatures. In the United States, papayas are commercially grown only in Hawaii and southern Florida.

Papaya is valued as a source not only of food but of an enzyme, papain. Papain is collected by scoring the unripe fruit, letting the copious latex-like sap drip into buckets, and then drying the latex into a powder, which is sold in supermarkets as a meat tenderizer. Papain is also used medicinally, especially for digestive ailments.

Papaya fruits are sometimes boiled green as a vegetable, but they cease to be a vegetable when their skins begin turning yellow or orange and they are slightly tender to the touch. The papaya flesh is then sweet and bright yellow, orange, or red. In the center are glistening black seeds that look like oversized fish eggs; they have a sharp, spicy taste and are sometimes dried and ground as a substitute for black pepper.

There are two main types of papayas, both of which are now available in markets. Hawaiian papayas weigh about 1 pound, Mexican papayas as much as 10 pounds. Hawaiian papayas have yellow skins when ripe and bright orange or pink flesh. Mexican papayas are generally less sweet, and their flesh may be yellow, orange, or pink.

Ripe papayas are rich in vitamin A but low in acid, so they are usually eaten with a squeeze of lime juice. They are also made into juice, served in fruit salads, dried, candied, and cooked into preserves.

The skin of the papaya is thin and tender. It peels off easily with a knife.

PAPAYA PRESERVES

MAKES 1 PINT

T HIS RECIPE makes a jarful of orange, partially gelled syrup laden with firm, darker orange chunks of papaya. To balance the sweetness, the limes provide acidity and a touch of bitterness.

1 pound peeled and seeded papaya
2 cups sugar
Zest of 2 limes, in thin shreds
¼ cup strained lime juice

1 Slice the papaya lengthwise into strips ½ to ¾ inch thick, and then cut the strips crosswise into approximate cubes.

2 In a preserving pan, layer the papaya pieces with the sugar. Top with the lime zest and juice. Cover the pan and let it stand at room temperature for 12 to 24 hours, until most of the sugar has dissolved.

3 Over medium heat, stir the contents gently until the sugar dissolves, and then raise the heat to medium-high. Bring the mixture to a boil. Remove the pan from the heat, cover it with a cloth, and let it stand at room temperature for 8 to 12 hours.

4 Return the pan to the heat and bring the mixture slowly to a simmer. Simmer the mixture for about 45 minutes, until the papaya pieces have darkened and are partially translucent.

5 Remove the pan from the heat and let the preserves cool for 5 minutes. Give them a stir and then pour the preserves into one pint or two half-pint mason jars. Add lids and rings, and process the jars in a boiling-water bath for 10 minutes.

PAPAYA JAM

MAKES ABOUT 2½ PINTS

To ENHANCE THE TROPICAL FLAVOR of papaya, you can use lime juice in place of lemon and add half a vanilla bean along with the juice and sugar. But this simple recipe lets the delicate flavor of papaya shine through.

2 pounds peeled and seeded papaya, cut into small pieces
3 cups sugar
½ cup lemon juice

1 Put the papaya pieces into a preserving pan and cover the pan. Simmer the fruit, stirring occasionally, until it is tender, about 15 minutes. Mash it with a potato masher and remove the pan from the heat.

2 Add the sugar and lemon juice to the pan. Cook the mixture over medium heat, stirring, for about 15 minutes, until it mounds slightly in a chilled dish.

3 Ladle the jam into pint or half-pint mason jars. Add lids and rings, and process the jars in a boiling-water bath for 10 minutes.

PEACH

Peach Jam   232

Peach-Fig Jam   233

Peaches in Syrup   234

Brandied Peaches with Vanilla   235

I F THE ONLY PEACHES you have ever eaten came from the supermarket, you have never eaten a fresh ripe peach. Peaches are soft, juicy, sweet, and incredibly aromatic—*if* they have ripened on the tree in hot weather. When they have, they are very perishable. They must be handled very gently and used within a few days. If you don't grow your own peaches, you'll want to beg them from a friend with a peach tree or buy them from a farmer.

Peaches originated in China and spread westward in ancient times. They arrived in Europe by way of Persia, where they so flourished that their botanical name is *Amygdalus persica*. In the United States, commercial cultivation of peaches began in the early nineteenth century. Today peaches are grown commercially in 29 states, but half of the production is in California. Peaches need hot summers and cool winters to thrive.

Peach cultivars are too numerous to discuss here, but they fall into two main categories: clingstone and freestone. Clingstone peaches are good for canning or pickling whole, if they are small, and you can cut them into narrow pieces by slicing toward the pit. They tend to be earlier and juicier than freestone peaches. Freestones are easily halved for canning, by cutting along the suture from the stem end to the blossom end and up the other side. There are excellent cultivars in each of these categories, and both types are good for eating fresh.

Although for many years peach breeders discarded white-fleshed crosses as too tender for commercial production, white-fleshed peaches are coming back. For this we can thank the Asians, who have paid top dollar for these very sweet, highly perfumed varieties. I highly recommend white-fleshed peaches for home orchards.

A special type of peach is the nectarine. You might think it a modern invention, but this naked peach has coexisted with the fuzzy one for 2,000 years, and it has been known by its English name since the seventeenth century or earlier. You can use nectarines in any way that you use peaches, although nectarines tend to have firmer flesh.

Another special type of peach is the "flat peach." Introduced to California from China in 1869, it lost favor until recently. New varieties such as Sweet Bagel and Stark Saturn (or Donut) are especially sweet and creamy, with yellow or white flesh and very small, freestone pits. These peaches, too, can be used as any others.

For all of the following recipes, peel the peaches by dipping them into boiling water for about a minute and then slipping off the skins. Process the peaches right away, or drop them into water acidulated with crushed vitamin C tablets (750 milligrams per quart of water) so that they do not brown.

"Of the gathering of peaches much might be said; let it suffice that they are neither pinched nor pulled off, but rather stroked off. A fond and delicate hand is applied, and a gentle rotatory movement should suffice if they are ripe."

—Edward A. Bunyard, The Anatomy of Dessert

PEACH JAM

P EACHES ARE WET!" I find this sentence in two places in my notes on this fruit. To quickly cook off excess water, make your Peach Jam in a wide pan—a large skillet works well—and don't try to work with a quantity larger than 2½ pounds.

> 2½ pounds peeled and pitted peaches
> 3¾ cups sugar
> 3 tablespoons lemon juice

1. Slice the peaches into a preserving pan and mash them lightly with a potato masher. Add the sugar and lemon juice. Heat the contents over medium heat, stirring, until the sugar is dissolved. Raise the heat to medium-high and boil the jam until a drop mounds in a chilled dish.

2. Ladle the jam into pint or half-pint mason jars. Add lids and rings, and process the jars for 10 minutes in a boiling-water bath.

PEACH AND GINGER JAM

If you want a fancier jam (though my children frown on this sort of adulteration), add ¼ cup chopped crystallized ginger (page 165) when you begin cooking your Peach Jam.

PEACH-FIG JAM

PEACHES, FIGS, and a little white wine make for an intriguing combination in this jam.

1 pound peeled and pitted peaches, thinly sliced
1 pound green-skinned figs, such as Desert King, cut into
    quarters or eighths depending on size
1 tablespoon lemon juice
3 cups sugar
⅓ cup white wine

1 Combine all of the ingredients in a preserving pan. Stir them over medium heat until the sugar dissolves, and then raise the heat to medium-high. Boil the jam until a drop mounds in a chilled dish.

2 Ladle the jam into pint or half-pint mason jars. Add lids and rings, and process the jars in a boiling-water bath for 10 minutes.

PEACHES IN SYRUP

....

MAKES 5 QUARTS

P EACHES ARE THE BEST REASON in the world to take up canning. Use just-ripe peaches, tender but not mushy. This recipe calls for small whole peaches, but you can substitute large peaches if you halve and pit them. The syrup here is light; if you like a heavier syrup, increase the quantity of sugar to as much as 8 cups.

> 2 quarts water
> 4 cups sugar
> 7 ½ pounds unpitted peaches,
>   about 2 inches in diameter

1 In a kettle, combine the water and sugar. Heat the contents to a boil, stirring until the sugar is dissolved. Remove the kettle from the heat and cover it to keep the syrup warm.

2 Loosen the skins of the peaches by dropping a few at a time into a kettle of boiling water. After 1 minute, take the peaches out with a slotted spoon and transfer them to a large bowl. When they are cool enough to handle, slip off the skins. Divide the juice that has collected in the bowl among 5 quart mason jars.

3 Return the kettle of syrup to the heat. With a slotted spoon, transfer the peaches, a few at a time, to the syrup. Bring the syrup to a boil, and then transfer the peaches to the jars.

4 When all the peaches have been heated in the syrup, ladle the syrup over the peaches, leaving ½ inch headspace. Run a narrow spatula around the inner surface of the jar to remove any bubbles. Add lids and rings, and process the jars in a boiling-water bath for 25 minutes.

....

BRANDIED PEACHES
WITH VANILLA

....

MAKES 5 QUARTS

R ECIPES FOR BRANDIED PEACHES call for anywhere from 2 tablespoons to 1 cup brandy per quart. Feel free to use more or less brandy than is called for here.

For extra vanilla flavor—and tiny black flecks in the syrup—slit the vanilla bean vertically before adding it to the syrup.

> 6 cups water
> 6 cups sugar
> 1 vanilla bean
> 7½ pounds unpitted peaches,
>   about 2 inches in diameter
> 1⅔ cups brandy

1 In a kettle, combine the water and sugar. Add the vanilla bean. Heat the contents to a boil, stirring to dissolve the sugar. Simmer the syrup, uncovered, for 10 minutes. Remove the kettle from the heat and remove the vanilla bean (rinse, dry, and save it, if you like, to flavor sugar). Cover the syrup to keep it warm.

2 While the syrup simmers, loosen the skins of the peaches by dropping a few at a time into a kettle of boiling water. After 1 minute, take the peaches out with a slotted spoon and transfer them to a large bowl. When they are cool enough to handle, slip off the skins. Divide any juice that has collected in the bowl among 5 quart mason jars.

3 Return the kettle of syrup to the heat. With a slotted spoon, transfer the peaches, a few at a time, to the syrup. Bring the syrup to a boil, and then transfer the peaches to the jars.

....

4 Divide the brandy evenly among the jars. Add syrup to fill the jars, leaving ½ inch headspace. Run a narrow spatula around the inner surface of the jar to remove any bubbles. Add lids and rings, and process the jars in a boiling-water bath for 25 minutes.

PEAR, EUROPEAN AND ASIAN

Pear Jam   241

Pear Preserves with Ginger   242

Pears in Red Wine   243

Pear–Red Wine Preserves   244

Pear-Apricot-Orange Preserves   245

Candied Asian Pears and Asian Pear
  Syrup   246

Pear Butter   248

Apple–Asian Pear Paste   249

Asian Pears in Honey Syrup   250

Sirop de Liège (Pear-Apple Syrup)   251

THE EUROPEAN PEAR, *Pyrus communis,* actually origi-nated in western Asia and made its way westward along with apples, quinces, and apricots. The trees thrived even in England, and over the centuries European breeders developed hundreds of cultivars (since pears don't grow true from seed, these were spread by grafting). In 1629 pear seeds were brought from England to Massachusetts, and Americans began selecting their own favorite varieties. In the 1900s, American grew thousands of kinds of pears, both native and European. They ranged from the size of a cherry to that of a grapefruit, and from green to yellow to red to maroon. Some were striped; some were speckled. Most were more or less pear shaped, but some were round and others long and thin.

Some were grown for special purposes—small varieties for pickling whole, astringent varieties for making perry, or pear cider. The earliest ripened in June, the latest in late November.

Many of these old varieties are still available for planting. Choices for supermarket shoppers, however, are very limited. Ninety-five percent of the commercial pear crop in the United States comes from Washington, California, and Oregon. Western farmers stick with just a few varieties, mainly big, juicy moderately early Bartlett; Anjou (or D'Anjou), a good keeper; russetted, slender, sweet Bosc; and my favorite—broad, firm, sweet, aromatic Comice, which ripens late in the season. Occasionally you may also find in markets red varieties of Bartlett and Anjou; long-necked, firm-fleshed Concorde; small, juicy Forelle; and very small, very sweet Seckel.

You may find still other pear varieties in nurseries. If you are planting pear trees, be sure to select varieties that will thrive where you live. In the South, where the branch-blackening disease fireblight is a problem, entirely different varieties are grown. Some, like Kieffer, are hybrids of European and Asian pears.

When European pears ripen, they should be eaten or cooked almost immediately. Most gardeners pick their pears just before they reach full ripeness and bring them indoors. Lower indoor temperatures slow the ripening, and having the pears laid out in boxes makes them easy to inspect. Signs of ripening are subtle; usually, even in red varieties, there is a slight yellowing of the skin. Sometimes, as with a russetted Bosc, the only clear sign of ripeness is a slight tenderness in the neck area. More than slight tenderness, in all pears, is a sign of overripeness.

Commercially grown pears are picked early and stored at a low temperature to supply markets through the winter and spring. Until recently, any supermarket pear sold in late winter or spring was likely to be beautiful on the outside but brown and mushy on the inside. In recent years, though, suppliers have better regulated picking and keeping times and temperature so that tasty pears are available most of the year.

Although they aren't as rich in pectin as apples, pears are very useful for preserving. Halve or quarter them for canning, if they are large; if not, can them whole. Slice them and dry them for tidy, lightweight snack food. You can use slightly overripe pears for jam and butter; just cut out and discard any mushy parts.

Sharing the genus *Pyrus* with European pears are Asian pears, related but very different fruits. Crisp rather than buttery, and usually round rather than pear shaped, Asian pears have been grown in eastern Asia for at least 2,500 years. Although they were first brought to California by Chinese miners during the Gold Rush, they have only recently become popular in this country. Asian pears are becoming well known by that name, but some people call them apple pears, because of the round shape of many varieties, and other people call them salad pears, because since they are typically low in acid their flavor is heightened by a little citrus juice or vinegar. Despite their low acidity, Asian pears are sweet and flavorful, and they often have a strong spicy or floral aroma.

"As it is, in my view, the duty of an apple to be crisp and crunchy, a pear should have such a texture as leads to silent consumption."

—Edward A. Bunyard, The Anatomy of Dessert

Asian pears come in many varieties. Japanese varieties are mostly derived from the sand pear, *P. pyrifolia*, a native Japanese tree with gritty fruits. But the grit under the skin is entirely or nearly absent in the best Japanese cultivars, which are generally round and russetted and often aromatic. Chinese varieties, hybrids of *P. ussuriensis* and other species, are often pear-shaped and usually yellow-green to yellow without russetting. Unrussetted Asian pear varieties tend to ripen earliest, in late summer, and the russetted varieties later, in the fall.

Asian pears are still relatively expensive in grocery stores, but they are easy to grow, although you need to plant two varieties that bloom at the same time to ensure good pollination. The trees are vigorous and very resistant to pests.

Unlike other pears, which are brought indoors for ripening, Asian pears ripen on the tree. Look for a color change—subtle in the russetted varieties—and a slight softening. I've found that the fruits keep for a long time in a cool room, although they gradually shrivel.

Since many Asian pear varieties are low in acid, they should be canned with added acid (lemon juice, lime juice, or citric acid) to prevent the growth of the bacteria that cause botulism.

Like European pears, Asian pears make good jam and butter.

For other recipes using pears, see *Cogna* (page 175) and Pear-Pineapple Marmalade (page 261).

PEAR JAM

....

MAKES ABOUT 3 PINTS

THIS PRESERVE OF PUREED PEARS is simple to make and simply delicious. I've made it with Bartlett pears, Seckel pears, and even Asian pears, and it's always a delight. Pear jam is a good use for pears that are slightly overripe.

> 3 pounds ripe pears, peeled, cored, and cut into chunks
> ¼ cup lemon juice
> 5 cups sugar

1. Combine the pears and lemon juice in a preserving pan, cover the pan, and set it over very low heat. Simmer the pears, stirring occasionally, until they are very soft, 20 to 30 minutes.

2. Press the pears with the juice through the medium screen of a food mill, or puree them in a food processor or blender.

3. Return the pear puree to the pan and stir in the sugar. Over low heat, stir until the sugar dissolves, and then raise the heat to medium-high. Bring the mixture to a boil and continue to boil it, stirring constantly, for about 15 minutes, until the jam falls heavily from a spoon and a drop of jam mounds in a chilled dish. Remove the pan from the heat and stir until the bubbling stops.

4. Ladle the jam into pint or half-pint mason jars and add lids and rings. Process the jars for 10 minutes in a boiling-water bath.

PEAR JAM WITH VANILLA

A hint of vanilla adds a different dimension to pear jam. Follow the directions above, but stir in 2 teaspoons vanilla extract just before ladling the jam into jars. If you make vanilla sugar, by burying a vanilla bean in a container of sugar, you can use the flavored sugar instead of plain sugar and vanilla extract.

PEAR PRESERVES
WITH GINGER

P EARS, LIKE QUINCES, turn red with long cooking. You'll witness the color change with this recipe. These preserves are wonderful over vanilla ice cream.

> 4 pounds just-ripe pears
> ¼ cup minced peeled ginger (the fresher the
>   better) or minced crystallized ginger, store-bought
>   or homemade (page 165)
> Grated or minced zest of 3 lemons
> 6 cups sugar
> ¼ cup strained lemon juice

1. Peel and core the pears and cut them into quarters if they are small or into eighths if they are large. As you work, layer the pear slices in a kettle with the ginger, lemon zest, and sugar; this will keep the pears from browning. Pour the lemon juice over all and let the kettle stand at room temperature, covered, for 6 to 12 hours, until most of the sugar has dissolved.

2. Set the kettle over low heat, and slowly bring the contents to a simmer. Keep them at a bare simmer for 1½ to 2 hours, until the pears are partially translucent and pink.

3. Remove the kettle from the heat and let the preserves cool for 5 minutes. Then ladle them into pint mason jars, add lids and rings, and process the jars in a boiling-water bath for 10 minutes.

PEARS IN RED WINE

MAKES 2 QUARTS

 USUALLY SERVED within a day or so of preparation, this classic dessert can also be preserved for last-minute use.

3 cups red wine (not too tannic)
¾ cup sugar
One 2-inch cinnamon stick
4 pounds small, firm ripe pears

1. In a nonreactive kettle, heat the wine and sugar with the cinnamon stick over medium heat until the sugar is dissolved.

2. While the wine and sugar heat, peel, halve, and core half of the pears. If you like, leave the stem attached to one half of each pear. Put the pear halves in the kettle; they should fit in a single layer. Cook them over low heat until they are tender, about 15 minutes.

3. While the first batch of pears cooks, prepare the rest of the pears in the same way.

4. When the first batch of pears are tender, transfer them with a slotted spoon to a quart mason jar. Put the rest of the pears into the cooking liquid and cook them over low heat until they, too, are tender.

5. Remove the kettle from the heat. With a slotted spoon, transfer the second batch of pears to another quart jar. Remove the cinnamon stick from the kettle and divide the cooking liquid between the jars, covering the pears well and leaving a ½-inch space at the top of each jar. Add lids and rings, and process the jars in a boiling-water bath for 25 minutes. Serve the pears as a dessert—cold, at room temperature, or gently reheated. If you plan to serve the pears hot, you might boil the syrup to thicken it.

PEAR–RED WINE PRESERVES

MAKES ABOUT 2 PINTS

IN THIS VERSION of the preceding recipe, the pears are cut into small pieces, and the syrup is much thicker. These preserves make a good topping for ice cream or cake.

    4 pounds just-ripe pears, peeled, cored, and cut into
        approximately ½-inch cubes
    4 cups sugar
    1 tablespoon strained lemon juice
    1 cup red wine (not too tannic)
    1 teaspoon vanilla extract

1 In a preserving kettle, layer the pear pieces with 2 cups of the sugar, and pour the lemon juice over. Cover the kettle and let it stand at room temperature for 6 to 12 hours, until most of the sugar has dissolved.

2 Add the remaining 2 cups sugar and the red wine to the kettle. Heat the contents over medium heat, stirring only as necessary, until all the sugar has dissolved. Raise the heat to medium-high and bring the contents to a boil. Boil rapidly for 5 minutes, skimming off any foam.

3 Remove the kettle from the heat and let the preserves cool for several minutes. Check the consistency of the syrup by dropping a little onto a chilled dish and letting it cool completely. If you like, return the kettle to the heat to thicken the syrup a little more. Stir in the vanilla extract when the boiling has stopped and the consistency is to your liking.

4 Ladle the preserves into pint or half-pint mason jars. Add lids and rings, and process the jars in a boiling-water bath for 10 minutes.

PEAR-APRICOT-ORANGE PRESERVES

 HESE PRESERVES OFFER a wonderful mix of flavors and aromas.

1 medium-size orange
¾ cup slivered dried apricots
½ cup water
One 3-inch cinnamon stick
1 pound peeled, cored, and diced just-ripe pears
3 cups sugar

1 Remove the zest from the orange in thin shreds. Peel the orange and dice the flesh. In a small saucepan, combine the orange zest and flesh with the apricots, water, and cinnamon stick. Bring the contents to a boil, cover the pan, and reduce the heat. Simmer the mixture for 5 minutes.

2 Transfer the contents of the saucepan to a preserving pan and add the pears and sugar. Heat the mixture over medium heat, stirring occasionally, until the sugar dissolves. Bring the mixture to a boil and boil it gently, occasionally stirring and skimming off the foam, for about 20 minutes, until the syrup thickens and reaches the thread stage (page 18) or 230°F on a jelly thermometer.

3 Remove the cinnamon stick and ladle the preserves into pint or half-pint mason jars. Add lids and rings, and process the jars for 10 minutes in a boiling-water bath.

CANDIED ASIAN PEARS AND ASIAN PEAR SYRUP

MAKES ABOUT 1½ CUPS CANDIED ASIAN PEARS
(AND 1½ CUPS SYRUP)

THIS IS MY FAVORITE WAY to preserve Asian pears. I especially like to use the fruits of my Seuri tree, which to me both smell and taste like bubblegum, only better. Preserved this way, the fruits retain their flavor and aroma and acquire the soft, chewy texture of jelly candies.

Over the years I have simplified this recipe repeatedly, but it's still a bit of work. You may find as I have, however, that candied Asian pears become your favorite treat for the winter holidays. Use the syrup on pancakes and waffles.

European pears can be preserved in the same way, although they will taste quite different.

> 2 cups water
> 2 tablespoons strained lemon juice
> 2½ pounds Asian pears, peeled, cored, and sliced 1 inch
>   thick (about 5½ cups)
> 2⅓ cups granulated sugar
> About ¼ cup extra-fine sugar

1 In a wide nonreactive pan, combine the water and lemon juice. Drop the pear slices into the pan and turn them to keep them from browning. Over low heat, simmer the pears until they are just tender, 15 to 20 minutes.

2 With a wire skimmer, transfer the pear slices to a bowl. Remove all but 1 cup liquid from the pan. Add the granulated sugar to the

pan and stir the contents over medium heat until the sugar dissolves. Raise the heat and boil the syrup without stirring until it reaches the thread stage (page 18) or 230°F on a jelly thermometer. Add the pears and cook them over low heat, without stirring, until they are partially translucent, about 1½ hours.

3 Remove the pan from the heat and cover it with a towel. Let the pan stand at room temperature for 8 to 12 hours.

4 With a wire skimmer, transfer the pear slices to a bowl. Boil the syrup until it again reaches the thread stage. Remove the pan from the heat and return the pear slices to the syrup. Return the pan to the heat, bring the syrup back to a boil, and then remove the pan from the heat again. Let the fruit cool in the syrup.

5 With a wire skimmer, transfer the pear slices to a rack or screen set over a dish to catch drips. Bring the syrup to a boil and boil it until it is thick. Pour it into a sterilized jar and cap the jar tightly. Store the jar in a cool, dry place, where the syrup should keep well for months.

6 Dry the fruit in a dehydrator or another warm place until the pears have lost most of their stickiness. This may take several days.

7 Roll the pear slices in the extra-fine sugar and then place them on a clean rack to finish drying.

8 Store the candied pear slices, layered in waxed paper, in an airtight container, where they will keep for months.

PEAR BUTTER

MAKES ABOUT 3½ PINTS

I USED TO MAKE THIS PRESERVE in great quantities when I lived in California's Santa Cruz Mountains, where I had a very productive Bartlett pear tree. Pear butter is every bit as delicious as apple butter, and a good use for pears that have begun to soften.

6 pounds cored and quartered pears (unpeeled)
About 4 cups light brown sugar
1 teaspoon ground cinnamon
1 teaspoon ground ginger
½ teaspoon ground cloves
½ teaspoon ground allspice

1 In a preserving pan, cook the pears over low heat, covered, until they are soft, about 20 minutes. If they are dense, you may need to add a little water at the start to keep them from scorching.

2 Using the coarse screen of a food mill, puree the pears. Measure the volume of the puree and add half as much light brown sugar. Add the cinnamon, ginger, cloves, and allspice and cook the mixture over low heat (or in an oven heated to 250°F), uncovered, until it is thick. This will probably take at least an hour or two. You'll need to stir occasionally at first and more frequently as the pear butter thickens.

3 Ladle the pear butter into pint or half-pint mason jars, and add lids and rings. Process the jars in a boiling-water bath for 10 minutes.

ASIAN PEAR BUTTER

My Asian pear trees are more productive than my regular pear trees, so Asian pears often stand in for regular pears in my kitchen. For Asian Pear Butter, I simplify the seasonings slightly to suit the flavor of the aromatic fruits.

Proceed exactly as for regular Pear Butter, but leave out the ginger and allspice, reduce the cloves to ¼ teaspoon, and add ½ teaspoon ground nutmeg.

APPLE–ASIAN PEAR PASTE

MAKES ABOUT 2½ POUNDS

T HIS IS ANOTHER RECIPE I developed to use some of my annual bounty of Asian pears. The paste is less grainy and a little softer than quince paste, slightly translucent, and a fine accompaniment to cheese.

1½ pounds quartered and cored Asian pears (unpeeled)
1½ pounds quartered and cored tart apples (unpeeled)
3 cups sugar

1. Over low heat, simmer the pears and apples together in a preserving pan, covered, until the Asian pears are soft (this may take as long as 1 hour). If necessary, add a tablespoon or two of water to avoid scalding the fruits before they release their juices.

2. Put the contents of the pan through the medium screen of a food mill. Return the fruit to the pan and add the sugar. Cook the mixture uncovered, stirring frequently, until the spoon leaves a bare trail in the pan. This may take an hour or more.

3. Remove the pan from the heat and pour the mixture into lightly oiled small, vertical-sided dishes. Let the top surface dry in a warm place, and then turn each block of paste over to dry on the other side.

4 Wrap the paste in waxed paper or plastic wrap and store the wrapped pieces in a heavy plastic bag in the refrigerator, where it should keep for several weeks or longer.

ASIAN PEARS
IN HONEY SYRUP

CANNING ASIAN PEARS in syrup is much like doing the same with other fruits. Since most Asian pear varieties are low in acid, however, it's important to include lemon juice or another acidic ingredient, such as citric acid. In this recipe I not only use ample lemon juice, I also replace the usual refined sugar with honey. Add spices to your liking, or leave them out. Serve these Asian pears for breakfast or a light dessert.

> 1¼ cups light honey (such as clover or blackberry)
> 3¼ cups water
> Grated zest of 1 lemon
> ½ cup strained lemon juice
> 8½ pounds Asian pears
> ¾ teaspoon anise seeds, ¾ teaspoon coriander seeds, or 6
>   slices ginger (optional)

1 In a preserving pan, combine the honey, water, lemon zest, and lemon juice. Bring the mixture to a simmer, stirring a bit to dissolve the honey.

2 Peel and core the Asian pears, slice them in half, and immediately drop the halves into the hot syrup. Simmer the fruit for 5 minutes, skimming off any foam.

3 While the fruit simmers, divide the spices, if you are using them, among quart or pint mason jars.

4 After the fruit has simmered for 5 minutes, remove it from the syrup with a slotted spoon and add it to the jars. Pour the hot syrup over the fruit, leaving ½ inch headspace in each jar. Add lids and rings, and process the jars in a boiling-water bath—pints for 20 minutes, quarts for 25 minutes.

SIROP DE LIÈGE
(PEAR-APPLE SYRUP)

MAKES ABOUT 1 PINT

MY DAUGHTER DISCOVERED THIS traditional preserve when she was living as an exchange student in Liège, Belgium. *Sirop de Liège* is much like boiled cider except that the fruits are cooked before they are pressed and the main ingredient is pears; only enough apples are added to ensure light gelling. The preserve has been made commercially since 1902, and today it is available with dates, plums, or prunes added. The oldest recipe, though, probably contained only pears and apples. I've found that Asian pears make a very good substitute for regular pears.

In Belgium, the dark, tart syrup is served with soft, strong-smelling Hervé cheese or other soft cheese and bread. The syrup is also enjoyed on crêpes and croissants and as an ingredient in both dessert and meat sauces.

2 pounds apples, quartered but not cored or peeled
6 pounds pears, quartered but not cored or peeled

1 Put the apples and pears into a very large kettle, cover the kettle, and place it over low heat. Let the fruit cook, stirring a few times, until it is soft and releases its juice. This will take several hours.

2 Drain and press out the juice. The ideal tool for this is a very small wine press, but you can use a sturdy strainer instead.

3 Pour the juice into a preserving pan. Boil the juice, stirring occasionally, until it is thick, dark, and glossy and falls from the spoon in big, slow drops. This will take at least 30 minutes.

4 Transfer the syrup to a sterilized jar and cap the jar tightly. Store it in the refrigerator, where it should keep for months.

PEPPER

Red Pepper Jam   255
Hot Red Pepper Jelly   256
Hot Green Pepper–Lime Jelly   257

Y *pepper* I mean *Capsicum*, a genus of problematic nomenclature. Columbus, greedy for spices, called the vegetable we know as pepper *pimiento*, likening it to black pepper, *pimienta* in Spanish—not to be confused with *Pimenta*, the scientific name for allspice. Caribbean islanders, though, called the pepper *ají*, as did most South Americans, and that name has stuck through the centuries in South America and the West Indies. Mexicans, meanwhile, have always called peppers *chiles*, and the Dutch spice traders tried to spread that name in Europe, to prevent confusion with their East Indian black pepper. Linnaeus cleared things up a bit with his generic term *Capsicum*—apparently from the Latin *capsa*, "box," although that seems a poor description of a pepper.

Considering the various pepper species and cultivars introduces a little clarity and a little more confusion. The pepper Columbus found in the West Indies came originally from South America. This species, which includes such aromatic but fiery members as the Scotch bonnet, is called *C. chinense*, though it has nothing to do with China. Popular in Asia, though, is the perennial *C. frutescens*, sometimes called bird pepper. One variety, Tabasco, was brought from Mexico to Louisiana, where it is still grown for fermented hot sauce. Most other peppers you're likely to know—sweet and hot, short or long, round or boxy or tapered—are *C. annuum*. One of my favorite *C. annuum* varieties is the sweet, thick-walled, heart-shaped pimiento, also called pimento. Such varieties as bell, Anaheim, cayenne, cherry, poblano, paprika, Fresno, and jalapeño are also *C. annuum*, the species domesticated in pre-Columbian Mexico and Central America and easiest to grow in northern climes.

If you grow your own peppers and plan to save the seeds, separate the varieties, or at least separate the sweet ones from the hot ones. Otherwise, you may be in for an incendiary surprise when varieties cross. You can't always tell a sweet pepper from a hot one by appearance.

RED PEPPER JAM

ONLY MILDLY PIQUANT, this jam is often served with cream cheese and crackers. Try it also in sandwiches made with smoked poultry or lamb.

> 1¼ pounds red bell or pimiento peppers, halved and seeded
> 2 to 4 small hot red peppers, such as jalapeño or Fresno,
>   halved and seeded
> 1 tablespoon salt
> 1 cup cider vinegar
> ½ cup Homemade Apple or Quince Pectin (page 17)
> 2½ cups sugar

1 Mince all the peppers. (You could use a food processor for this task, but a knife will provide a better appearance. Wear rubber or plastic gloves when handling the hot peppers to avoid burning your fingers, and be sure not to touch your eyes.) Toss the peppers in a bowl with the salt and let them stand for 1 hour. Drain them, rinse them with cold water, and then drain them again thoroughly.

2 Combine the minced peppers with the vinegar, homemade pectin, and sugar in a preserving pan. Stir the mixture over medium heat until the sugar is dissolved, and then raise the heat to medium-high. Bring the mixture to a boil and boil it until a drop mounds in a chilled dish.

3 Remove the pan from the heat. Ladle the mixture into pint or half-pint mason jars, and add lids and rings. Process the jars for 10 minutes in a boiling-water bath.

HOT RED PEPPER JELLY

THIS IS A HOTTER, more translucent spread than Red Pepper Jam (page 255).

¼ pound small hot red peppers, such as jalapeño or Fresno
1 tablespoon salt
2¾ cups Homemade Apple or Quince Pectin (page 17)
⅓ cup white wine vinegar
2¾ cups sugar

1 Mince the peppers without seeding them (wear rubber or plastic gloves for this task). Toss them with the salt in a small bowl. Let them stand for 1 to 2 hours, until they have released some liquid. Drain and rinse them, and then drain them again.

2 Combine the peppers with the homemade pectin, vinegar, and sugar in a preserving pan. Stir the contents over medium heat until the sugar is dissolved. Raise the heat to medium-high, and boil the jelly until it passes the spoon test (page 18).

3 Immediately remove the pan from the heat and let the jelly cool for 5 minutes. Then give it a stir and pour it into hot sterilized half-pint mason jars. Add lids and rings, and process the jars for 10 minutes in a boiling-water bath.

HOT GREEN PEPPER–LIME JELLY

MAKES 2 HALF-PINTS

SWEET, HOT, BITTER, and a little salty, this is much more flavorful than most spicy lime jellies. It will be especially bitter if you use Mexican limes. If you like, you can substitute lemons for the limes.

½ pound limes
3½ cups water
2 ounces green jalapeño peppers
1 teaspoon salt
2 minced garlic cloves
2 cups sugar

1. Remove half of the zest of one lime in thin shreds, and put the shreds into a small bowl. Peel the rest of the lime, and all of the remaining limes, with a vegetable peeler, leaving most of the pith on the fruit. Halve all the limes, squeeze out their juice, and strain the juice. Reserve the strained juice in a covered container and put the seeds and pulp into a large saucepan. Chop the rinds coarsely and add them to the saucepan. Add the 3½ cups water to the saucepan and bring the contents to a boil. Simmer the contents for 1¼ hours.

2. Meanwhile, cover the lime zest in the small bowl with water. Let the bowl stand while you simmer the lime rinds.

3. As the lime rinds begin to simmer, mince the peppers without seeding them (wear rubber or plastic gloves for this task). Toss them in a small bowl with the salt and let them stand while the lime rinds simmer.

4 When the lime rinds are ready, strain the liquid first through a colander and then through a damp jelly bag. You should have 2 cups. Pour the liquid into a preserving pan and add the reserved lime juice.

5 Drain the lime zest, and add it to the pan.

6 Drain and rinse the peppers. Drain them again thoroughly, and add them to the pan.

7 Add the garlic and sugar to the pan. Stir the contents over medium heat until the sugar is dissolved. Raise the heat to medium-high and boil the mixture until it reaches 220°F on a jelly thermometer. Remove the pan from the heat. If the jelly doesn't pass the spoon test (page 18), let it cool for a few minutes. As soon as you see any sign of gelling, give the jelly a stir and immediately pour it into half-pint mason jars. Add lids and rings, and process the jars in a boiling-water bath for 10 minutes.

PINEAPPLE

Pineapple Preserves   260

Pear-Pineapple Marmalade   261

Candied Pineapple and Pineapple
    Syrup   262

INDIGENOUS TO SOUTHERN BRAZIL, this herbaceous perennial spread to the West Indies sometime before Columbus arrived. The pineapples Columbus found, unlike their wild relatives, were seedless; the natives propagated them vegetatively, with cuttings. Starting new plants from the crowns of fruits carried on their ships, Europeans spread pineapple cultivation around the tropics and subtropics and even grew them in greenhouses at home.

In the United States, pineapples can be grown in southern Florida and coastal southern California. Fruits sold in markets, however, come from Hawaii, Mexico, and Central America.

Pineapples don't ripen after picking, and when they are fully ripe they don't keep long. So they are picked when just slightly underripe and quickly taken to market. Only a few varieties, with both high sugar and high acid content, keep well enough for long-distance shipping. You may have to travel to the tropics to taste fully ripe pineapple and low-acid varieties that don't ship well. Some of these varieties have white rather than yellow flesh and are amazingly aromatic.

If you live in a frost-free area and want to grow your own pineapple, you can start by twisting the crown out of a store-bought fruit, letting the crown dry for two days, and then planting it in the ground or starting it in water. Once a plant is established, you can start new ones by cutting and planting slips or suckers.

In the market, choose pineapples with green, fresh-looking leaves and no soft spots, dark spots, or mold on the stem end. Green-skinned pineapples can be just as ripe as yellow-skinned ones, so, instead of fussing about color, sniff the pineapple: A ripe one will smell good.

To trim a pineapple for fresh eating or for preserving, cut off both ends, including the crown of leaves at the top end. Stand the pineapple on end and cut off the thick peel in wide strips from top to bottom. With the tip of a vegetable peeler or a small knife, cut out the "eyes." Then cut the pineapple in half and into wedges, and trim the hard, fibrous core from each wedge.

For other recipes using pineapple, see Apricot-Pineapple Jam (page 54) and Yellow Tomato–Pineapple Preserves (page 344).

PINEAPPLE PRESERVES

MAKES ABOUT 3 PINTS

BECAUSE PINEAPPLES are very low in pectin, these preserves won't set. But the fruit-and-syrup combination is lovely over cake or ice cream. If you like, add the zest of a lemon or orange to the pan along with the listed ingredients.

> 2½ pounds peeled and cored pineapple, cut into
>   approximately ⅜-inch cubes
> ⅓ cup strained lemon juice
> 4¼ cups sugar

In a preserving pan, combine all of the ingredients. Gently stir the contents over medium heat until the sugar is dissolved. Raise the heat to medium-high and boil the contents until the syrup is slightly thickened and the pineapple is translucent. Remove the pan from the heat and let the preserves cool for 5 minutes. Give them a stir and ladle them into pint or half-pint mason jars. Add lids and rings, and process the jars in a boiling-water bath for 10 minutes.

PEAR-PINEAPPLE MARMALADE

MAKES ABOUT 2 PINTS

 MOOTH, SWEET PEARS and tangy pineapple combine well in these simple marmalade-like preserves.

1¾ cups chopped peeled just-ripe pears
1¾ cups chopped pineapple
2¾ cups sugar

1 Combine all of the ingredients in a preserving pan. Stir them over medium heat until the sugar dissolves. Raise the heat to medium-high and boil the mixture until a drop mounds in a chilled dish.

2 Ladle the marmalade into pint or half-pint mason jars, and add lids and rings. Process the jars in a boiling-water bath for 10 minutes.

CANDIED PINEAPPLE AND PINEAPPLE SYRUP

MAKES ABOUT 1½ CUPS CANDIED PINEAPPLE
(AND ABOUT 1½ PINTS PINEAPPLE SYRUP)

CANDIED PINEAPPLE has always been a favorite treat of mine, so I had to learn to make my own. I bottle the syrup to mix with water or soda water as a hot-weather drink.

This recipe uses approximately half a medium-size pineapple.

1¼ cups water

3¼ cups sugar

½ cup light corn syrup

1 pound peeled and cored pineapple, sliced
about ¾ inch thick

1 In a preserving pan, combine the water, ½ cup of the sugar, and the corn syrup. Heat the mixture slowly until the sugar dissolves, and then bring the syrup to a boil. Add the pineapple pieces. Heat the mixture to between 180° and 185°F, and then remove the pan from the heat. Cover the pan with a cloth and let the mixture stand at room temperature for 18 to 24 hours.

2 With a wire skimmer, transfer the pineapple pieces to a bowl. Add ¾ cup of the sugar to the pan. Bring the syrup to a boil and skim off any foam. Remove the pan from the heat and return the pineapple pieces to the pan. Cover the pan with a cloth and let the mixture stand for another 18 to 24 hours.

3 With a skimmer, transfer the pineapple pieces to a bowl. This time, add 1⅓ cups of the sugar to the pan. Bring the syrup to a boil and skim off any foam. Remove the pan from the heat and return the pineapple pieces to the pan. Cover the pan with a cloth

and let the mixture stand at room temperature for 18 to 24 more hours.

4. Once more, use a skimmer to transfer the pineapple pieces to a bowl. Add the remaining ⅔ cup sugar to the pan. Bring the syrup to a boil and skim off any foam. Remove the pan from the heat and return the pineapple pieces to the pan. Cover the pan with a cloth and let the mixture stand at room temperature for a final 18 to 24 hours.

5. With a skimmer, transfer the pineapple pieces to a rack or screen set over a dish to catch drips. Bring the syrup to a boil and boil it until it is thick. Pour it into pint or half-pint mason jars, add lids and rings, and process the jars for 10 minutes in a boiling-water bath.

6. Place the rack of pineapple pieces in a warm, dry place. Let them dry until they are leathery; this may take several days. Then store the pieces in an airtight container. They should keep well for several months.

PLUM

Japanese Plum Jam   267

Prune Plum Jam   268

Refrigerator Prune Plum Jam   269

Damson Jam   270

Greengage Plum Jam   271

Prune Plum Preserves with Kumquat   272

Prune Plum Preserves with Port   274

Greengage Plum Preserves   275

Plum-Apple Conserve   276

Prune Plum Conserve   277

Japanese Plum–Apple Paste   278

Prune Plum Paste   279

Damson Plum Paste   280

Plum-Apple Leather   282

THIS DIVERSE GROUP OF STONE-FRUIT species produces round and oblong fruits that range in size from that of a cherry to that of a small peach, in flavor from tart to very sweet, and in color from green to yellow to red to purple to blue.

In the United States, the favorite plum for fresh eating is *Prunus salicina*, which originated in China but is generally known as the Japanese plum. The plant breeder Luther Burbank began importing Japanese plum trees to California in 1885, and he eventually released 113 varieties, the most popular of which is the Santa Rosa. The tart, juicy fruits can't be dried unless they are pitted, but they make good jams, sauces, and pastes.

P. domestica is the European plum, which is oblong, yellow fleshed, and blue skinned, with a silver bloom. Because in the right conditions these very sweet plums can be dried without pitting, they were highly valued in the years before refrigeration. Best-known varieties in the United States include Italian, French, Brooks, Seneca, and

Stanley, but other cultivars may be better for preserves or fresh eating.

Native to western Asia is *P. insititia* (or *P. domestica insititia*), the damson, so named for Damascus, where the plum was probably first bred. The Romans introduced the damson to England, and the English brought it to the American colonies. Since damsons naturally form thickets, they have for hundreds of years been grown in hedgerows, often along with hazelnuts. The small, oval plums, with dark blue skins and greenish yellow flesh, were once used to make a blue dye. Because they are usually tart and often a little bitter, they are still favored in England for jams and other sweet preserves. Improved varieties are available, but damsons grow more or less true from seed. They are common in hedgerows on old farms, like mine, in western Oregon.

Also growing wild in rural Oregon is the greengage plum, or, more accurately, the gages—a family of small, round, sweet, mostly green or yellow plums that may have originated in Armenia. They were developed in France, where they became known in the early

A PRUNE BY ANY OTHER NAME

In the 1970s my parents bought a "prune ranch." It was called a ranch because *any* California farm was called a ranch, and the trees were called prune trees because *prune* is French for "plum" and the plum variety came from France. Unfortunately, prunes were already out of style; people associated them with old folks and digestive ailments. The lovely old trees were soon replaced with a vineyard.

In other areas of California, prune production continues, but the word *prune* still provokes smirks. So in 2000 the prune-plum growers decided they would no longer use *prune* for the dried fruit, much less the fresh. They got permission from the U.S. Food and Drug Administration to rename prunes "dried plums." And the growers decided to attempt, for the first time, large-scale marketing of fresh prune plums. Look for them in the supermarket under another new name, Sugar Plums.

sixteenth century as Reine Claude, after the wife of François I. Perhaps owing to a lost label, they were renamed in England for Sir Thomas Gage, who imported one or more of the French trees in the early eighteenth century. The best of these plums is said to be the true Greengage cultivar, which is described by various writers as melting, juicy, spicy, luscious, and "pure nectar," with a skin that is slightly bitter. George Washington and Thomas Jefferson both grew the Greengage, but since the eighteenth century, sadly, U.S. production has greatly declined. The French think so highly of gage plums, however, that various gage cultivars together make up about 40 percent of French plum production. Gages are favored for eating out of hand as well as poaching in syrup, pureeing for mousses or fools, and making into jam.

Also deserving mention is the cherry plum, *P. cerasifera*, a Eurasian native valued in California mostly as a rootstock and ornamental tree; numerous cultivars with purple foliage have been developed. Cherry plums grow wild in California, and the small, tart, round fruits are delicious. Most of the plum jam I had a child was made from wild cherry plums that my little brother and I picked.

None of the species I've mentioned grows well in the coldest and hottest parts of North America. But there are native plums in these regions, and some of them have been improved or hybridized with Japanese plums. Local nursery owners should be able to tell you more.

How do you judge when to pick plums? European, gage, and damson plums are ripe and ready for harvest when they come away from their stems with the gentlest tug. Japanese plums are ripe when they are aromatic and slightly tender.

JAPANESE PLUM JAM

WHEN YOU PIT THE PLUMS, be sure to save any juice they release. If you prefer a smooth rather than a lumpy jam, press the cooked plums through the medium screen of a food mill.

When made with Santa Rosa plums, this recipe produces a tart, lovely beet-red jam.

> 2 pounds pitted Japanese plums, cut into small pieces
> 3 cups sugar

1. Put the plums into a preserving pan and bring them to a simmer, stirring. Cover the pan and simmer the plums in their own juice until they are tender, about 10 minutes.

2. Remove the pan from the heat and stir in the sugar. Stir the contents over medium heat until the sugar is dissolved. Raise the heat to medium-high and bring the mixture to a boil. Boil the jam until a drop mounds in a chilled dish.

3. Pour the jam into pint or half-pint mason jars, and add lids and rings. Process the jars for 10 minutes in a boiling-water bath.

PRUNE PLUM JAM

MAKES ABOUT 2 PINTS

ECAUSE PRUNE PLUMS are so sweet, you can use less sugar to make them into jam, but you'll want to add lemon juice for a good set and flavor balance.

2 pounds prune plums, pitted and cut into small pieces
3 tablespoons lemon juice
2½ cups sugar

1 In a preserving pan, combine the cut plums with the lemon juice. Cover the pan and simmer the plums for about 10 minutes, until they are tender and have released their juice.

2 Remove the pan from the heat and add the sugar. Stir the contents over medium heat until the sugar is dissolved. Raise the heat to medium-high and boil the jam until a drop mounds in a chilled dish.

3 Ladle the jam into pint or half-pint mason jars, add lids and rings, and process the jars for 10 minutes in a boiling-water bath.

PRUNE PLUM JAM WITH HONEY

Honey complements prune plums without overwhelming their flavor.

Make Prune Plum Jam, but substitute light honey, such as clover or blackberry, for the sugar. Honey tends to cause a lot of foaming, so be sure to skim the jam well before putting it into jars.

REFRIGERATOR
PRUNE PLUM JAM

I F YOU'D LIKE TO MAKE a small quantity of prune plum jam for more or less immediate use, I suggest reducing the proportion of sugar even more than for Prune Plum Jam (opposite page), as in this recipe.

1 pound prune plums, pitted and cut into small pieces
1 cup sugar
2 tablespoons lemon juice

1. Combine all of the ingredients in a large skillet (10 to 12 inches is preferable). Over medium heat, stir the contents until the sugar is dissolved. Raise the heat to medium-high and then boil the jam, stirring, until a drop mounds in a chilled dish. Pour the jam into a pint jar.

2. Store the jar in the refrigerator, where the jam should keep for several weeks or longer.

DAMSON JAM

DAMSON PLUMS are tedious to pit raw; it's easier to cook the plums first, as in this recipe. Expect the jam to set very quickly, because damsons are rich in pectin.

2 pounds damson plums (unpitted)
¼ cup water
About 2 cups sugar

1. Put the plums and water into a preserving pan, saucepan, or large skillet, and simmer the plums, covered, for about 15 minutes, until their skins have burst and their juice runs out. Uncover the pan, and continue to simmer the plums for about 10 minutes, stirring, until the pits are well separated from the flesh.

2. Remove the pan from the heat and transfer the plums to a colander set over a bowl. Press the damson flesh through the colander, discarding the pits and skins. Measure the volume of the pulp.

3. Put the pulp into a preserving pan and add ¾ cup sugar for each cup of pulp. Over medium heat, stir the contents until the sugar is dissolved. Raise the heat to medium-high and boil the jam until a drop mounds in a chilled dish.

4. Ladle the jam into pint or half-pint mason jars, and add lids and rings. Process the jars for 10 minutes in a boiling-water bath.

GREENGAGE PLUM JAM

OR JAM, YOU WANT GREENGAGES that are fully ripe—
they should pull away from their stems with a gentle tug—
but that are not yet very soft. Greengages have a strong bloom, so
wipe them clean with a damp cloth. To pit each plum, slice through
the stem end and along the valley on one side. This is easier to do
with some cultivars than others. If you have trouble pitting the plums
raw, boil them with their pits, and then skim off the pits when they
separate from the flesh and rise to the top.

> 2¼ pounds greengage plums, pitted (if this isn't too
>   difficult)
> ⅓ cup water
> 1½ tablespoons lemon juice
> 3 cups sugar

1 Combine the plums and water in a preserving pan. Gently boil
the plums, covered, until they are tender; this should take about
10 minutes. If you didn't pit the plums before cooking them,
skim off the pits now.

2 Add the lemon juice and sugar to the preserving pan. Stir the
contents over medium heat until the sugar is dissolved. Raise the
heat to medium-high and boil the jam until a drop mounds in a
chilled dish.

3 Ladle the jam into pint or half-pint mason jars. Add lids and
rings, and process the jars for 10 minutes in a boiling-water bath.

GREENGAGE PLUM JAM WITH VANILLA

I first tasted greengage jam with vanilla at the home of a friend; a Spanish friend of hers had made it and brought it from Spain as a gift.

Make Greengage Plum Jam according to the recipe above, but add half a vanilla bean to the pan with the plums and water, and then remove the bean just before putting the jam into jars. Alternatively, add 2 teaspoons vanilla extract to the jam when the cooking is finished and the boiling has stopped.

GREENGAGE PLUM JAM FLAVORED WITH GREENGAGE SEEDS

In past centuries, jams made from greengages and other stone fruits were often flavored with their own bitter almond–like kernels.

When you pit your greengages for jam, crack about 16 of the pits and take out the kernels. Simmer the kernels in a cup of water for 10 minutes. Discard the water, and then cook the kernels along with the jam.

PRUNE PLUM PRESERVES WITH KUMQUAT

MAKES 2 TO 2½ PINTS

THIS RECIPE AND THE VARIANTS that follow are a sort of cross between preserves and jam. If you like bigger pieces of fruit, halve the plums instead of quartering them.

Although prune plums have deep blue skins and golden flesh, jam or preserves made from them turns out a beautiful dark red.

I love to use aromatic kumquat peel in this recipe, but you can use orange peel instead.

> 2 pounds just-ripe prune plums, pitted and quartered
> 3 cups sugar
> ½ teaspoon chopped dried kumquat peel (page 184) or
>   grated orange zest
> 3 tablespoons strained lemon juice

1 In a preserving pan, layer the plums and sugar. Sprinkle the kumquat peel or orange zest, and then the lemon juice, on top. Let the pan stand at room temperature, covered, for 12 to 24 hours.

2 Set the pan over medium heat and stir the contents gently until the sugar has dissolved. Simmer the plums in the syrup until they are tender. Raise the heat to medium-high and boil the mixture without stirring until the syrup is thick. When you put a little into a chilled dish, you should be able to draw a clear path through the syrup with your finger.

3 Ladle the preserves into pint or half-pint mason jars. Add lids and rings, and process the jars for 10 minutes in a boiling-water bath.

PRUNE PLUM PRESERVES WITH RED WINE

Red wine such as Cabernet or Merlot subtly enhances prune plum preserves.

Follow the recipe above, but substitute ½ cup red wine for the lemon juice and one 3-inch cinnamon stick for the kumquat peel.

PRUNE PLUM PRESERVES WITH BROWN SUGAR

The brown-sugar flavor comes through clearly in these preserves, without overwhelming the flavor of the plums.

Follow the recipe, but substitute light brown sugar for half of the granulated sugar in the recipe.

PRUNE PLUM PRESERVES
WITH PORT

MAKES ABOUT 3 PINTS

HAS IT EVER OCCURRED TO YOU that tawny port tastes like prunes? It's natural to try combining these two, and many cooks have, using either fresh or dried prune plums. These preserves are an excellent accompaniment to vanilla ice cream.

> 3 pounds just-ripe prune plums, each
> pierced twice with a fork
> 3 cups sugar
> ¼ cup water
> About 1½ cups tawny port

1 Combine the plums, sugar, and water in a kettle over very low heat. Stir very gently until the sugar is completely dissolved. Raise the heat slightly and simmer the plums, uncovered, for 10 minutes. Remove the kettle from the heat. Cover it with a cloth and let it stand at room temperature for 12 to 24 hours.

2 With a slotted spoon, transfer the plums to a bowl. Bring the syrup to a boil and boil it briskly until it is slightly thickened. Reduce the heat, add the plums, and heat them very gently for 5 minutes. Divide the plums and syrup evenly among 3 pint mason jars. Add lids and rings, and process the jars in a boiling-water bath for 20 minutes.

GREENGAGE PLUM PRESERVES

MAKES ABOUT 2 PINTS

REENGAGES make a luscious spoon sweet. Served with a bit of crème fraîche, these preserves are heavenly.

2 pounds greengage plums, each pierced
   about 4 times with a fork
1⅔ cups water
2 tablespoons strained lemon juice
3¼ cups sugar
1 vanilla bean

1 In a nonreactive kettle over medium-high heat, heat the plums and water to a simmer. Remove the kettle from the heat. With a slotted spoon, transfer the plums to a bowl. Add the lemon juice, sugar, and vanilla bean to the kettle. Stirring to dissolve the sugar, bring the mixture slowly to a boil. Raise the heat, and boil the syrup until it reaches the thread stage (page 18) or 230°F.

PRUNES IN PORT

Years ago, at the Eugene Saturday Market, a farmer trying to sell me some of his prunes insisted that I sample his prunes in port, and I was glad I did. I later found a recipe that combined pitted prunes with sugar and port, but I've since found that prunes (and port!) are so sweet that they need no added sugar. You simply put prunes, pitted or not, into a jar, cover them well with tawny port, and wait about 3 months for a fine dessert and cordial combined.

2 Return the plums to the kettle and bring the syrup back to a boil. Remove the kettle from the heat. Cover the kettle with a cloth and let the mixture stand at room temperature for 8 to 12 hours.

3 With a slotted spoon, transfer the plums to a bowl. Boil the syrup until it reaches thread stage again. Return the plums to the kettle and bring the syrup back to a boil. Remove the kettle from the heat. Cover the kettle with a cloth and let the mixture stand at room temperature for another 8 to 12 hours.

4 Return the kettle to the heat and slowly bring the preserves to a boil. Boil them gently for 5 minutes and then ladle the plums and their syrup into pint or half-pint mason jars. Add lids and rings, and process the jars in a boiling-water bath for 20 minutes.

PLUM-APPLE CONSERVE

MAKES ABOUT 3 PINTS

ALTHOUGH THIS PRESERVE has few ingredients, I call it a conserve because the apple pieces keep their shape and provide textural contrast. I use only prune plums for this recipe, but you might try it with Japanese plums instead, omitting the lemon juice.

2 pounds just-ripe prune plums, halved and pitted
3 tablespoons lemon juice
1 cinnamon stick
1 pound firm, tart apples, such as Fuji, cut into pieces
approximately $\frac{1}{4} \times \frac{1}{4} \times \frac{1}{2}$ inch
$4\frac{1}{2}$ cups sugar

1. Put the plums, lemon juice, and cinnamon stick into a preserving pan. Stir the contents over low heat until the plums are soft, about 10 minutes. Add the apples and simmer the contents about 15 minutes more, until the apples are tender.

2. Add the sugar to the pan and stir the contents over medium heat until the sugar is dissolved. Raise the heat to medium-high and boil the jam until a drop mounds in a chilled dish.

3. Remove the pan from the heat, and remove the cinnamon stick from the pan. Ladle the conserve into pint or half-pint mason jars. Add lids and rings, and process the jars in a boiling-water bath for 10 minutes.

PRUNE PLUM CONSERVE

MAKES ABOUT 5½ PINTS

FOR PEOPLE WHO PREFER a complex preserve, this one combines bitter, chewy citrus and crunchy nuts with sweet plums and raisins.

2 small oranges
1 lemon
1 cup water
4 pounds prune plums, halved and pitted
½ pound (about 1½ cups) raisins
6 cups sugar
1 cup coarsely chopped walnuts

1. If the oranges and lemon were store-bought and not labeled organic, put them in a colander in the sink and pour boiling water over them to remove any wax. Scrub them well.

2. Squeeze the juice from the oranges and lemon, and reserve it. Scrape and discard the pulp and excess pith from the inside of the rinds, and chop the rinds. In a saucepan, combine the chopped rinds with the water and simmer the rinds for 30 minutes.

3. Empty the contents of the saucepan into a nonreactive kettle and add the reserved juice, plums, raisins, and sugar. Simmer the mixture, stirring occasionally, until it begins to thicken, about 1 hour. Stir in the walnuts and bring the mixture to a boil.

4. Ladle the conserve into pint or half-pint mason jars. Add lids and rings, and process the jars for 10 minutes in a boiling-water bath.

JAPANESE PLUM–APPLE PASTE

MAKES ABOUT 1½ POUNDS

HERE IS A BRIGHTLY COLORED, sprightly flavored alternative to quince or guava paste for serving with cheese or nuts.

1 pound tart apples, such as Gravenstein, halved (unpeeled and uncored)
½ cup water
1 pound Japanese plums, halved and pitted
1½ cups sugar

1. Put the apples into a kettle with the water. Simmer the apples for about 12 minutes, until they are tender. Remove the kettle from the heat. Pick the seeds out of the apples and discard the seeds.

2. Add the plums to the kettle. Simmer the apples and plums together for about 15 minutes, until the plums are quite tender.

3. Put the contents of the kettle through the medium screen of a food mill. Put the puree into the kettle and add the sugar. Heat the mixture over low heat, stirring, until the sugar is completely dissolved. Simmer the mixture, stirring often at first and almost constantly toward the end, for 40 minutes or more. When the paste is ready, you'll have to hold onto the kettle to keep it from sliding around, and your spoon will leave a clear path across the bottom.

4. Pour the paste about ¾ inch thick into lightly oiled dishes with vertical sides. Let the paste cool, and then turn it out of the dishes to dry in a warm place, such as near a stove, in a food dehydrator, or, if your climate allows, in the sun.

5. When the paste is dry to the touch, cut it into smaller pieces, if you like, and wrap the pieces in plastic. Unless you'll be eating the paste soon or you're sure that it is thoroughly dry, store it in the refrigerator, where it will keep for months.

PRUNE PLUM PASTE

MAKES ABOUT 2¼ POUNDS

 ENHANCED WITH acid- and pectin-rich crabapple juice, prune plums make an excellent dark, sweet paste.

3 pounds prune plums, pitted
1 cup Homemade Crabapple Pectin (page 17)
2½ cups sugar
2 tablespoons lemon juice

1. Put the plums and juice into a nonreactive kettle. Simmer the contents, covered, until the plums are tender, about 20 minutes. Remove the pan from the heat and let the mixture cool.

2 Put the plums and homemade pectin through the medium screen of a food mill. Put the puree into the kettle along with the sugar and lemon juice. Heat the mixture over low heat, stirring, until the sugar is completely dissolved. Simmer the mixture, stirring very often at first and constantly as the mixture thickens, for 30 minutes or more. When the paste is ready, your spoon will briefly leave a clear path across the bottom of the kettle.

3 Pour the paste about ¾ inch thick into lightly oiled dishes with vertical sides. Let the paste cool and then turn it out of the dishes to dry in a warm place, such as near a stove, in a food dehydrator, or, if your climate allows, in the sun.

4 When the paste is dry to the touch, cut it into smaller pieces, if you like, and wrap the pieces in plastic. Unless you'll be eating the paste soon or you're sure that it is thoroughly dry, store it in the refrigerator, where it will keep for months.

DAMSON PLUM PASTE

MAKES ABOUT 1½ POUNDS

NEARLY CONSTANT STIRRING is required to avoid scalding paste when you're making it from soft fruits without the addition of apple or quince, but the result is worth the trouble. Damsons make a dark red, tart paste with a slightly spicy flavor.

> 2 pounds ripe damson plums
> 1½ cups sugar
> Extra-fine sugar (optional)

1 Preheat the oven to 250°F. Spread the plums in a nonreactive baking pan and put the pan in the oven for 1 to 1½ hours, until

the fruit is soft, most of the skins have split, and some of the juice has run out into the pan.

2. Push the fruit through a coarse-mesh sieve, leaving behind the skins and pits. Put the pulp into a preserving pan with the sugar. Heat the mixture over low heat, stirring, until the sugar is completely dissolved. Simmer the mixture, stirring very often at first and constantly as the mixture thickens, for 30 minutes or more. When the paste is ready, your spoon will briefly leave a clear path across the bottom of the kettle.

3. Pour the paste about ¾ inch thick into lightly oiled dishes with vertical sides. Let the paste cool, and then turn it out of the dishes to dry in a warm place, such as near a stove, in a food dehydrator, or, if your climate allows, in the sun.

4. When the paste is dry to the touch, cut it into smaller pieces, if you like, and wrap the pieces in plastic. Unless you'll be eating the paste soon or you're sure that it is thoroughly dry, store it in the refrigerator. Or cut the paste into bite-size pieces, roll them in extra-fine sugar, if you like, and store them in an airtight container. Either way, the paste should keep for several weeks, at least.

PLUM-APPLE LEATHER

 PPLES PROVIDE BODY in this tangy Japanese-plum fruit leather.

1 pound apples of your choice, cored and sliced
3 pounds Japanese plums, pitted

1 Put the apple slices into a saucepan and simmer them until they are tender, stirring often and adding a few spoonfuls of water if necessary. Puree the apples and plums in a blender.

2 Secure plastic wrap over dehydrator screens, leaving an uncovered margin for air circulation, or use heavy-duty plastic sheets made to fit into your dehydrator. Spread the puree in a ¼-inch layer.

3 Dry the puree for approximately 1 day, rotating the screens for even drying and reducing the heat, if possible, after the first few hours.

4 When the leather is ready, it will no longer be wet or sticky, but it will still be pliable, not brittle. If it cracks or breaks when you try to roll it, mist it lightly with water from a spray bottle and dry it a little longer.

5 Roll each piece of leather with the plastic wrap on which it has dried. Store the rolls in a sealed plastic bag or tightly closed glass jar in a cool place. They will keep for at least 1 year.

POMEGRANATE

Pomegranate Syrup   284

T HIS "GRAINY APPLE" or "grainy fruit" originated in the Near East and is probably still most popular there, although it is also widely grown in France, Spain, California, the southern United States, and other warm regions of the world. The bright red (or sometimes white) flowers of this shrub are followed in autumn by apple-size, leathery skinned fruits, each filled with edible seeds encased in transparent crimson flesh—like garnets, who took their name from this fruit (as did grenades). The seeds are sprinkled over such dishes as *baba ghanoush* (pureed eggplant with lemon juice and sesame paste), added to salads, and, most often, turned into juice. The juice can be boiled down to pomegranate molasses (which is similar to Grape Molasses, page 173) or combined with sugar to make a syrup. The syrup is added to all sorts of dishes for its color as well as its flavor, and it is used as a base for brilliant red drinks.

POMEGRANATE SYRUP

AT ONE TIME THIS SYRUP was called *grenadine*, from the French word for pomegranate, *grenade*. Today, commercial grenadine can contain any assortment of sweeteners, colorings, and flavorings. This is sad, because real *sirop de grenadine* is a cinch to make.

In this recipe you don't cook the fruit, so its substantial vitamin C content and flavor are preserved. Use Pomegranate Syrup in alcoholic beverages, drink a little straight as a winter tonic, or pour the syrup over crushed ice.

> 2 pounds pomegranates (about 4)
> About 2½ cups sugar

1. Cut the pomegranates into quarters, bend the segments backward, and, with your fingers, push the "berries" into a bowl. Discard any pith and membranes that come off with the berries. To avoid splattering your clothes and kitchen with pomegranate juice, you can do this work with your hands and the fruit submerged in a big basin of water. Drain the berries well when you finish.

QUICK POMEGRANATE SORBET

In a powerful blender, mix 1 cup Pomegranate Syrup, ¼ cup strained lemon juice, ¾ cup cold water, and the ice cubes from two trays. Serve immediately.

2 Measure the volume of the berries; you should have about 2½ cups. Combine the berries with an equal volume of sugar in a heavy-weight, gallon-size, zipper-top plastic bag. Seal the bag and, keeping one hand on the seam so it doesn't come open, crush the berries by squeezing the bag, rolling a rolling pin over it, or gently smacking it with a hammer or other tool.

3 Transfer the contents of the bag to a quart jar. Tightly cap the jar and shake it twice a day.

4 After 3 days, all of the sugar should be dissolved. Pour the contents of the jar though a strainer and collect the syrup in a pint jar. Store the jar in the refrigerator. The syrup should keep well for several weeks.

PUMPKIN AND WINTER SQUASH

Pumpkin Jam   287
Pumpkin Butter   289
Cabello de Ángel   290

U NLIKE OLD WORLD GOURDS, the annual fruits we call pumpkins and squashes are indigenous to the New World, where they have been cultivated for thousands of years. Wonderfully diverse, they range in size from a few ounces to 50 pounds or more, in skin color from white to tan to salmon to orange to green to blue-gray, and in shape from round or oblate to long and thin to acorn-, pear-, or turban-shaped. They can be deeply ribbed, striped, warty, or none of these. And in taste they range from bland, watery, and fibrous to dense, sweet, and creamy. Generally, they have bright orange flesh that is loaded with vitamin A.

The pumpkin and squash varieties gardeners know best fall into three species. *Cucurbita pepo*, native to North America, includes spaghetti squash, turban squash, acorn squash, little orange pie pumpkins, and big, fibrous Halloween pumpkins as well as zucchini (page 353) and other summer squashes. *C. maxima*, native to South America, includes sweet, dense-fleshed winter squashes such as buttercup and Hubbard. *C. moschata*, which was cultivated in Mexico from about 3400 B.C. and almost as early in Peru, includes butternut and crookneck squashes.

Pumpkins and squashes are easy to grow from seed outdoors, and if your growing season is short you can easily transplant seedlings started indoors. Harvest the fruits after their rinds are hardened and preferably after the vines have died, but before the first frost. After harvest, wash the fruits; you might also rinse them with a weak chlorine bleach solution to discourage rot.

Store pumpkins and squashes in a cool, dry place; an attic is generally better than a basement or garage. I keep mine in large baskets in my dining room until my family finishes them off in March or April. If we have too many to eat in one winter, I bake some, mash the flesh, and freeze it. Or I make preserves, using such recipes as the three that follow.

PUMPKIN JAM

MAKES ABOUT 1½ PINTS

WITH SUBTLE SEASONINGS that never hide the bold flavor of sweet pumpkin or winter squash, jams like this one are used as pastry fillings in Spain, Mexico, and Mexican bakeries in the United States. If you prefer a spicier, pumpkin-pie taste, feel free to add another cinnamon stick or two or even ground spices.

To bake winter squash, cut it in half and lay it cut side down in a greased baking pan. Cook the squash in a 400°F oven until the flesh is tender.

Some winter squashes have been bred to be free of fiber, but others need straining after they're cooked. Whatever variety of squash you use, I suggest putting it through a food mill or another sort of strainer.

1½ cups sugar

1 cup water

Zest of 1 lemon, in thin shreds

2 cinnamon sticks

4 cups baked and pureed winter squash,
    such as butternut, buttercup, or sweet meat,
    or pie pumpkin

1 In a kettle, combine the sugar and water. Put the lemon zest and cinnamon sticks into a spice bag and add it to the kettle. Over low heat, heat the mixture, stirring gently, until the sugar is dissolved.

2 Add the pureed squash. Cook the mixture over medium heat, stirring often at first and constantly toward the end, until the jam is very thick, about 20 minutes.

3 Remove the pan from the heat and spoon the jam into glass or plastic containers. When they are cool, store them in the refrigerator or freezer. In the refrigerator, the jam will keep for a few weeks.

PUMPKIN BUTTER

T HIS BUTTER has a much richer, spicier flavor than Pump-kin Jam (page 287). Try Pumpkin Butter on toast or as a filling for cookies.

3 cups baked and pureed winter squash,
    such as butternut, buttercup, or sweet meat,
    or pie pumpkin (page 287)
1 cup pure maple syrup
1½ cups light brown sugar
¼ cup strained lemon juice
1 teaspoon ground cinnamon
¼ teaspoon ground allspice
⅛ teaspoon ground cloves

1 In a kettle, combine all of the ingredients. Cook the mixture over medium heat, stirring very frequently, until it is boiling and quite thick.

2 Remove the pan from the heat and spoon the pumpkin butter into glass or plastic containers. When they are cool, store them in the refrigerator or freezer. In the refrigerator, the butter will keep for several weeks.

CABELLO DE ÁNGEL

T HIS "ANGEL HAIR" preserve from Spain combines stringy spaghetti squash with aromatic honey. *Cabello de ángel* is typically used for filling or topping pastries.

1 pound seeded spaghetti squash
⅔ cup honey
1 cinnamon stick
Zest of ½ lemon

1. Cut the squash into large pieces, remove the seeds, and steam the pieces until they are tender, about 45 minutes. Let them cool.

2. Scrape the squash flesh out of the rind and combine the flesh in a small nonreactive skillet with the honey, cinnamon stick, and lemon zest. Simmer the mixture for about 35 minutes, stirring occasionally, until the excess liquid has evaporated and the squash strands are partially translucent.

3. Pack the preserve into a jar and cap the jar tightly. When it has cooled, store it in the refrigerator, where it should keep for at least 2 weeks.

QUINCE

Quince Jelly 293

Quince Jam 296

Quince Paste 297

Quince-Apple Paste 300

Quince Preserves 301

Golden Quince Marmalade 302

Quince Preserves with Grated
   Quince 304

Quince Syrup 305

Raw Quince Syrup 307

G ARDENERS APPLY THIS NAME to two plants, the tree called *Cydonia oblonga* or fruiting quince, and its cousin *Chaenomeles*, a shrub commonly known as flowering or Japanese quince or, in many old books, simply Japonica. Both plants produce attractive flowers and edible fruits.

Flowering quince is a spiky, fast-growing shrub native to eastern Asia and grown in North America for its lovely red, pink, or white early-spring flowers. Most gardeners ignore the plant's few fruits, which are bright yellow when fully ripe. About the size of apples, these round, hard fruits are useful in preserving, since they contain more vitamin C than lemons and more pectin than even the fruit of *Cydonia oblonga*.

C. oblonga is the tree that North American gardeners call simply quince. Now hard to find, quince trees were once very popular in American gardens, for good reason. The spreading, well-formed trees are petite—they grow no more than 15 feet tall—and especially ornamental when they are covered with pink blossoms in midspring. The large, bright yellow, pear-shaped fruits, with their strong pineapple-like fragrance, have abundant acid and pectin and combine well with other fruits to brighten flavors and to ensure good gelling. Best of all, from a gardener's point of view, quinces are too hard to be attacked by codling moth larvae.

Native to the Near East, the quince has been treasured throughout Western history. The fruit was a fertility symbol in ancient Greece, where it was a ritual offering at weddings. Romans stewed quinces with honey and combined them with leeks. The French, whose name for the fruit, *coing*, in its plural form became the English singular *quince*, added the trees to their orchards under orders from Charlemagne. *Cotignac*, quince paste or jelly, became a specialty of Orléans and was the first gift offered Joan of Arc when she lifted the siege of that city. In the fifteenth and sixteenth centuries, many recipes for preserving quinces with honey appeared in English cookbooks, usually under the name *chardequynce*. In the sixteenth century, too, the English and other Europeans began importing quince paste from Portugal. This *marmalade*, whose name came from the Portuguese word for quince, *marmelo*, was preserved with sugar rather than honey, in a style learned from the Arabs. The meaning of *marmalade* gradually changed, but quince paste stuck around. Still very popular in Spain, Italy, and the Near East, it is the ancestor of Latin America's ubiquitous guava paste, which is often made partially of quince.

Quinces of most varieties commonly available in the United States (such as Pineapple, Orange, Smyrna, and Van Deman) are too hard and astringent to eat raw, but some less common varieties require no cooking. Jim Gilbert has brought several of these from Russia and sells them through his mail-order nursery, One Green World.

Green quinces are covered with a woolly substance, much of which comes off on its own as the fruits ripen. Rub off the remainder before cutting your quinces.

Because the quince is a very hard fruit, you should cut it with a heavy blade. Despite their high acid content, quinces brown immediately when cut. Steam or sugar or both will generally restore their color, but if you like you can hold the slices in water acidulated with lemon juice or ascorbic acid (crushed vitamin C lozenges work well for this purpose).

In addition to their uses in preserves, quinces are delicious baked whole, sliced and sautéed, and combined with sweet apples in applesauce, apple butter, and apple pie.

For other quince recipes, see Blackberry-Quince Paste (page 68), Cranberry-Quince Jelly (page 112), and Cranberry-Quince Preserves (page 115).

QUINCE JELLY

MAKES ABOUT 3 HALF-PINTS

QUINCES MAKE A PINK, firm, clear tart jelly, much loved by people who grow up eating these fruits. Quinces cooked for jelly can be cored and used for Quince Paste (page 297).

This recipe works well with quince juice from a steam juicer (page 14). Seven pounds of quinces should produce enough rosy juice for two batches of jelly (doubling the recipe is *not* a good idea). The fruit will need to steam for about an hour and a half, so be sure to refill the base with water as needed. Leave the fruit in the steam juicer for about 8 hours after the cooking is through to allow the juice to finish dripping.

3½ pounds quinces, stems and blossom ends removed
2¼ cups sugar
1 tablespoon strained lemon juice

1 Slice the quinces into quarters, but do not peel or core them. Put them into a kettle with just enough water to cover them. Bring the contents to a boil, and then reduce the heat to a simmer.

Simmer the quinces for 1 to 1½ hours, partially covered, until they are tender and pink.

2. Strain the juice through a coarse-mesh strainer and then through a damp jelly bag. Do not squeeze the bag. Measure the volume of the juice; you should have 3 cups. The juice may already be softly gelled.

3. In a preserving pan, combine the quince juice, sugar, and lemon juice. Heat the mixture over medium heat, stirring gently, until the sugar is completely dissolved. Raise the heat to medium-high and boil the mixture until it passes the sheet test (page 18).

4. Remove the pan from the heat and pour the mixture into half-pint mason jars. Add lids and rings, and process the jars in a boiling-water bath for 10 minutes.

QUINCE-GERANIUM JELLY

Greeks traditionally flavor their quince jelly with rose geranium leaves. To try this variant, make Quince Jelly as above. When the jelly passes the spoon test (page 18), gently swish 3 geranium sprigs through the liquid for 20 seconds or so, and then press them with a spoon against the side of the pan. Put the jelly into jars and process them as directed.

QUIDDANY

In England and her American colonies, quince jelly was once known as *quiddany* or *quidony,* from the French *cotignac,* "quince paste or jelly." The liquid jelly was often poured into molds in the shapes of fruits, animals, and birds and then turned out of the molds for drying and storage. Just as *marmalade* came to mean any sort of jam, *quiddany* came to be applied to many kinds of jelly.

It never turns out clear for me, but I love this jelly anyway. It is firm, quite tart, pleasingly tannic, and a beautiful milky pink. (For a clear jelly from flowering quinces, see the next variation.)

Follow the instructions for Quince Jelly, but use flowering quince fruits instead of regular quinces.

CLEAR FLOWERING QUINCE JELLY

Follow the instructions for Quince Jelly, but use flowering quince fruits instead of regular quinces, and use the following method to clarify the juice:

After straining the juice through a coarse-mesh strainer, pour it into a saucepan. Tear about 15 squares of 2-ply undyed, unscented toilet paper, or 7 undyed, unscented facial tissues into small pieces. Put the paper into a bowl, cover it well with boiling water, and let the bowl stand for 1 minute.

Break up the paper with a fork, put it into a strainer, and drain the paper thoroughly without pressing. When the paper has stopped dripping, put it into the pan with the quince juice. Bring the juice to a full boil, stirring to break up the mass of paper.

Pour the juice with the paper into a damp jelly bag set over a bowl. When the jelly bag is cool enough to handle, squeeze it to extract all the juice from the paper. The paper will act as a filter, and so produce a clear pink juice in very little time. Finish making the jelly as directed.

QUINCE JAM

THIS SIMPLE JAM requires minimal cooking of the quinces and therefore turns out a pale golden color, like apple-sauce.

> 2 pounds quinces, peeled, quartered,
>   cored, and thinly sliced
> 1¼ cups water
> 2 cups sugar

1 Combine the quince slices and water in a preserving pan. Simmer the quince slices, covered, until they are just tender, about 5 minutes.

2 With a slotted spoon, remove the slices to a bowl. Add the sugar to the preserving pan. Heat over medium heat, stirring gently, until the sugar is dissolved, and then boil the syrup gently until it reaches the thread stage (page 18) or 230°F.

3 Return the quince slices to the pan. Over medium heat, bring the contents to a simmer. Continue to simmer the quinces until they are very soft, about 10 minutes, and then mash them with a potato masher. Simmer the jam for 2 to 3 minutes more, until it is very thick and mounds in a saucer.

4 Ladle the jam into pint or half-pint mason jars. Add lids and rings, and process the jars in a boiling-water bath for 10 minutes.

QUINCE PASTE

THIS PRESERVE is the original English marmalade: a jam so thick that you cut it with a knife to serve it. The first written record of marmalade in England occurred in 1524, when Henry VIII wrote of receiving some from Hull of Exeter. Hull's gift probably came from Portugal, where the quince was called *marmelo* and quince paste *marmelada* (in those days quince paste was usually packed in small wooden boxes, very handy for long-distance trade). But soon the English were making their own quince paste; Martha Washington's *Booke of Sweetmeats*, handwritten by her forebears, has eight recipes for quince *marmalet*. Only later did the English start applying the term *marmalade* to preserves made from other fruits, and not until the nineteenth century did they reserve it for citrus jams. Today the English call the original marmalade *quince cheese*, and in 1981, at England's insistence, the European Economic Community issued an edict that preserves labeled *marmalade* had to be made of oranges, lemons, limes, or grapefruits.

Nowadays the original marmalade is less popular in England than farther south. In France quince paste is *cotignac*, a specialty of Orléans. In Spain it is known as *dulce de membrillo* or *carne de membrillo* and eaten with cheese, usually from sheep's milk. Quince paste is eaten in the Middle East with blanched almonds—whole almonds are laid on the hot paste after it is poured into a mold, so that when the paste is cut each piece is topped by a nut, or halved almonds are laid between layers of paste.

In the United States, apparently, quince paste is growing in popularity. At a chic wine tasting in California recently, I was served thin slices of quince paste atop small pieces of roast duck.

The color of quince paste can vary from pale gold to deep crimson, depending on the degree of oxidation. Benign neglect—that is, repeated heating and cooling—produces a prettier preserve, especially if you cover the kettle as the mixture cools.

Centuries ago Europeans added flavorings such as rose water and cinnamon to their quince paste, and this practice continues today in the Middle East. My own favorite spice for quince paste is cardamom. To try quince paste with rose water or cardamom, see the variations that follow.

> 2 pounds quinces (about 3), quartered but
>   not seeded or peeled
> 1 cup water
> 2 cups sugar

1. Combine the quinces and water in a kettle. Over low heat, simmer the quinces, covered, until they are quite tender, about 20 minutes. Remove the kettle from the heat, and let the quinces cool a bit. For a redder paste, let the kettle stand at room temperature for 8 to 12 hours.

2. Scoop out the seeds from each quince piece and discard the seeds. Pass the fruit and any juice in the kettle through the medium screen of a food mill.

3. Put the puree into the kettle along with the sugar. Heat the mixture over low heat, stirring, until the sugar is completely dissolved. Simmer the mixture, stirring often at first and almost constantly toward the end, for 40 minutes or more. When the paste is ready, you'll have to hold onto the kettle to keep it from

sliding around, and your spoon will leave a clear path across the bottom.

4. Pour the paste about ¾ inch thick into lightly oiled dishes with vertical sides. Let the paste cool and then turn it out of the dishes to dry in a warm place, such as near a stove, in a food dehydrator, or, if your climate allows, in the sun.

5. When the paste is dry to the touch, cut it into smaller pieces, if you like, and wrap the pieces in plastic or waxed paper. Unless you'll be eating the paste soon or you're sure that it is thoroughly dry, store it in a heavy-duty plastic bag in the refrigerator, where it should keep for several months.

QUINCE PASTE FROM QUINCES USED FOR JELLY OR SYRUP

If you use the juice of the quinces for jelly or syrup, your quince paste will be a little bland. To avoid this, follow the recipe for Quince Paste, but add 2 tablespoons lemon juice to the kettle along with the pureed fruit and sugar.

QUINCE PASTE WITH CARDAMOM

The exotic flavor of cardamom is a wonderful complement to sweet, tart quince. Follow the recipe for Quince Paste, but add the seeds from 7 cardamom pods (less than ¼ teaspoon), crushed in a mortar, to the kettle along with the quince puree and sugar.

QUINCE PASTE WITH ROSE WATER

Available in Middle Eastern markets, rose water adds a lovely flavor and fragrance to quince paste. The first *marmalada* brought to England from Portugal was probably flavored with rose water.

To make your own rose-scented paste, stir in ½ teaspoon rose water just before spreading the hot paste in dishes.

QUINCE-APPLE PASTE

MAKES ABOUT 1¾ POUNDS

 PPLES COMBINE WELL with quince to make a paste slightly milder in flavor. I like it with a hint of added cinnamon.

1 pound apples, quartered but not seeded or peeled
1 pound quinces, quartered but not seeded or peeled
1 cup water
Two 3-inch cinnamon sticks
2⅓ cups sugar

1 Combine the apples, quinces, water, and cinnamon sticks in a kettle. Over low heat, simmer the fruit, covered, until it is quite tender, about 20 minutes. Remove the kettle from the heat and let the fruit cool a bit.

2 Core each piece of fruit. Pass the fruit and any juice in the kettle through the medium screen of a food mill. Remove the cinnamon stick from the kettle.

3 Put the puree into the kettle along with the sugar. Heat the mixture over low heat, stirring, until the sugar is completely dissolved. Simmer the mixture, stirring often at first and almost constantly toward the end, for 40 minutes or more. When the paste is ready, you'll have to hold onto the pot to keep it from sliding around, and your spoon will leave a clear path across the bottom.

4 Pour the paste about ¾ inch thick into lightly oiled dishes with vertical sides. Let the paste cool and then turn it out of the dishes to dry in a warm place, such as near a stove, in a food dehydrator, or, if your climate allows, in the sun.

5 When the paste is dry to the touch, cut it into smaller pieces, if you like, and wrap the pieces in plastic or waxed paper. Unless

you'll be eating the paste soon or you're sure that it is thoroughly dry, store it in a heavy-duty plastic bag in the refrigerator, where it should keep for several months.

QUINCE PRESERVES

MAKES ABOUT 2 PINTS

T HE FIRST RECIPE I TRIED for quince preserves came from Ana Bégué de Packman's *Early California Hospitality*. Like Mission grapes and Mission figs, quinces were among the fruits planted by the Spanish padres, who then distributed cuttings among the pueblos and rancheros of Old California, California *de antes*.

Before preserving quinces and other fruits in syrup, the Californios treated them as they treated corn, with a soak in lime water, or *ensernada*. A lime soak gives fruit or vegetables a hard, almost brittle texture. Personally, I find this treatment unnecessary, for quinces if not for other fruits. Quince slices remain quite firm provided you keep the heat low during most of the cooking.

Inspired by a similar Persian recipe, I've added vanilla here. I've also tried this recipe with star anise and sliced ginger. With any of these flavorings, the preserves are delicious on pancakes.

4 cups water
4 cups sugar
2 pounds quinces (about 4), peeled, cored, and cut into
    quarters or smaller slices
½ vanilla bean, in a spice bag

1. In a kettle, combine the water and 2 cups of the sugar. Place the kettle over medium heat and heat the contents, stirring gently, until the sugar is completely dissolved. Continue heating until the liquid comes to a boil and then add the quince slices and the spice bag with the vanilla bean. Simmer the quinces uncovered for 1 hour. Remove the kettle from the heat and let the quinces cool in their syrup.

2. With a slotted spoon, remove the quince slices from the syrup. Add the remaining 2 cups sugar to the kettle. Heat the syrup over medium heat, stirring gently, until the sugar is completely dissolved. Return the quince slices to the kettle, reduce the heat, and cook at a bare simmer until the quince slices are red and partially translucent. This will probably take at least 1½ hours.

3. Remove the kettle from the heat, press the spice bag against the side of the kettle, and remove the bag. Divide the quince slices and syrup among pint or half-pint mason jars. Add lids and rings, and process the jars for 10 minutes in a boiling-water bath.

GOLDEN QUINCE MARMALADE

MAKES ABOUT 1½ PINTS

I BASED THIS RECIPE on an old one from May Byron's *Jams and Jellies*. Byron called her version quince honey, probably because it resembled crystallized honey in both color and texture. Today, however, we are most familiar with honey in liquid form, so the old name doesn't fit as well as it once did. I'm calling this preserve marmalade to suggest its coarse texture—even though the original marmalade was quince paste, a smooth finger food.

The fast cooking here keeps the quince pale. If you grate the quinces even a few minutes before adding the gratings to the syrup, they will oxidize to a rust-red. If you'd prefer a red marmalade, by all means let the grated quince redden before cooking it. It will redden even more if you lengthen the cooking time by boiling the syrup only until it reaches the thread stage (page 18) or 230°F, covering the pot after adding the quince, and cooking the quince for a long period over low heat. Don't let the marmalade get too thick, though, because it will thicken even more as it cools.

> 2¼ cups water
> 2¼ cups sugar
> 1½ pounds quinces (about 3 medium-size)

1. In a preserving pan, combine the water and sugar. Heat them over medium heat, stirring gently, until the sugar is completely dissolved. Raise the heat to medium-high and boil the syrup for about 10 minutes to the soft-ball stage (page 19) or 235°F.

2. Immediately remove the pan from the heat, peel the quinces, and then coarsely grate the quince flesh into the syrup, leaving behind the cores (use the skins and cores for jelly, if you like). Over low heat, boil the mixture gently, stirring constantly, for about 10 minutes or until the marmalade is thick.

3. Ladle the marmalade into pint or half-pint mason jars. Add lids and rings, and process the jars for 10 minutes in a boiling-water bath.

QUINCE PRESERVES WITH GRATED QUINCE

MAKES 1½ TO 2 PINTS

I WAS INSPIRED BY the preceding recipe to develop this one; I wanted to see the grated quince suspended in syrup or jelly rather than packed tightly in a jar. The first test batch was beautiful, but my husband, not a great quince fan, thought the flavor a little boring. So I added lemon zest and ginger. If you love quince unadorned, you might leave out these extras.

> 3½ cups sugar
> Zest of 1 lemon, in thin shreds
> ¼ cup strained lemon juice
> 2 pounds quinces (about 4 medium-size)
> ¼ cup thin strips of crystallized ginger, store-bought or
>   homemade (page 165)

1. Put the sugar, lemon zest, and lemon juice into a bowl. Peel the quinces, coarsely grating the flesh around the core, and combining the peels and cores in a large saucepan; weigh the grated flesh as you work. When you have ½ pound, immediately put the grated quinces into the bowl with the sugar and lemon. Mix the contents well and set the bowl aside. Don't bother peeling or grating any remaining fruits; cut them into eighths and add them to the pan.

2. Barely cover the quince peels, cores, and pieces with water. Bring the mixture to a boil, cover the pan, and reduce the heat. Simmer the contents until the quince is tender.

3. Drain the liquid from the pan and measure the volume of the liquid. If there is more than 3 cups, pour it into a preserving pan and boil the liquid until it is reduced to 3 cups.

4 Add the grated quince mixture and the crystallized ginger to the pan. Heat the mixture over medium heat, stirring, until the sugar is completely dissolved. Raise the heat to medium-high and boil the mixture until the syrup has thickened.

5 Ladle the preserves into pint or half-pint mason jars, add lids and rings, and process the jars for 10 minutes in a boiling-water bath.

QUINCE SYRUP

MAKES ABOUT 1 PINT

T HERE ARE VARIOUS WAYS to make syrup from quinces. You can, for example, combine sugar with the liquid from quinces cooked for quince paste and then simmer the mixture until it is as thick as you like, but in doing so you'd rob your quince paste of flavor. I like the simplicity of this recipe, in which the sugar is cooked with the fruit. If you cook the mixture very slowly, it will turn a beautiful dark red.

Like other fruit syrups, quince syrup can be poured over pancakes and ice cream and the like, but it is more often added to water or tea for a cold or hot drink.

> 2 pounds quinces or flowering quinces,
> stems and blossom ends removed
> 4 cups water
> 2½ cups sugar

1 Quarter the quinces, but do not peel or seed them. Combine the quinces, water, and sugar in a large saucepan. Over medium heat,

bring the contents to a boil, stirring until the sugar is completely dissolved. Reduce the heat so that the liquid barely simmers. Place a lid from a slightly smaller pan on top of the fruit to keep it submerged but to allow steam to escape. Let the contents simmer for at least 1 hour, until the liquid has reddened and thickened to a thin syrup.

2 Drain off the syrup through a fine-mesh strainer. Pour the syrup into a jar and cap the jar. Store the syrup in the refrigerator, where it should keep for several months.

QUINCE SYRUP WITH LIME

Iranians like to add lime juice to their quince syrup, combine the syrup with water (about one part syrup to three parts water), and serve the mixture over ice.

Make the syrup as directed. Just before or after pouring the syrup into the jar, stir in 2 tablespoons lime juice.

QUINCE GRANITA

Quince Syrup makes a tart, tasty granita. Follow the recipe for Floral Ice (page 160), but substitute Quince Syrup for the rose or violet syrup and omit the lemon juice.

RAW QUINCE SYRUP

MAKES ABOUT 1½ CUPS

THIS UNUSUAL BUT VERY SIMPLE recipe preserves the ample vitamin C and fresh flavor of uncooked quince. Combine the syrup with cold water or soda for a refreshing drink, or pour it over cake or ice cream.

You'll need approximately 2 quinces to fill a quart jar. Skin the fruits with a vegetable peeler and cut out the hard flesh at the core along with the seeds.

My friend Susan Yoder-Guardipee makes quince syrup this way, but instead of cutting the quinces into cubes, she slices them very thinly. In three weeks or so, the slices become soft and sweet, and her family eats them as candy. If you try this, I suggest using an additional ¼ cup sugar to keep the quince slices from oxidizing.

> 1 pound peeled and cored quinces, cut into
> approximately ¾-inch cubes
> 2 cups sugar

1. Layer the quince cubes and sugar in a quart jar. Cap the jar tightly and let it stand at room temperature for 2 weeks. Shake the jar several times a day until all the sugar is dissolved, and once a day thereafter.

2. After 2 weeks, drain off the syrup and pour it into jars. Cap the jars and store them in the refrigerator, where the syrup should keep for several weeks. (You can turn the shriveled cubes of quince into a lovely treat by cooking them at a bare simmer for about 1 hour in white or rosé wine or grape juice. They make an outstanding accompaniment to roast goose or pork.)

I invented this variation to exploit the antioxidant, antibiotic, and otherwise health-promoting properties of honey. Take a spoonful of this aromatic syrup straight to relieve a sore throat or cough, boost your energy, and warm your body in winter.

Because honey (in liquid form) contains water, this syrup will turn out thinner than the version made with granulated sugar, the quince pieces won't shrink as much, and the total volume of quince and syrup will be about 50 percent greater. The syrup should cover the fruit in a matter of hours rather than days.

Follow the recipe as directed, but layer the quince pieces with 2 cups honey instead of sugar. You'll end up with about 2½ cups syrup.

RASPBERRY

Raspberry Jam   311

Smooth Raspberry Jam   312

Raspberry–Red Currant Jam   313

Cristina's Raw Raspberry Jam   314

Raw Raspberry Puree   315

Raw Raspberry Sauce   315

Raspberry Vinegar   317

Raspberry Shrub   318

T HIS FRAGILE, VELVETY, highly perfumed cousin of the blackberry grows wild over much of North America. Wild species include *Rubus strigosus*, the American red raspberry, and the nearly identical *R. idaeus*, the European red raspberry; some botanists consider these two the same species. There are two North American species of black raspberries, or blackcaps: *R. leucodermis*, of the West, and the inaptly named *R. occidentalis*, of the East. Because the fruits leave behind their central cores when picked, you might also classify with raspberries such other native species of *Rubus* as the salmonberry, with its soft, yellow or red, usually blandly flavored fruits; the thimbleberry, with its round, hairy red fruits; and the low-growing, cool-climate, bog-loving cloudberry, whose flavorful little golden fruits enliven the diets of both Canadians and northern Europeans.

Whereas blackberries grow with abandon over the countryside and neglected areas of cities, raspberries tend to hide in cool, moist woodlands. To enjoy raspberries regularly, therefore, you may have to plant your own. Cultivars have been developed for various characteristics, such as spineless canes, extension of the harvest season, resistance to root rot and other diseases, and color. Golden or yellow raspberries, which have lost their red color through a mutation, taste like other varieties. Although raspberries have perennial roots and biennial canes, fall or "everbearing" raspberries fruit on primocanes, so the berries ripen mainly in late August or September. By planting both summer and fall varieties suited to your region, you can harvest raspberries for much of the summer.

In the garden, raspberries are a little fussier than blackberries. Raspberries need plenty of water but also good drainage to avoid root rot, so a raised bed may be necessary. They prefer cool temperatures and will tolerate partial shade. They can be grown in hedgerows or on hills, and some sort of trellis is recommended even for black and purple raspberries, which have stiff canes. Pruning requirements depend on the variety.

Raspberries are ripe when they slip off their "receptacles," or central cores, with a slight tug. Berries falling off their receptacles are overripe. If you are going to make your berries into jam, pick them just-ripe for a relatively high pectin content.

As you pick your berries, avoid letting grass seeds and other debris fall on them. Because raspberries are so delicate, you want to avoid having to rinse them.

If you can't use your berries right away, spread them in a shallow layer and refrigerate them for a few hours. Or freeze them in a single layer on baking pans and then transfer them to freezer bags or rigid containers.

RASPBERRY JAM

MAKES ABOUT 2 PINTS

I ONCE OVERHEARD a young woman tell her fiancé that, although he had several jars of jam in his cupboard, his home wouldn't be ready for her until he had stocked up on raspberry jam—the best jam, the One True Jam. I must have grimaced, because since I'd spent my thirteenth summer picking raspberries for pay ("Another day, another dollar!" my father would say jocularly, and accurately, as he dropped my sister and me at the bus stop at six in the morning), I was still on a 25-year raspberry hiatus. But I've since regained my love of raspberries, and now I agree that raspberries make one of the best jams, if not the very best.

2 pounds raspberries
3 cups sugar
2 tablespoons lemon juice

1 In a preserving pan, mash the raspberries with a potato masher. Add the sugar and lemon juice. Over medium heat, heat the mixture, stirring gently, until the sugar is dissolved. Raise the heat to medium-high and boil the mixture, stirring frequently, until a drop of the jam forms a mound in a chilled dish.

2 Ladle the jam into pint or half-pint mason jars, add lids and rings, and process them in a boiling-water bath for 10 minutes.

SMOOTH
RASPBERRY JAM

MAKES ABOUT 2 PINTS

T HIS IS AN INTERESTING CHANGE from raspberry jam with its seeds. I recommend this recipe especially if your berries are small and seedy.

> 2 pounds raspberries
> 3 cups sugar
> 2 tablespoons lemon juice

1 Puree the raspberries. You can pass them through the fine screen of a food mill, but some of the seeds might be small enough to escape. For a totally seedless jam, you might whirl the berries briefly in a blender and then pass them through a tamis, or drum sieve, with a fine stainless-steel or nylon screen. A tomato strainer with a berry screen is probably the best tool of all for pureeing raspberries.

2 In a preserving pan, combine the berry puree, sugar, and lemon juice. Over medium heat, heat the mixture, stirring gently, until the sugar is dissolved. Raise the heat to medium-high and boil the mixture, stirring frequently, until a drop of the jam forms a mound in a chilled dish.

3 Ladle the jam into pint or half-pint mason jars, add lids and rings, and process them in a boiling-water bath for 10 minutes.

RASPBERRY–
RED CURRANT JAM

SUMMER RASPBERRIES and red currants ripen at about the same time and, when cooked, share a brilliant red color. In this jam, the tart, spicy flavor of currant juice enhances the headily aromatic, uncrushed raspberries.

1½ cups red currant juice (page 120)
6½ cups sugar
3 pounds raspberries

1. In a preserving pan, combine the currant juice and sugar. Heat the mixture over medium heat, stirring gently, until the sugar is dissolved.

2. Add the raspberries to the pan. Over medium heat, stirring occasionally, boil the jam until a drop of it mounds in a chilled dish.

3. Ladle the jam into pint or half-pint mason jars. Add lids and rings, and process the jars for 10 minutes in a boiling-water bath.

CRISTINA'S
RAW RASPBERRY JAM

MAKES ABOUT 1 PINT

T HIS SIMPLE RECIPE comes from my young Moldovan friend Cristina Nicoară, who makes the jam in large quantities every summer with her family at their village home. The jam doesn't set, of course, but it is thick enough for many purposes, and it has a wonderfully fresh raspberry flavor. In Moldova the jam is often served over crêpes, and you might like it over pancakes, waffles, or ice cream.

The jam must be refrigerated, and it will keep for no more than a few weeks. For a raw raspberry jam to keep in the cellar, Cristina and her family use, by weight, two parts sugar to one part fruit.

¾ pound raspberries
1½ cups sugar

1 In a bowl, mash the raspberries with a potato masher. Stir in the sugar until it has dissolved. Pour the jam into a jar and tightly cap the jar.

2 Store the jam in the refrigerator. Provided your berries were fresh-picked and free from mold, the jam should keep for a few weeks.

RAW RASPBERRY PUREE

MAKES ABOUT 1 PINT

 MAKE THIS PUREE for the freezer, to use later in ice creams, smoothies, and the like.

1 pound raspberries
2 tablespoons sugar

1 Puree the berries through the fine screen of a food mill into a bowl. Stir in the sugar.

2 If you'll be using the puree very soon, store it in the refrigerator. Otherwise, store it in the freezer, in a well-sealed plastic or glass container with about 1 inch headspace.

RAW RASPBERRY SAUCE

MAKES ABOUT 1 PINT

THIS IS THE KIND OF SAUCE that chefs in chic restaurants drizzle on dessert plates. The recipe is the same as the one for Raw Raspberry Puree (above) except that you add more sugar. The sauce is a tart, fragrant counterpoint to chocolate desserts.

1 pound raspberries
1 cup sugar

1. Puree the berries through the fine screen of a food mill into a bowl. Stir in the sugar.

2. If you'll be using the sauce within a week or so, store it in the refrigerator. Otherwise, store it in the freezer, in a well-sealed plastic or glass container with about 1 inch headspace. Serve the sauce cold, at room temperature, or briefly heated, as you prefer.

RASPBERRY ICE CREAM

Makes about 2½ cups

Because I keep my own chickens and ducks, I often use raw eggs in ice cream and mayonnaise without worrying about salmonella. If you must avoid raw eggs, make a cooked version of this ice cream: Beat the yolks lightly, stir them into the warmed cream and sugar, and heat the mixture into a custard sauce—that is, until it coats the back of a wooden spoon (if you insert an instant-read thermometer into the sauce, it will read 160°F at this point). Chill the custard before combining it with the Raw Raspberry Puree. Since the raspberries need no cooking, your ice cream will still taste delightfully of fresh summer fruit.

You can also vary this recipe by adding a few drops of vanilla extract or kirsch, but I prefer giving the raspberries the whole spotlight.

1 cup cream
3 egg yolks
1 cup Raw Raspberry Puree (page 315)
⅔ cup sugar

Whirl all of the ingredients together in a blender. Freeze the mixture in an ice-cream freezer according to the manufacturer's directions.

RASPBERRY VINEGAR

THIS VINEGAR, combined with olive oil and a little salt, is my favorite dressing for a butter lettuce salad, with or without such additions as sliced oranges, radishes, and avocados. The flavor and fragrance of homemade raspberry vinaigrette is *nothing* like that of the chemical-tasting raspberry dressing served so often in restaurants.

> 1 pound raspberries
> 2 cups white wine vinegar

1. Put the raspberries into a sterilized quart jar and cover them with the vinegar. Let the jar stand, tightly covered with a plastic cap, for 3 to 4 weeks.

2. Strain the vinegar through a sieve and then through a damp jelly bag. Funnel the vinegar into sterilized bottles. Cap or cork the bottles and then store them in a cool, dark place. The vinegar should keep for 4 to 6 months. Save the raspberries, if you like, and use them in salads without added vinegar. I especially like them with sliced Asian pear and arugula.

RASPBERRY SHRUB

MAKES ABOUT 2 QUARTS

T HE WORD *shrub*, meaning a sweetened, acidulated fruit juice mixed with ice water, comes from the same Arabic root as *syrup*. Before the advent of commercial soft drinks, shrubs were quite popular, and friends of mine still treat themselves to raspberry shrub once a year while haying. No drink could be more welcome when you're working hard on a hot summer day.

To serve the shrub, mix 1 part syrup with about 3 parts combined water and ice. You can use soda water instead of plain water, if you like, but I think you'll find that the vinegar in the shrub provides plenty of tingle.

> 2 quarts Raspberry Vinegar (page 317)
> 2 cups sugar
> 1 cup brandy (optional)

1 Make Raspberry Vinegar according to the instructions on page 317, but don't bottle the vinegar. After straining it through a damp jelly bag, combine it in a saucepan with the sugar. Stirring, bring the mixture to a boil over medium heat. Let the mixture boil for 5 minutes and then let it cool. Stir in the brandy, if you are using it.

2 Funnel the shrub into sterilized bottles and tightly cap or cork the bottles. Store them in a cool, dry, dark place, where the shrub should keep well for at least 1 year.

RHUBARB

Rhubarb-Orange Jam   321

Rhubarb-Ginger Preserves   322

Rhubarb-Rose Preserves   323

Rhubarb Cordial   324

NATIVE TO RIVERBANKS in southern Siberia, this hardy perennial of the genus *Rheum* grows 2 to 4 feet tall from large rhizomes. In cooler climates, the plant dies back to the ground in winter, and the leaves emerge from crown buds in the spring.

Rhubarb was used medicinally, as a laxative and cathartic, for thousands of years before the easy availability of sugar prompted the English to begin using the plant as food. Although the level of oxalic acid in the leaves is high enough to make people sick, the stalks are safe to eat, though quite tart, and they are so delicious when sweetened that some people refer to rhubarb as pie-plant. Rhubarb came to the Americas with English colonists before 1800, and gardeners and cooks still prize it as one of the first "fruits" of spring, useful for wines, cordials, jams, jellies, sauces, and chutneys as well as for pies.

Since the plant sometimes reproduces from seed, there are many varieties of rhubarb, and most of them are known by multiple names. The varieties can be generally grouped by color: Although most rhubarb stalks have red skins, most have green interiors, and some have green or speckled skins as well as green interiors. A few varieties, such as Cherry Red, Strawberry, Valentine, and Crimson Red, are red inside and out. These varieties may also be sweeter and less prone to sending up seed stalks, which take energy from the produc-

WILD RHUBARB

Over much of Alaska grows a wild plant, *Polygonum alaskabanum*, that locals call wild rhubarb. Growing 3 to 6 feet tall, the plant tastes like rhubarb and is used in the same ways.

tion of edible stalks. Red-fleshed varieties are treasured where they thrive.

If you want to plant rhubarb, give it compost-rich soil, plenty of water, and good drainage. Let your plant establish itself for a year before you begin cutting the stalks. Once the plant is thriving, you can divide it by cutting pieces from the crown, each with at least one strong bud.

When you harvest rhubarb, choose stalks that are firm, not spongy. Twist the stalks and snap them off the base of the plant instead of cutting them. For the health of the plant, always leave a few stalks standing. Cut the leaves off the harvested stalks and lay them close to the plant to help retain soil moisture and to eventually nourish the plant. Peel away any tough strings from the stalk before using them.

For another recipe using rhubarb, see Strawberry-Rhubarb Jam (page 330).

RHUBARB-ORANGE JAM

I BASED THIS RECIPE on an old Pennsylvania Dutch one. The jam turns out a pretty red if you have a well-colored rhubarb variety such as Cherry Red, Valentine, or Crimson Red. If your rhubarb doesn't cook up red, you might use blood-orange juice instead of regular orange juice, or even substitute red currant juice. Or simply enjoy your greenish jam!

2½ pounds rhubarb stalks, cut into pieces
    about ⅜ inch square
½ cup water
Grated zest of 1 orange
½ cup orange juice
3 cups sugar

1 In a preserving pan, combine the rhubarb, water, and orange zest. Cover the pan and simmer the contents for about 20 minutes, until the rhubarb is tender.

2 Remove the pan from the heat and add the orange juice and sugar. Over medium heat, stir the contents until the sugar is dissolved. Raise the heat to medium-high and boil the jam until it mounds in a chilled dish.

3 Ladle the jam into pint or half-pint mason jars. Add lids and rings, and process the jars for 10 minutes in a boiling-water bath.

RHUBARB-GINGER PRESERVES

INGER BRINGS OUT the flavor of rhubarb, and cooking the rhubarb in sugar keeps the pieces intact.

As with Rhubarb-Orange Jam (page 321), these preserves will be prettier if you have a rhubarb variety that cooks up red.

2 pounds rhubarb stalks, cut crosswise
    into ½-inch pieces
3 cups sugar
¼ cup water
½ cup coarsely chopped crystallized ginger, store-bought or
    homemade (page 165)

1. In a preserving pan, toss together the rhubarb and sugar. Cover the pan and let it stand for 6 to 12 hours, until the sugar is dissolved.

2. Add the water and crystallized ginger to the pan. Stir the contents over medium heat until the sugar is completely dissolved. Raise the heat to medium-high and boil the mixture, stirring only as necessary to prevent scalding, until the syrup has thickened and the rhubarb is partially translucent.

3. Remove the pan from the heat and let the preserves cool for 5 minutes. Stir them and ladle them into pint or half-pint mason jars. Add lids and rings, and process the jars for 15 minutes in a boiling-water bath.

RHUBARB-ROSE
PRESERVES

A FEW MINUTES BEFORE writing these words, I opened a six-year-old jar of Rhubarb-Rose Preserves, and for a moment I thought that the roses were blooming in the garden. These preserves can raise you out of midwinter blues into happy plans for spring.

Dark red rose petals may enhance the color of this jam a bit, but they won't turn a green jam red.

> 2 pounds rhubarb stalks, cut crosswise
> into ½-inch pieces
> 3 cups sugar
> 2 tablespoons strained lemon juice
> ½ packed cup unsprayed fragrant rose petals,
> preferably red

1 In a preserving pan, toss together the rhubarb and sugar. Cover the pan and let it stand at room temperature for 6 to 12 hours, until much of the sugar is dissolved.

2 Add the lemon juice and rose petals to the pan. Stir the contents over medium heat until the sugar is completely dissolved. Raise the heat to medium-high and boil the mixture, stirring only as necessary to prevent scalding, until the syrup has thickened, about 10 minutes.

3 Remove the pan from the heat and let the preserves cool for 5 minutes. Stir them and ladle them into pint or half-pint mason jars. Add lids and rings, and process the jars for 15 minutes in a boiling-water bath.

RHUBARB CORDIAL

IKE CURRANTS and other soft fruits, rhubarb easily renders its juice in a steam juicer (page 14). If you don't have a steam juicer, you can make rhubarb juice by the jelly-bag method (page 15) instead. Mellow the rhubarb flavor and enhance the color, if you like, by cooking about one part red fruit juice to two parts rhubarb juice in this syrup.

For a refreshing hot-weather drink, mix one part of this concentrate with two parts chilled plain water or soda water.

> Rhubarb juice
> Strawberry, raspberry, or
>   red currant juice (optional)
> Sugar

Measure the volume of the rhubarb juice, if you're using only rhubarb, or measure the combined juices. Pour the juices into a saucepan, and add ½ cup sugar for each pint of juice. Heat the mixture to a boil and boil it for 1 minute. Pour the mixture into pint or quart mason jars. Add lids and rings, and process the jars for 10 minutes in a boiling-water bath.

STRAWBERRY

Small-Batch Strawberry Jam   327

Main-Crop Strawberry Jam   328

Strawberry-Orange Jam   329

Strawberry-Rhubarb Jam   330

Strawberry Preserves   331

Sunshine Strawberry Jam   332

Strawberry Syrup   333

VARIOUS SPECIES OF STRAWBERRIES are indigenous to Eurasia, North America, and South America. Wild strawberries can be very fragrant and delicious, but the berries are small and scant. So, since the early seventeenth century, strawberries have been bred and interbred—first in France, then in England, then in the eastern United States, the southern states, the Pacific Northwest, and, ultimately, California. The modern cultivated strawberry derives from an accidental cross, in France, of two species: *Fragaria virginiana*, of eastern North America, and *F. chiloensis*, of the west coasts of both North America and South America.

Today, California's central and southern coastal counties produce at least 85 percent of all strawberries sold in the United States. You probably know these berries from the supermarket. They are very large, durable, and pale on the inside even when they're fully red on the outside. They are available from March through November.

Outside of California, farmers and gardeners produce very different strawberry varieties, developed for regional growing conditions. In Oregon, for example, most strawberries ripen in June or early July. They are usually red throughout, very fragrant, and very fragile.

They must be used the day they are picked or, at least, refrigerated and used the day after.

In most regions of the United States, including coastal California, strawberries are easy to grow but hard to grow well. Their shallow roots need irrigation and, often, mulching; their straying habit makes cultivation difficult; and the plants are susceptible to many pests and diseases. To many gardeners, though, strawberries are worth the trouble of growing them, if only in pots.

Modern strawberry varieties fall into three general types: June-bearers, which produce one crop in early summer; everbearers, which produce a crop in early summer and another in the fall; and day-neutrals, which produce more or less continuously through the growing season. June-bearers are most productive, but having some plants of the other types allows for a longer harvest season.

Pick strawberries when they are fully red but before they turn dark and soft. If you want to serve the berries raw—with cream or sour cream or perhaps red wine—do so the same day, when they are at their sweetest. If you're making jam or other preserves with sugar, you can chill the berries overnight. To preserve all their juice, rinse and drain the berries before hulling them.

To keep strawberries for later use, rinse, drain, and hull them, slice them if you like, and then spread them on trays and freeze them. When they are frozen, pack them into freezer bags and return them to the freezer. Depending on how you plan to use the berries, you might coat them with sugar before freezing them (Oregon State University Extension advises combining 3 cups sugar with a package of powdered pectin; the thawed berries should keep in the refrigerator for several days without getting mushy). Strawberries will keep well in the freezer for as long as a year.

Since strawberries are low in both pectin and acid, they tend to make a soft jam. I think this is one of their charms.

For another recipe using strawberries, see Strawberry-Kiwi Jam (page 183).

SMALL-BATCH
STRAWBERRY JAM

H ERE'S A RECIPE for using those first spring strawberries in the garden or market, to brighten your mornings until the main harvest.

> 1 pound strawberries, hulled and sliced thin or mashed
> 1 cup sugar
> 2 tablespoons lemon juice

1. In a 12-inch nonreactive skillet, combine all of the ingredients. Stir the contents over medium heat until the sugar is dissolved. Raise the heat to medium-high and boil the mixture, stirring and skimming off the foam, until a drop mounds slightly in a chilled dish.

2. Store the cooled jam in a tightly capped jar in the refrigerator, where it should keep well for a few weeks.

MAIN-CROP
STRAWBERRY JAM

MAKES ABOUT 3½ PINTS

 F YOU USE SMALL, tender berries, you may not need to mash them at all.

3 pounds strawberries, hulled
6 tablespoons lemon juice
Seeds and membranes of 2 lemons
4½ cups sugar

1 Put the strawberries into a preserving pan and mash them if they are quite firm. Add the lemon juice. Put the lemon seeds and membranes into a spice bag, add it to the pan, and cover the pan. Simmer the strawberries until they are soft.

2 Remove the pan from the heat and add the sugar. Stir the contents over medium heat until the sugar is dissolved. Raise the heat to medium-high and boil the jam, stirring and skimming off foam, until a drop mounds slightly in a chilled dish.

3 Press the spice bag against the side of the pan, and remove the bag. Ladle the jam into pint or half-pint mason jars. Add lids and rings, and process the jars for 10 minutes in a boiling-water bath.

STRAWBERRY-ORANGE JAM

I F THE ORANGE HAS SEEDS, you can increase the pectin content of this jam by putting them into a spice bag and heating the bag along with the jam.

> 1 medium-size orange
> 3 pounds strawberries, hulled
> 4½ cups sugar

1. Remove the zest of the orange in thin shreds. Squeeze out the juice and put it and the zest into a preserving pan. Add the strawberries to the pan and mash them if they are firm. Cover the pan and simmer the strawberries until they are soft.

2. Remove the pan from the heat and add the sugar. Stir the contents over medium heat until the sugar is dissolved. Raise the heat to medium-high and boil the jam, stirring and skimming off the foam, until a drop mounds slightly in a chilled dish.

3. Ladle the jam into pint or half-pint mason jars. Add lids and rings, and process the jars for 10 minutes in a boiling-water bath.

STRAWBERRY-RHUBARB JAM

MAKES ABOUT 3 PINTS

 TRAWBERRIES HIDE THE COLOR of green rhubarb, which gives body to this jam.

1 large lemon
2 pounds strawberries, hulled
¾ pound rhubarb stalks, cut into
approximately ⅜-inch cubes
4¼ cups sugar

1 Squeeze the juice from the lemon. Put the seeds into a spice bag, and put the bag and juice into a preserving pan. Add the strawberries, and slice or mash them if they are large and firm. Add the rhubarb. Over low heat, simmer the contents until the rhubarb is tender, about 30 minutes.

2 Remove the pan from the heat and add the sugar. Stir the mixture over medium heat until the sugar is dissolved. Raise the heat to medium-high and boil the jam, stirring and skimming off the foam, until a drop mounds in a chilled dish.

3 Ladle the jam into pint or half-pint mason jars. Add lids and rings, and process the jars for 10 minutes in a boiling-water bath.

STRABERRY PRESERVES

 IF YOUR STRAWBERRIES are very large, cut them in half for preserves. If they are small, leave them whole.

2½ pounds strawberries, hulled
4 cups sugar
¼ cup strained lemon juice

1. In a preserving pan, layer the strawberries and sugar. Pour the lemon juice over them. Cover the pan and let it stand at room temperature for 8 to 12 hours.

2. Place the pan over medium heat. Stirring gently, heat the contents until the sugar is completely dissolved. Raise the heat to medium-high and boil the mixture for 3 minutes, skimming off any foam. Remove the pan from the heat and cover it with a cloth. Let the pan stand at room temperature for 8 to 12 hours.

3. With a skimmer, transfer the strawberries to a bowl. Boil the syrup until it drops slowly and heavily from a spoon. Return the strawberries to the pan and bring the preserves to a full boil. Ladle the fruit and syrup evenly into pint or half-pint mason jars. Add lids and rings, and process the jars for 10 minutes in a boiling-water bath.

STRAWBERRY-ROSE PRESERVES

In June the scents of strawberries and roses mingle deliciously in the air. They will do the same whenever you open a jar of these preserves.

Make Strawberry Preserves in the usual way, except include 5 ounces unsprayed fragrant red or pink rose petals (about 3 quarts, loosely packed) with the strawberries when you layer them with the sugar.

SUNSHINE
STRAWBERRY JAM

MAKES 1 TO 1¼ CUPS

IF YOU HAVE WARM, dry summers, try cooking your jam in the sun for a change. This is an enjoyable project to share with children.

Many recipes for sun-cooked jam start with stovetop cooking and have you finish the cooking—or drying, actually—in the sun. This recipe calls for no stovetop cooking at all and very little sugar.

If this method works well for you, you might try it with other fruits, such as blackberries, raspberries, apricots, peaches, and plums.

> 1 pound strawberries, hulled
> 1 tablespoon lemon juice
> ¼ cup sugar

1 Puree the strawberries in a blender, food mill, or food processor, or, for a coarser texture, mash them briefly with a potato masher. Blend in the lemon juice and sugar. Pour the mixture into a glass or stainless-steel pan, 9 inches square or larger. If you're using an electric dehydrator (it should be equipped with a fan), make sure the pan will fit inside with enough space around it to allow air to circulate.

2 If you're making your jam in the sun, cover the pan with cheese-cloth or window screening, and set the pan where ants won't reach it.

3 If you're using a food dehydrator with a thermostat, set it to 130°F.

4 "Cook" the jam, stirring it about every 2 hours, until it is as thick as you'd like; keep in mind that it will thicken as it cools. Depending on the pan size, air temperature, air circulation, humidity, and how thoroughly you have pureed the berries, the jam will be ready in 4 to 12 hours. (Using a potato masher may nearly double the drying time, but I like the coarse texture that results.) If you're cooking your jam in the sun and it isn't ready by nightfall, refrigerate the pan overnight.

5 Pour the finished jam into a jar and store it in the refrigerator. Since this jam is very low in sugar, you'll want to use it up within a week or two.

STRAWBERRY SYRUP

MAKES ABOUT 1½ PINTS

THIS RECIPE comes from the Caucasus. Serve the syrup over pancakes or vanilla ice cream, or mix about 3 tablespoons with a cup of cold soda water or plain water and pour the mixture over crushed ice.

> 1½ pounds strawberries, hulled
> 4¾ cups sugar
> 2 tablespoons strained lemon juice

1 In a bowl, layer the strawberries with 2½ cups of the sugar. Crush the berries with a potato masher to release the juices. Let the mixture stand at room temperature for 8 to 12 hours.

2 Puree the mixture with a blender or food mill. Combine the puree in a kettle with the remaining 2¼ cups sugar. Heat the mixture slowly, stirring until the sugar is dissolved, and then raise the heat to medium-high. Bring the mixture to a boil, reduce the heat, and boil the mixture gently for 5 minutes, skimming off the foam.

3 Remove the pan from the heat and strain the syrup through a strainer fine enough to catch the strawberry seeds, stirring as needed. You can use the pulp remaining in the strainer as jam.

4 Pour the strained syrup into the kettle. Add the lemon juice and heat the syrup to a boil. Immediately pour it into pint or half-pint mason jars. Add lids and rings, and process the jars for 10 minutes in a boiling-water bath.

STRAWBERRY TREE

Strawberry Tree Jam   336

*A*rbutus unedo is native to the Mediterranean region and western Europe as far north as Ireland. Like madrone, a species of *Arbutus* whose shiny orange bark decorates the coastal hills from California to British Columbia, strawberry tree is an evergreen with glossy dark green leaves and little bell-shaped flowers (the name madrone comes from *madroño*, the Spanish word for strawberry tree). The English name for *A. unedo* describes its fruit, which looks something like a round strawberry and, like a strawberry, has many tiny seeds. Some people find the fruit mealy and let the birds have it, but others love its tart flavor, which they describe as being between that of a guava and a nectarine. In the Mediterranean countries, the fruit is valued for its high vitamin C content and used in jam and jelly. The Portuguese make the fruit into a kind of liquor, by first fermenting the fruit in water and then distilling the liquid.

Like madrone, the strawberry tree thrives in areas with mild winters, moderate summers, and light, well-drained soil. More often a shrub than a tree, *A. unedo* makes a good tall hedge; it grows as high as 25 feet in the San Francisco Bay area. (If you're thinking of planting one or more of your own strawberry trees, beware that this species, like manzanita and other members of the Ericaceae family, is a host for Sudden Oak Death fungus.)

The fruit of the strawberry tree is ripe when it turns soft and dark red.

STRAWBERRY TREE JAM

MAKES ABOUT 2½ CUPS

THIS RECIPE comes from my daughter, Rebecca, who bore strangers' stares as she gathered the fruit on the Mills College campus, and then cooked the fruit into a jam in the dark basement kitchen of a dormitory. Although the jam was tart and tasty, she didn't like the many tiny seeds. If they bother you, press the pulp through an extra-fine-mesh sieve before adding the sugar.

> 1 pound (about 3 cups) mashed ripe strawberry-tree fruit
> 1 cup sugar

1. Put the mashed fruit into a preserving pan or nonreactive skillet. Heat the fruit briefly, stirring, and then remove the pan from the heat and stir in the sugar. Heat the mixture over medium heat, stirring, until the sugar is dissolved. Raise the heat to medium-high and boil the jam, stirring often, until a drop of it mounds in a chilled dish.

2. Pour the jam into one or more jars and cap the jars tightly. When the jam has cooled, store the jars in the refrigerator, where the jam will keep for several weeks.

TOMATILLO AND GROUND CHERRY

Tomatillo or Ground Cherry Jam 339
Tomatillo-Lime Marmalade 340

T HESE TWO TART, aromatic fruits grow on annual plants in the genus *Physalis*. Each fruit is enclosed in a paper-like husk (*physalis* means "bladder" in Greek), which starts out green and turns straw yellow as the fruit ripens. Both species grow wild in gardens and elsewhere throughout much of the Americas.

Tomatillo, *P. ixocarpa*, grows as tall as 5 feet, although without staking or caging it tends to sprawl. The smooth, somewhat sticky, and slightly oblate fruits grow to 1 to 2½ inches and fill their husks so well when ripe that the husks sometimes burst a seam. In Mexico, the fruits are used for salsa when at or near full size but still green, and this is the way you'll find them in supermarkets. When tomatillos ripen, their green husks become tan, and the green- or purple-skinned fruits become golden or purple-gold. At this stage, the fruit is quite sweet and may begin to soften. It may fall from the plant to the ground, protected from bruising by its husk. Ripe tomatillos are thought too cloying for salsa, but they are perfect for sweet preserves.

Ground cherry, *P. peruviana*, is a compact, low-growing plant that is native to the Andes. The smooth, round fruit, approximately

In England, ground cherries are served whole as a dessert, dipped in sugar syrup and fondant, their husks folded back like wings.

½ inch in diameter, is sometimes called the Cape gooseberry, because once introduced to the Cape region of South Africa it became valued there more than in its homeland. The fruit has become naturalized on mountain slopes of the Hawaiian Islands, where it is called *poha* and collected for jam, jelly, and pie and cookie fillings.

You may well have ground cherries, tomatillos, or both in your garden even if you have never planted them. If not, buy the seed from a seed company, and you'll probably never have to do this again. The plants self-sow abundantly, although if your growing season is very short you may have to save seeds and start them indoors. Plant (or keep) at least two tomatillo plants, since they are self-sterile.

You can grow tomatillos and ground cherries wherever you grow tomatoes, but with a lot less care. Tomatillos and ground cherries tolerate drought better and have few problems with insects or disease. Do harvest ripe fruits before they split from the rain or excessive overhead irrigation.

TOMATILLO OR GROUND CHERRY JAM

MAKES 2 TO 2½ PINTS

SOME PEOPLE THINK ground cherries make better jam, but tomatillos, because they are bigger, are much less trouble to pick and husk. With either fruit, you'll get a translucent, golden jam flecked with many tiny seeds. Serve it with cornbread, or try a dab alongside roast pork.

3 pounds husked ripe tomatillos or ground cherries
4 cups sugar

1. If you're using tomatillos, halve or quarter them.

2. Put the fruit into a preserving pan, set the pan over low heat, and cover the pan. Cook the fruit, stirring occasionally, until it is soft. Mash it briefly with a potato masher. Remove the pan from the heat.

3. Stir in the sugar. Over medium heat, heat the mixture until the sugar is dissolved. Raise the heat to medium-high and boil the jam until a drop mounds in a chilled dish.

4. Ladle the jam into pint or half-pint mason jars. Add lids and rings, and process the jars for 10 minutes in a boiling-water bath.

TOMATILLO-LIME
MARMALADE

MAKES ABOUT 2½ PINTS

L ime and ginger complement the tropical-fruit flavor of tomatillos. Like old-fashioned green-tomato marmalade, this preserve might be served with meat.

4 large limes
4 pounds sliced ripe or green tomatillos
½ teaspoon salt
½ cup water
3 tablespoons peeled and minced fresh ginger
4 cups sugar

1. If the limes were store-bought and not labeled organic, put them in a colander in the sink and pour boiling water over them to remove any wax. Scrub them well.

2. Combine the tomatillos and salt in a nonreactive kettle. Remove the zest of the limes in thin shreds and add it to the kettle along with the water and ginger. Bring the mixture to a boil, and boil it gently, stirring occasionally, for 10 minutes.

3. Slice the limes as thinly as possible, discarding any seeds (there is no need to peel them). Add the lime slices to the kettle with the sugar. Over medium heat, stir until the sugar dissolves. Then boil the mixture gently, stirring often, for about 50 minutes, until a drop of the marmalade mounds in a chilled dish.

4. Ladle the marmalade into pint or half-pint mason jars. Add lids and rings, and process the jars for 10 minutes in a boiling-water bath.

TOMATO

Tomato Marmalade   342

Yellow Tomato–Pineapple Preserves   344

Green Tomato Preserves   346

Tomato-Apple Butter   347

T HE LOVE-APPLE (*pomme d'amour*), as the French called it, or the golden apple (*pomodoro*), as the Italians still call it, originated in South America and was being cultivated by the Aztecs when Cortes arrived in Mexico in 1519. Because the plant clearly belonged to the nightshade family, some of whose members are poisonous, Europeans viewed the tomato, along with its cousins the potato and the eggplant, with initial suspicion; perhaps the tomato could be safe as an occasional aphrodisiac, but you wouldn't eat it regularly. By the eighteenth century, though, tomatoes were common fare in Spain and Italy, and by the end of the century they were popular in the United States. Mary Randolph, in her *Virginia House-Wife* (1824), includes numerous tomato recipes, including one for green tomato marmalade.

Perhaps because tomatoes marry well with meats and vegetables, they have always been used more with savory foods than in desserts or breakfast sweets. American tomato jams and marmalades—green, red, or yellow—are typically spiced and made bitter with citrus peel. Serving the same function as sweet chutneys in England, these preserves have generally been served with meats, though they are also good on toast.

Tomatoes make fine simple sweet preserves, too, without bitter ingredients. Recipes in old books include tomato butter with apple, tomato jelly, and plain tomato jam. Tomatoes combine well with pineapple in the preserves recipe on page 344.

To preserve ripe tomatoes, make sure they are just-ripe—firm and sound. They will not only be free of disease organisms at this stage, but their pectin content will be at its maximum.

Use green tomatoes when they have reached full size and have just begun to change color.

TOMATO
MARMALADE

MAKES ABOUT 2½ PINTS

T HIS IS A WONDERFUL USE for the last of fall's tomatoes and the first of winter's citrus. You can use either red or yellow tomatoes. Try this marmalade with pot roast.

> 1 medium-size orange
> 1 lemon
> 2½ cups water
> 2 pounds ripe tomatoes
> One 3-inch cinnamon stick
> ½ teaspoon whole cloves
> 2 teaspoons chopped fresh ginger
> 2 cups sugar

1 If the orange and lemon were store-bought and not labeled organic, put them in a colander in the sink and pour boiling water over them to remove any wax. Scrub them well.

2 Halve the fruit, squeeze out and reserve the juice, and place the seeds and membranes on a square of cheesecloth. Cut the lemon

rind halves in half again, and quarter the orange rind halves. Put the rinds into a small saucepan with the water. Simmer the rinds, covered, for about 30 minutes, until they are tender.

3 Remove the rinds with a slotted spoon and set them aside to cool. Reserve the cooking liquid.

4 Dip the tomatoes into boiling water for 30 to 60 seconds, until their skins begin to crack. Let them cool briefly, slip off their skins, and squeeze the skins dry before discarding them. Using a strainer, drain off the tomato juice into a preserving pan. Add the cooking liquid from the citrus rinds and the juice from the orange and lemon. Add the cinnamon, cloves, and ginger to the cheesecloth square, tie the square into a bundle, and add it to the preserving pan. Bring the mixture to a boil, and boil it until it is reduced by half, about 30 minutes.

5 Scrape the excess pith from the citrus rinds and cut the rinds into thin crosswise strips. Chop the tomatoes coarsely. Turn off the heat under the preserving pan and add the tomatoes and citrus rinds. Stir in the sugar. Boil the mixture gently until it looks glossy and a drop of the marmalade mounds in a chilled dish, about 40 minutes. Squeeze the cheesecloth bundle and remove it.

6 Ladle the marmalade into pint or half-pint mason jars, leaving ¼ inch headspace. Add lids and rings, and process the jars for 10 minutes in a boiling-water bath.

YELLOW TOMATO–
PINEAPPLE PRESERVES

....

MAKES ABOUT 3 PINTS

YELLOW TOMATOES are popular with gardeners partially because they tend to be less acidic than red tomatoes, but mostly because they add to the palate of colors in the garden and kitchen. Here is one way to show them off.

In my experience, these preserves do not gel at all; in fact, they turn out very syrupy. But they taste wonderful. A person who tries to guess their contents may succeed with the pineapple but strike out with the tomato. Try these preserves as a finishing glaze for chicken, or spread them on chicken or pork sandwiches.

> 2¼ pounds yellow tomatoes
> 4½ cups sugar
> ½ medium-size pineapple
> 4 thin slices fresh ginger

1 Dip the tomatoes into boiling water for 30 to 60 seconds. Let them cool briefly and then slip off their skins. Cut them into wedges about 1 x 1½ inches and put the wedges into a bowl. Add the sugar and gently mix. Cover the bowl and let it stand for 6 to 12 hours, gently turning the tomatoes once or twice in the meantime.

2 Peel and core the pineapple and chop it coarsely, reserving all juice. Weigh the chopped pineapple; you should have ¾ pound.

3 Strain the syrup from the tomatoes into a nonreactive kettle. Add any sugar from the bottom of the bowl and any juice from chopping the pineapple. Put the ginger slices into a spice bag and add

it to the kettle. Stir the mixture over medium heat until the sugar has completely dissolved. Raise the heat to high and boil the syrup until it reaches the thread stage (page 18) or 230°F. Add the tomato wedges and chopped pineapple. Reduce the heat and barely simmer the mixture until the tomato wedges are partially translucent, at least 30 minutes. Skim off any foam. Press the spice bag against the side of the kettle, and remove the bag. Ladle the preserves into pint or half-pint mason jars. Add lids and rings, and process the jars for 10 minutes in a boiling-water bath.

GREEN TOMATO PRESERVES

MAKES ABOUT 3 PINTS

WHEN FROST THREATENS, this is a fine way to use some of your unripe tomatoes. The almost relish-like preserves go well with meats and other savory foods.

> 2 pounds green tomatoes, cut into wedges
>   about 1 × 1½ inches
> 3 tablespoons lime juice
> Grated zest of 2 limes
> 1 tablespoon grated fresh ginger
> 3 green jalapeño or Fresno peppers,
>   cut into thin rounds
> 3 cups sugar

1. Combine all of the ingredients in a nonreactive kettle. Cover the kettle and let it stand at room temperature for 8 to 12 hours, turning the mixture a few times.

2. Bring the mixture slowly to a simmer, stirring gently until the sugar is completely dissolved. Simmer the mixture for 1 to 1½ hours, until the tomatoes are partially translucent. Remove the pan from the heat and cover it with a cloth. Let it stand at room temperature for another 8 to 12 hours.

3. Strain the mixture through a colander set over a bowl. Return the syrup to the pan and boil it briefly, until it has noticeably thickened. Return the fruit to the pan, bring the preserves to a boil, and ladle them into pint or half-pint mason jars. Add lids and rings, and process the jars for 15 minutes in a boiling-water bath.

TOMATO-APPLE BUTTER

THIS DEEP RUST-RED, spicy butter is traditionally served with roast pork, chicken, or ham; you might love it on hamburgers, too. The smell of it cooking seems the very aroma of autumn.

I make this butter with applesauce and tomato puree from my pantry. To start from scratch, make applesauce by cooking peeled cored apples in a covered pan until they're soft, or cook them with the skins on and then puree the apples with a food mill. To make tomato puree, heat tomatoes in a covered pan until they're soft, and then strain them through a tomato strainer or food mill.

1 quart applesauce
1 quart seeded, skinned, and pureed tomatoes
1⅓ cups light brown sugar
½ cup cider vinegar
½ teaspoon ground cinnamon
½ teaspoon ground allspice
½ teaspoon ground ginger
¼ teaspoon ground cloves
1 teaspoon salt

Combine all of the ingredients in a preserving pan. Simmer the mixture, stirring often, for about 40 minutes, until it is thick. If you'll be serving it with meat, you'll probably want the butter a little less thick than apple butter. Ladle the butter into pint or half-pint mason jars. Add lids and rings, and process the jars for 15 minutes in a boiling-water bath.

WATERMELON

Watermelon Preserves   349

Watermelon Molasses   350

Watermelon Rind Preserves   351

itrullos lanatus developed in southern Africa, probably in the Kalahari Desert, where it still grows wild and is valued as a source of clean water. From there watermelons spread throughout Africa; Egyptians were cultivating them before 2000 B.C. Sixteenth-century European slave traders, or the slaves themselves, brought seeds to North America, where both white and Native American farmers began cultivating the melons. But they weren't widely available in markets until a South Carolina breeder, Charles Fredric Andrus, developed disease-resistant, tough-skinned varieties in the 1950s. His cultivars are the ancestors of the varieties popular in the United States today.

Preferred for pickling is the round, white-fleshed, pectin-rich watermelon called the citron melon, which grows wild in the San Diego area and Baja California. In the southeastern United States, a wild cross between the citron melon and modern watermelon is called pie melon; it is usually pickled or cooked in some way.

The Chinese have bred special watermelon varieties that are extra seedy. Rich in fat and protein, watermelon seeds are one of the most popular snack foods in China. In West Africa, the seeds are pressed for oil.

Seedless watermelons, which have dominated the U.S. market since the 1990s, are produced through a method involving genetic manipulation. That the technique requires interplanting with seeded watermelons may ensure, I hope, that we always have tasty watermelons. To me, seedless watermelons always seem lacking in flavor.

Like other melons, watermelons grow as annual vines, but they are easily distinguished by their deeply lobed, grayish leaves. Watermelons are planted at about the same time as other melons and cucumbers. Where summers aren't both long and hot, the smaller, round varieties such as Sugar Baby and the yellow-fleshed Yellow Doll are most likely to ripen.

A watermelon is ripe when its skin looks dull rather than shiny, the pale patch on the underside has yellowed, and the tendril near where the stem attaches to the vine has shriveled and turned brown.

WATERMELON PRESERVES

MAKES ABOUT 3 PINTS

 OU CAN USE EITHER red or yellow watermelon in this unusual recipe.

4½ pounds prepared watermelon (see below)
5 cups sugar
1 cup light corn syrup
Grated zest of 2 lemons
⅓ cup strained lemon juice

1 Prepare the watermelon: Slice the colored flesh away from the pale rind. Cutting out and discarding seedy areas, cut the flesh into pieces no larger than ¾ inch in any dimension. Weigh the pieces as you work.

2 When you have 4½ pounds watermelon pieces, layer them with the sugar and corn syrup in a nonreactive kettle. Add the lemon

zest and juice. Cover the kettle and let it stand at room temperature for 8 to 12 hours, gently turning the mixture two or three times.

(3) Set the kettle over low heat and slowly bring the mixture to a simmer. Simmer the mixture for several hours, until the fruit is dark and translucent and the syrup is thick. Remove the kettle from the heat and let the preserves cool for 5 minutes.

(4) Stir the preserves gently, and then ladle them into pint or half-pint mason jars. Process the jars for 10 minutes in a boiling-water bath.

WATERMELON MOLASSES

MAKES ABOUT ½ PINT

I INVENTED THIS RECIPE partially because I was tired of eating watermelon and partially to see if the idea would work. Watermelon Molasses, I discovered, tastes remarkably like Grape Molasses (page 173).

20 pounds watermelon

(1) Scoop the red or yellow watermelon flesh from the rind into a steam juicer (page 14) or stockpot, and heat it until the juice is rendered. If you've used a stockpot, strain the juice to eliminate the seeds.

(2) Boil the juice to a thick brown syrup; this will probably take at least 2 hours. Reduce the heat as the syrup begins to thicken, and stir to prevent caramelization. Pour the syrup into a sterilized jar and cap the jar tightly. Store the jar in a cool, dark place for up to 1 year.

WATERMELON RIND PRESERVES

MAKES 1½ PINTS

THIS TREAT WAS MORE COMMON in the days when watermelons had thicker skins. Even today, though, it's well worth the trouble to make. Start by cutting a watermelon into thin slices, and slice the white rind away from the pink or yellow flesh before serving the melon. To prepare the rind, cut the green skin from each long piece, trim off any remaining flesh, and then cut the piece into equal-size rectangles, triangles, parallelograms, or other shapes. One medium-size thin-skinned watermelon should provide enough rind for this recipe.

> ¼ cup salt
> 4 quarts cold water
> 1¾ pounds (about 6 cups) prepared watermelon rind
>   (see above)
> One ¾-inch piece fresh ginger, thinly sliced
> 2 cups sugar
> ¼ cup strained lemon juice
> 1 small lemon (optional), thinly sliced

1. Combine the salt with 1 quart of the water; stir until the salt dissolves. Place the rind in a bowl, and pour the brine over the rind. Let the rind stand at room temperature for 5 to 6 hours.

2. Drain and rinse the rind, and drain it again. Cover it again with 1 quart of the cold water. Let the rind stand for 30 minutes, then drain it.

3 Place the rind in a preserving pan with 1 quart of the cold water. Bring the water to a boil, and simmer over low heat until the rind is tender, about 15 minutes. Drain the rind in a colander.

4 Tie the ginger in a spice bag, and place the bag in the preserving pan. Add the sugar, lemon juice, remaining 1 quart water, and lemon slices, if you are using them. Heat the syrup, stirring, until the sugar dissolves. Add the rind. Simmer, uncovered, until the rind is translucent, 1 to 1½ hours. (If the syrup seems thin or overabundant at this point, remove the rind with a slotted spoon, and boil the syrup until it has thickened a bit. Return the rind to the pan.)

5 Squeeze the spice bag against the side of the pan, and remove it. Ladle the rind and syrup into pint or half-pint jars. Add lids and rings, and process the jars for 10 minutes in a boiling-water bath.

ZUCCHINI
(MARROW)

Marrow (Zucchini) Preserves   354

ALSO KNOWN AS VEGETABLE MARROW, the fruit the English call marrow is really an overgrown zucchini, although preferred varieties are more often golden than dark green. Marrows are often baked and stuffed, but around the time of World War I they became popular for use in sweet preserves. Marrow preserves were even made in America for a time; I found a recipe in Marion H. Neil's *Canning, Preserving and Pickling,* published in Philadelphia in 1914. But the biggest assortment of recipes for marrow preserves must be in *May Byron's Jam Book,* published in England in 1917. These recipes variously include dry chile, canned pineapple, cinnamon, apple, lemon slices, and "spirits" in addition to the lemon juice, lemon rind, and ginger you'll find in my basic recipe. Feel free to experiment with these enhancements and more, because marrow or zucchini, on its own, is low in flavor and nutritional value.

Although American gardeners favor zucchini about 1 inch in diameter, the fruits tend to hide under leaves and to grow to massive proportions in a few days' time. Zucchini growers are notorious for placing their overgrown fruits on neighbors' porches and sneaking away. If you don't want your monster zucchini ending up in a compost heap, try this recipe instead.

MARROW (ZUCCHINI) PRESERVES

MAKES ABOUT 2 PINTS

THESE CLEAR, GOLDEN preserves are a beautiful sight, and the lemon and ginger make them tasty, too. Although the quantities may seem small in this recipe, you'll want to use your biggest pan, because the zucchini produces a lot of water that must be boiled off. Try these preserves atop biscuits or white yeast bread.

2½ pounds peeled, seeded very large zucchini,
   cut into approximately ¾-inch cubes
¼ cup strained lemon juice
Grated zest of 1 lemon
1 tablespoon minced fresh ginger, in a spice bag
3½ cups sugar

1. Toss all of the ingredients together in a preserving pan and let the mixture stand at room temperature for 24 hours. Most of the sugar will dissolve during this period.

2. Place the pan over medium heat and heat the mixture until the sugar is completely dissolved.

3. Raise the heat to medium-high and boil the mixture uncovered until it reaches the thread stage (page 18) or 230°F; this will probably take about 20 minutes. Remove the pan from the heat and stir until the boiling stops. Remove the spice bag holding the ginger. Let the preserves cool in the pan; the zucchini chunks will plump as they cool.

4. Ladle the preserves into pint or half-pint mason jars. Add lids and rings, and process the jars for 10 minutes in a boiling-water bath.

MEASUREMENT EQUIVALENTS

Please note that all conversions are approximate.

Liquid Conversions

U.S.	Metric	U.S.	Metric
1 tsp	5 ml	1 cup	240 ml
1 tbs	15 ml	1 cup + 2 tbs	275 ml
2 tbs	30 ml	1¼ cups	300 ml
3 tbs	45 ml	1⅓ cups	325 ml
¼ cup	60 ml	1½ cups	350 ml
⅓ cup	75 ml	1⅔ cups	375 ml
⅓ cup + 1 tbs	90 ml	1¾ cups	400 ml
⅓ cup + 2 tbs	100 ml	1¾ cups + 2 tbs	450 ml
½ cup	120 ml	2 cups (1 pint)	475 ml
⅔ cup	150 ml	2½ cups	600 ml
¾ cup	180 ml	3 cups	720 ml
¾ cup + 2 tbs	200 ml	4 cups (1 quart)	945 ml
			(1,000 ml is 1 liter)

Weight Conversions

U.S. / U.K.	Metric	U.S. / U.K.	Metric
½ oz	14 g	7 oz	200 g
1 oz	28 g	8 oz	227 g
1½ oz	43 g	9 oz	255 g
2 oz	57 g	10 oz	284 g
2½ oz	71 g	11 oz	312 g
3 oz	85 g	12 oz	340 g
3½ oz	100 g	13 oz	368 g
4 oz	113 g	14 oz	400 g
5 oz	142 g	15 oz	425 g
6 oz	170 g	1 lb	454 g

Oven Temperature Conversions

°F	Gas Mark	°C
250	½	120
275	1	140
300	2	150
325	3	165
350	4	180
375	5	190
400	6	200
425	7	220
450	8	230
475	9	240
500	10	260
550	Broil	290

SELECT REFERENCES

Bunyard, Edward. *The Anatomy of Dessert: With a Few Notes on Wine.* New York: Modern Library, 2006. (First published by Dulau, London, in 1929.)

Byron, May. *Jams and Jellies: 543 Recipes.* New York: Dover 1975. (First published as *May Byron's Jam Book* by Hodder and Stoughton, London, in 1917.)

California Rare Fruit Growers. Plant/Tree Descriptions. www.crfg.org

Confitures à la Lorraine. La Confiture de Groseilles de Bar-le-Duc. www.groseille.com

Davidson, Alan. *The Oxford Companion to Food.* Oxford: Oxford University Press, 1999.

Edmonds, Jennifer M., and James A. Chweya. Solanum nigrum *L. and Related Species.* Rome: International Plant Genetic Resources Institute, 1997.

Heiser, Charles B., Jr. *The Fascinating World of the Nightshades: Tobacco, Mandrake, Potato, Tomato, Pepper, Eggplant, etc.* New York: Dover, 1987. (First published as *Nightshades: The Paradoxical Plants* by W. H. Freeman & Co., San Francisco, in 1969.)

Hess, Karen, transcriber. *Martha Washington's Booke of Sweetmeats and Booke of Cookery.* New York: Columbia University Press, 1981.

Kamp, David. *The United States of Arugula: How We Became a Gourmet Nation.* New York: Broadway Books, 2006.

Neil, Marion Harris. *Canning, Preserving, and Pickling.* Philadelphia: David McKay, 1914.

de Packman, Ana Bégué. *Early California Hospitality: The Cookery Customs of Spanish California, with Authentic Recipes and Menus of the Period.* Fresno, California: Academy Library Guild, 1952.

Purdue University Center for New Crops and Plant Products. New Crops Resource Online Program. www.hort.purdue.edu/newcrop

Purvis, Bob. "Apricots—a Wider Geographic Possibility?" *POMONA* XXXIV (Fall 2006).

Reich, Lee. *Uncommon Fruits Worthy of Attention: A Gardener's Guide.* Reading, Massachusetts: Addison-Wesley, 1991.

Rombough, Lon. *The Grape Grower: A Guide to Organic Viticulture.* White River Junction, Vermont: Chelsea Green, 2002.

Siroperie Meurens S.A. Sirop de Liège: Belgian Speciality. www.sirop-de-liege.com

Waters, Alice, and the Cooks of Chez Panisse. *Chez Panisse Fruit.* New York: HarperCollins, 2002.

Wilson, C. Anne. *The Book of Marmalade: Its Antecedents, Its History and Its Role in the World Today, Together with a Collection of Recipes for Marmalades and Marmalade Cookery.* New York: St. Martin's/Marek, 1986. (First published by Constable and Company, London, in 1985.)

INDEX

A

Acid for gelling, 8, 9–10
  and copper pans, 25
  overabundant, 16
  testing for, 10, 15
  in various fruits, 13, 15
Acidulated water, 231, 292
Actinidia, 180–81
Almond(s)
  in Fig-Almond Cake, 148–49
Alum, 105, 106
American Gardener, The (Cobbett), 95, 200
Amygdalin, 104
Amygdalus persica, 230–31
Apple(s). *See also* Crabapple(s)
  about, 35–38
  –Asian pear paste, 249–50
  -blackberry leather, 70–71
  butter, 38–41, 88, 347
    low-sugar, 39–40
    no-sugar-added, 40–41
    with carrots, 88
    with tomatoes, 347
  -carrot butter, 88
  cider, 36
    jelly, 42
    syrup, 41–42
  in *Cogna,* 175–76
  in conserve, 175–76, 276–77
  -elderberry jelly, 135
  -ginger preserves, 43
  jam, with caramel, 44–45
  jelly, 41–42, 48–49
    from cider, 42
    with mint, 48–49

juice, 69
pectin, homemade, 15, 17, 134
-plum conserve, 276–77
-plum leather, 282
-plum paste, 278–89
paste, 278–79, 300–301
  with plums, 278–89
  with quince, 300–1
preserves, with ginger, 43
-quince paste, 300–1
-tomato butter, 347
syrup, 41–42
in *Sirop de Liège,* 250–51
-tomato butter, 347
Apricot(s)
  about, 51–52
  jam, 53
    with pineapple, 54
    with pineapple and ginger, 54
  kernels, 53, 104
  nectar, 56
  paste, 55
  sorbet, 52
Arbutus unedo, 335–36
Asian pears. *See* Pear(s), Asian

B

Banana(s)
  about, 57–58
  jam, with ginger, raisins, and rum,
    58–59
Bar-le-Duc preserves, 122
Bars, Fig, 145
Batch size, 10, 11, 12

Bilberry, 75
Blackberry(ies)
    about, 60–62
    compared with raspberries, 60–61
    jam, 63–67
        with black currants, 66
        with brandy, 64
        with grappa and juniper berries,
            64–65
        raw, 67
        seedless, 64–65
        small-batch, 65–66
    jelly, 62–63
    leather, with apple, 70–71
    paste, 69–70
        with quince, 68–69
    shrub, 74
    syrup, fermented, 72
    vinegar, 73
        in Blackberry Shrub, 74
Blackcaps, 309
Black currant. *See* Currant(s), black
Black nightshade. *See* Garden huckle-
    berry(ies)
Bletting medlars, 199–200
Blood orange, 214, 219
    marmalade, 219–20
Blueberry(ies)
    about, 75–77
    -citrus preserves, 78
    jelly, 80
    syrup, fermented, 81
Boiling-water processing, 22–23
    at high elevations, 23
    steps in, 23
Book of Marmalade, The (Wilson), 219
Brandied Cherries, 95
Brandied Cranberry Preserves, 116
Brandied Peaches with Vanilla, 235
Brandy
    cherries in, 95
    cranberries in, 116
    flavored with cherries, 93–94
    peaches in syrup with, 235
Breba (fig), 140–41, 175
Bunyard, Edward A., 142, 206, 231
Butter(s), 4
    apple, 38–40, 88, 347
        low-sugar, 39
        no-sugar-added, 40
        quick, 40

    carrot-apple, 88
    medlar, 202
    pear, 248–49
    pumpkin, 289
    rose hip, 156–57
    squash, winter, 289
    tomato-apple, 347
    winter squash, 289
Byron, May, 199, 302, 353

C

Cabello de Ángel, 290
Candied fruits, 20
    Asian pears, 246–47
    cherries, 99–100
    cranberries, 117
    lemon peel, 224
    orange peel, 223
    pineapple, 262–63
Caneberry(ies), 60. *See also*
        Blackberry(ies), Raspberry(ies)
Canning, 20–25
    equipment for, 20–21
    open-kettle, 24
    tools for, 21
Canning, Preserving and Pickling (Neil),
    353
Cantaloupe(s)
    about, 82–83
    jam, 84, 85
        with mint, 84
        with vanilla, 85
    preserves, with cinnamon, 86
Caramel
    -apple jam, 35
    -coconut jam, 108–9
    taste, from scorching, 31
Carrot(s)
    about, 87
    -apple butter, 88
    marmalade, 89
Castanea, 203–5
Chaenomeles, 291
Chardequynce, 292
Cherry(ies)
    about, 90–91
    brandied, 95
    candied, 99–100
    compot, Cristina's, 91–92

-currant jam, 98
-currant preserves, 97
-flavored brandy, 93–94
how to pit, 94
jam, 98
kernels, 104
maraschino, 105–6
Montmorency, 90–91, 94, 97, 98, 99
Morello, 93, 105
paste, 102–3
preserves, 96–97
sour, 90–91
spiced, 103–4
sweet, 90
syrup, 99–100, 101
Cherry plums, 266
Chestnut(s)
    about, 203–5
    cream, 210–11
    how to roast, 204
    how to store, 204–5
    in syrup, 208–10
Cider, 36
    jelly, 42
    syrup, 41–42
Citron melon, 348
Citrullos lanatus, 348–49
Citrus
    aurantifolia, 189
    aurantium, 213
    latifolia, 189
    medica, 188
Cleanup, 24–25
Cloudberry, 309
Cobbett, William, 95, 200
Coconut(s)
    about, 107–8
    -caramel jam, 108–9
Cogna, 175–76
Compot, Cherry, 91–92
Cotignac, 292, 294
Concord grape. *See* Grape(s), Concord
Conserve(s), 4
    fig, 146
    mixed fruit and nut, 175–76
    plum-apple, 276–77
    prune plum, 277–78
Copper pans, 25
Cordial
    black currant, 125
    rhubarb, 324

Corylus, 205–6
Cotignac, 292, 297
Cowberry, 110–11
Crabapple(s)
    about, 35, 37
    jelly, 45–47, 49–50
        with cloves and red wine
            vinegar, 47
        with geranium leaves, 49–50
        with ginger, 45–46
    juice, 69
    pectin, 15, 17
Cranberry(ies)
    about, 110–11
    candied, 117
    highbush, 114
    jam, 113
    jelly, 112
    marmalade, 114
    -quince jelly, 112
    -quince preserves, 115
    preserves, brandied, 116
    sauce, simple, 111–12
    syrup, 117
    uses for, 110
Cristina's Cherry *Compot,* 91–92
Cristina's Raw Raspberry Jam, 314
Crystallized fruits, 20
Cucumis melo, 82–83
Cucurbita, 286–87
Cumberland Sauce, 121
Curd
    lemon, 193–94
    lime, 194
    orange, 222
Currant(s)
    about, 118–19
    black, 118, 119, 130
        -blackberry jam, 66
        cordial, 125
        jam, 66, 124, 126
        jelly, 121–22
        juice, 120–21
    growing of, 119
    juice, 120–21, 313
    outlawing of, 118–19
    red, 118, 119
        in Bar-le-Duc preserves, 122
        -cherry jam, 98
        -cherry preserves, 97
        in Cumberland Sauce, 121

Currant(s), red (*continued*)
    jelly, 121–22
    juice, 97, 120–21, 313, 324
    preserves, 123
    -raspberry jam, 313
    white, 118, 119, 122
    preserves, 123
Cydonia oblonga, 5, 291–92

D

Damson plum(s)
    about, 265
    jam, 270
    paste, 280–81
Davidson, Alan, 107, 151
Drop test, 18

E

Eggplant(s)
    about, 127
    preserves, 128–29
Elderberry(ies)
    about, 130–32
    -apple jelly, 135
    black, American, 131
    black, European, 130–31
    blue, 131
    jam, 132
    jelly, 134, 135
    juice, 133
    red, 131
    rob, 136
    syrup, 137
Elder flowers
    about, 130
    in gooseberry jam, 166
English marmalade, 213, 217–19
Equipment for preserving, 25, 26–27, 28
Ericaceae, 75

F

Feijoa (pineapple guava)
    about, 138
    jam, 139
Fermented Blackberry Syrup, 72

Fermented Blueberry or Huckleberry
    Syrup, 81
Fig(s)
    about, 140–42
    -almond cake, 148–49
    bars, 145
    jam, 142–44, 145, 233
      in bar cookies, 145
      low-sugar, 144
      no-sugar-added, 144
      smooth, 143–44
    -peach jam, 233
    preserves, 146
      with fennel and bay, 147
    varieties, 141–42
    whole, in vanilla-flavored syrup, 148
Filbert. *See* Hazelnut(s)
Floral Ice, 160
Flowering quince
    about, 291
    jelly, 295
      clear, 295
Flowers
    about, 150–52
    elder, 130, 167
    roses, 150–55, 160
    violets, 150, 151, 159, 160
Foaming, 11
Food mill, 25, 26
Fortune, Robert, 184–85
Fortunella, 184–85
Fragaria, 325–26
Fruit leather
    blackberry-apple, 70–71
    plum-apple, 282

G

Gage, Sir Thomas, 266
Gage plums. *See* Greengage plum(s)
Garden huckleberry(ies) (*Solanum* species)
    about, 161–62
    jam, 162
    as medicine, 162
Garden nightshade. *See* Garden huckle-
    berry(ies)
Gaylussacia, 75
Gelling, 6–9, 11, 80
    copper pans and, 25

of jelly, 11, 13, 16–18
tests for, 18
Geranium, in crabapple jelly, 49
Ginger
    about, 163
    crystallized, 165
        in lemon marmalade, 192–93
        in low-sugar fig jam, 144
        in mango-orange jam, 198
        in peach jam, 232
        in pear preserves, 242
        in rhubarb preserves, 322
        in quince preserves, 304–5
    in syrup, 164–65
Gooseberry(ies)
    about, 166
    jam, 167
        with elder flowers, 167
Grape(s)
    about, 168–69
    Concord, 168, 169, 170–71
        jam, 170–71
        jelly, 172–73
    conserve, 175–76
    juice, 172
    molasses, 173–74, 350
    muscadine, 169
    uses for, 168, 169
Grapefruit
    about, 177
    marmalade, 178–79
Grape Grower, The (Rombough), 171
Green Walnut Preserves, 207–8
Greengage plum(s)
    about, 265–66
    jam, 271–72
        with vanilla, 272
        with greengage kernels, 272
    preserves, 275
Green Tomato Preserves, 346
Ground cherry(ies)
    about, 337–38
    in fondant, 338
    jam, 339

H

Hazelnut(s)
    about, 205–6

in Cogna, 175–76
in Rebecca's Hazelnut-Chocolate
    Spread, 211–12
Highbush cranberry(ies), 114
Homemade pectin, 15, 17
    apple, 134
    orange, 221
    quince, 102
Honey, 9
    in kumquat preserves, 185–86
    in Orange Honey, 217
    in Raw Elderberry Syrup, 137
    in Rose Hip Syrup, 158
    syrup, Asian pears in, 250–51
    syrup, orange slices in, 216–17
Hot Green Pepper–Lime Jelly, 257–58
Hot Red Pepper Jelly, 256
Huckleberry(ies)
    about, 75–77
    garden. See Garden huckleberry(ies)
    syrup, fermented, 81
    in syrup, 79

I

Ice Cream, Raspberry, 316

J

Jam(s), 3, 6, 11–12
    apple-caramel, 44–45
    apricot, 53, 54
        with pineapple, 54
    Asian pear, 241
    banana, with ginger, raisins, and rum,
        58–59
    blackberry, 63–67
        with black currant juice, 66
        with brandy, 64
        with grappa and juniper berries,
            64–65
        raw, 67
        seedless, 64–65
        small-batch, 65–66
    black currant, raw, 126
    cantaloupe, 84, 85
        with mint, 84
        with vanilla, 85

Jam(s) (*continued*)
  caramel-apple, 44–45
  caramel-coconut, 108–9
  cherry–red currant, 98
  Concord grape, 170–71
    spiced, 171
  coconut-caramel, 108–9
  cranberry, 113
  crystallization of, 10–11, 30
  damson, 270
  darkening of, 31
  defined, 3
  elderberry, 132
  faded, 31
  feijoa, 139
  fig, 142–44, 233
    low-sugar, 144
    no-sugar-added, 144
    with peaches, 233
    smooth, 143
  garden huckleberry, 162
  gooseberry, 167
    with elder flowers, 166
  grape, Concord, 170–71
  greengage, 271–72
    with greengage kernels, 272
    with vanilla, 272
  ground cherry, 339
  history of, 6
  Japanese plum, 267
  kiwi, 181–82, 183
    with strawberries, 183
  mango-orange, 198
  papaya, 229
  peach, 232, 233
    with figs, 233
    with ginger, 232
  pear, 241
    with vanilla, 241
  pepper, red, 255
  pineapple guava, 139
  prune plum, 268, 269
    refrigerator, 269
  pumpkin, 287–88
  quince, 296
  raspberry, 311–14
    raw, 314
    with red currant juice, 313
    smooth, 312
  red pepper, 255

  rhubarb-orange, 321
  squash, winter, 287–88
  strawberry, 183, 327–30, 332–33
    main-crop, 328
    with orange, 329
    with rhubarb, 330
    small-batch, 327
    sun-cooked, 332–33
  tomatillo, 339
  winter squash, 287–88
Japanese plum(s)
  about, 264, 266
  -apple conserve, 276–77
  -apple leather, 282
  -apple paste, 278–79
  jam, 267
Japonica, 291
Jelly(ies), 3, 13–14
  acid in, 15, 16, 17–18
  apple, 42, 48–49
    cider, 42
    mint, 48–49
  bag, described, 13–14, 15
  blackberry, 62–63
  blueberry, 80
  cider, 42
  cloudy, 15, 30
  Concord grape, 172–73
  crabapple, 45–46, 47, 49–50
    with cloves and red wine vinegar,
      47
    with geranium leaves, 49–50
    with ginger, 45–46
  cranberry-quince, 112
  crystallization of, 10–11, 30
  currant, 121–22
  darkening of, 31
  defined, 3
  elderberry, 134, 135
  elderberry-apple, 135
  faded, 31
  flowering quince, 295
  gelling of, 13, 16, 17–18
  grape, 172–73
  hot green pepper–lime, 257–58
  hot red pepper, 256
  lemon, 190–91
    with rosemary, 191
  lime, 191, 257–58
    –hot green pepper, 257–58

medlar, 200–1
mint, 48–49
orange, 221
   with cinnamon, 221
   with vanilla, 221–22
pectin for, 13
Oregon grape, 226
pepper, 256, 257–58
quince, 293-94
   -cranberry, 112
   from flowering quince, 295
   with geranium leaves, 294
red currant, 121–22
red pepper, 256
remaking of, 17–18
rose, 152–53
rubbery, 30
Sirop de Liège, 250–51
soft, 30
sticky, 30
syneresis of, 16, 30
weeping of, 16, 30
Jostaberry, 118
Juglans regia, 205

K

Kamp, David, 180
Kernels, stone-fruit, 53, 104, 272
Kiwi(s)
   about, 180–81
   jam, 181–82, 183
   preserves, 182
   -strawberry jam, 183
Kumquat
   about, 184–85
   marmalade, 187
   peels, 184
   preserves with honey, 185–86

L

Leather(s), fruit, 4
   blackberry-apple, 70–71
   plum-apple, 282
Lemon(s)
   about, 188–90
   curd, 193–94

-ginger marmalade, 192–93
jelly, 190–91
   with rosemary, 191
juice, to prevent browning, 190
marmalade, 192–93, 217–19
pectin in, 190, 217
peel, candied, 224
–sweet orange marmalade, 217–19
syrup, 195
   with ginger, 195
tips for juicing, 192
Lime
   curd, 194
   –hot green pepper jelly, 257–58
   jelly, 191, 257–58
   Key, 189
   -mango jam, 197–98
   Mexican, 189, 194
   syrup, 194–95
      with ginger, 195
   tips for juicing, 192
   -tomatillo marmalade, 340
Lingonberry, 110–11
Loquat, 199
Low-Sugar Apple Butter, 39
Low-Sugar Fig-Ginger Jam, 144

M

Mahonia, 2215
Madroño, 335
Malus, 35–38
Mango(es)
   about, 196–97
   -lime jam, 197–98
   -orange-ginger jam, 198
Maraschino cherries, 105–6
Marmalade(s), 3
   bitter orange, 213, 217
   blood orange, 219–20
   carrot, 89
   chunky, 219
   cranberry, 114
   dark, 218–19
   English, 5, 213, 217, 218–19
   ginger-lemon, 192–93
   grapefruit, red, 178–79
   history of, 5, 217, 218–19, 292,
      297–98

Marmalade(s) (*continued*)
  kumquat, 187
  lemon-ginger, 192–93
  Moro orange, 219–20
  orange, 5, 217–19
    bitter, 217
    blood, 219–20
    chunky, 219
    dark, 218–19
    sweet, with lemon, 217–19
  pear-pineapple, 261
  quince, 302–3
    golden, 302–3
  Scottish, 5, 213, 217
  sweet orange–lemon, 217–19
  tomatillo-lime, 340
  tomato, 342
Marrow (zucchini)
  about, 353
  preserves, 354
Martha Washington's Booke of Sweetmeats and Booke of Cookery (Hess), 150, 297
Mason jar(s), 20–21, 28
  lids, 21, 28
    checking seals of, 23–24
  rings, 21, 24, 28
May Byron's Jam Book (Byron), 199, 353
Medlar(s)
  about, 199–200
  bletting, 199–200
  butter, 202
  jelly, 200–201
Membrillo, dulce de, 5, 297
Meyer lemon, 188–89
Mint jelly, 48–49
Molasses (condensed fruit syrup)
  grape, 173–74
  pomegranate, 283
  watermelon, 350
Mold in jars, 31
Moro orange, 214, 219
  marmalade, 219–20
Morus, 67
Mostarda, 173–74
  dulce d'uva, 175–76
Mulberries, 67
Muskmelon, 82. *See also* Cantaloupe(s)

N

Nectar, apricot, 56
Nectarine, 231
Neil, Marion H., 353
Nightshade, black. *See* Garden huckleberry(ies)
Nightshade, garden. *See* Garden huckleberry(ies)
Nonreactive, defined, 28
No-Sugar-Added Fig Jam, 144
Nuts, 203–6. *See also* Almond(s), Chestnut(s), Hazelnut(s), Walnut(s)

O

One Green World nursery, 181, 292
Open-kettle canning, 24
Orange(s)
  about, 213–15
  bitter, 15, 213, 217
  blood, 214
    marmalade, 219–20
  curd, 222
  honey, 215
  jelly, 221–22
    with cinnamon, 221
    with vanilla, 221–22
  marmalade, 5, 213, 217–18, 219–20
  Moro, 214, 219
    marmalade, 219–20
  navel, 214
  -pear-apricot preserves, 245
  pectin, homemade, 17, 221
  pectin in, 15, 213, 215, 217
  peel, 214–15
    candied, 223–24
  -rhubarb jam, 321
  Seville, 213, 217
  slices, in honey syrup, 216–17
  sour, 213, 217
  -strawberry jam, 329
  sweet, 213, 214
    -lemon marmalade, 217–18
  Valencia, 214
Oregon grape(s)
  about, 225

jelly, 226
pectin in, 225
Oxalic acid, 319

P

Pans for preserving, 25, 28
Papain, 227
Papaya(s)
about, 227–28
Hawaiian, 227–28
jam, 229
Mexican, 227–28
preserves, 228–29
Paste(s), 4
apple–Asian pear, 249–50
apricot, 55
blackberry, 69–70
with quince, 68–69
cherry, 102–3
damson plum, 280–81
Japanese plum–apple, 278–79
prune plum, 279–80
quince, 292, 297–301
with apples, 300–1
as by-product of jelly making, 293, 299
with cardamom, 299
with rose water, 299
Peach(es)
about, 230–31
brandied, 235–36
clingstone, 230–31
-fig jam, 233
flat, 231
freestone, 230–31
how to peel, 231
jam, 232, 233
in syrup, 234, 235
Pear(s)
about, 237–40
Asian, 239–40
acid in, 239, 240
–apple paste, 249–50
candied, 246–47
in honey syrup, 250–51
jam, 241
syrup, 246–47
when to harvest, 239

butter, 248–49
European, 237–39
-apricot-orange-preserves, 245
butter, 248–49
in *Cogna,* 175–76
jam, 241
pectin in, 239
-pineapple marmalade, 261
preserves with ginger, 242
preserves with red wine, 244
in red wine, 243
in *Sirop de Liège,* 251-52
varieties, 238
when to harvest, 238
jam, 241
with vanilla, 241
Pectin, 6, 8, 9, 12, 13
apple, homemade, 15, 134
concentrating, 15
crabapple, homemade, 15, 17
in currants, 119
homemade, using, 15
in lemons, 190
orange, homemade, 15, 17, 217
in oranges, 15, 213, 217
in Oregon grape, 225
quince, homemade, 15, 17, 102
in quinces, 291–92
in strawberries, 326
packaged, 6–7
types of, 7
testing for, 15, 16
in various fruits, 12, 13
Peel, candied
lemon, 224
orange, 223–24
Pepper *(Capsicum)*
about, 253–54
jam, red, 255
jelly
hot green–lime, 257–58
hot red, 256
Persian walnut. *See* Walnut(s), Persian
Physalis, 327–28
Pie melon, 348
Pie-plant, 319
Pineapple(s)
about, 259–60
-apricot jam, 54
candied, 262–63

Pineapple(s) (*continued*)
  -pear marmalade, 261
  preserves, 260–61
  syrup, 262–63
Pineapple guava (feijoa)
  about, 138
  jam, 139
Plum(s)
  about, 264–66
  -apple leather, 282
  cherry, 266
  conserve, 276–78
  damson, 265
    jam, 270
    paste, 280–81
  European, 264–65, 275. *See also*
      Prune plum(s); Prunes
    conserve, 276–78
    jam, 268, 269
    paste, 279–80
    preserves, 272–74
  greengage, 265–66. *See also* Green-
      gage plum(s)
    jam, 271–72
    preserves, 275
  Japanese, 264, 266
    -apple conserve, 276–77
    -apple leather, 282
    -apple paste, 278–79
    jam, 267
  paste, 278–81
  prune, 265, 275. *See also* Prune
      plum(s); Prunes
    conserve, 276–78
    jam, 268, 269
    paste, 279–80
    preserves, 272–74
  when to harvest, 266
Pomegranate
  about, 283
  molasses, 283
  sorbet, 284
  syrup, 284–85
POMONA magazine, 52
Preserved Pears with Ginger, 242
Preserves (proper), 4, 18–20
  apple-ginger, 43
  apricot-orange-pear, 245
  Bar-le-Duc, 122
  blueberry-citrus, 78

cantaloupe, with cinnamon, 86
cherry, 96, 97, 116
  brandied, 116
  with currant juice, 97
cranberry, brandied, 116
cranberry-quince, 115
currant, 123
eggplant, 128–29
fig, 146, 147
  with fennel and bay, 147
floating fruit in, 31
gelling of, 19, 20
greengage plum, 275
green walnut, 207–8
kiwi, 182
kumquat, 185–86
marrow, 354
orange-pear-apricot, 245
papaya, 228–29
pear-ginger, 242
pear-orange-apricot, 245
pear–red wine, 244
pineapple, 260–61, 344–45
  with tomato, 344–45
plum, 272–75
prune plum, 272–74
  with brown sugar, 273
  with port, 274
  with red wine, 273
quince, 115, 301–2, 304–5
  with cranberries, 115
  with ginger and grated quince, 304–5
  with star anise, 301
  with vanilla, 301–2
rhubarb, 322, 323
  with ginger, 322
  with rose petals, 323
rose, 153–54
shriveled, 31
spaghetti squash, 290
strawberry, 331
  with rose petals, 331
sugar in, 19
tomato, 344–45, 346
  green, 346
  yellow, with pineapple, 344–45
walnut, green, 207–8
watermelon, 349–50, 351–52
  rind, 351–52
zucchini, 354

Preserves (sweetmeats)
   history of, 4–7
   kinds of, 3–4
Preserving equipment, 25, 26–27, 28
Preserving pan, defined, 25, 28
Prune plum(s). *See also* Prunes
   conserve, 276–78
     with apples, 276–77
   jam, 268, 269
     refrigerator, 269
   preserves, 272–74
     with brown sugar, 273
     with port, 274
     with red wine, 273
Prunes, 265
   in port, 275
Prunus
   cerasifera, 266
   cerasus, 90
   domestica, 264–65
   instititia, 265
   salicina, 264
Pumpkin
   about, 286–87
   butter, 289
   jam, 287–88
Puree, raspberry, 315
Pyrus, 237–40

Q

Quick Apple Butter with No Sugar Added, 40
Quiddany, 294
Quince(s)
   about, 291–95
   -apple paste, 300–1
   -blackberry paste, 68–69
   candy, raw, 307
   -cranberry jelly, 112
   -cranberry preserves, 115
   flowering, 291
     granita, 306
     jelly, 295
   jam, 296
   jelly, 293–94
     with cranberry juice, 112
     with geranium leaves, 294

   juice, 69, 102
   marmalade, 302–3
     golden, 302–3
     red, 303
   paste, 297–98
     as by-product of jelly making, 293, 299
     with apples, 300
     with blackberries, 68–69
     with cardamom, 299
     with rose water, 299
   pectin, homemade, 15, 17, 102
   pectin in, 291–92
   preserves, 301–302, 304–5
     with cranberries, 115
     with ginger, 301
     with grated quince, 304–5
     with star anise, 301
     with vanilla, 301–2
   syrup, 305–8
     in granita, 306
     with lime, 306
     raw, with honey, 308
     raw, with sugar, 307
   uses for, 293
   varieties, 293
   and wine relish, 307–8

R

Randolph, Mary, 341
Raspberry(ies)
   about, 309–10
   black, 309
   fall, 310
   freezing, 310
   golden, 309–10
   growing, 310
   ice cream, 316
   jam, 311–14
     raw, 314
     with red currant juice, 313
     smooth, 312
   juice, in Rhubarb Cordial, 324
   puree, 315
     in ice cream, 316
   –red currant jam, 313
   sauce, 315–16
   shrub, 318

Raspberry(ies) (*continued*)
  vinegar, 317
    in shrub, 318
Raw Blackberry Jam, 67
Raw Black Currant Jam, 126
Raw Elderberry Syrup, 137
Raw Quince Syrup, 307–8
Rebecca's Hazelnut-Chocolate Spread,
    211–12
Red currants. *See* Currant(s), Red
Red Grapefruit Marmalade, 178–79
Red Pepper Jam, 255
Refrigerator Prune Plum Jam, 269
Rheum, 319–20
Rhubarb
  about, 319–20
  Alaskan, 320
  cordial, 324
  -ginger preserves, 322
  -orange jam, 321
  -rose preserves, 323
  varieties, 319–20
Ribes, 118–20, 166
Rob, elderberry, 136
Rombough, Lon, 171
Rose(s)
  about, 150–52
  hip(s), 151, 156–57, 158
    butter, 156–57
    syrup, 158
  jelly, 152–53
  petal(s), 150–51, 152–55, 323, 331
    jelly, 152–53
    preserves, 153–54
    in rhubarb preserves, 323
    in strawberry preserves, 331
    syrup, 155, 160
  preserves, 153–54
  -rhubarb preserves, 323
  -strawberry preserves, 331
  syrup, 155, 158, 160
  varieties for preserving, 151, 156
Rubus, 60–62, 309–10

S

Salal, 225
Salmonberry, 309
Sambucus, 130–31

Sand pear, 239
Sauce, raspberry, 315–16
Saucer test, 18
Seedless Blackberry Jam, 64–65
Seville orange, 213, 219
Sheet test, 18
Shrub, 318
  blackberry, 74
  raspberry, 318
Simmering, defined, 28
Simple Cranberry Sauce, 111
Sirop de Liège, 250–51
Skimming, 11, 28
Small-Batch Blackberry Jam, 65–66
Small-Batch Strawberry Jam, 327
Smooth Fig Jam, 143
Smooth Raspberry Jam, 312
Sorbet
  apricot, 52
  pomegranate, 284
Sour orange, 213, 217
Spaghetti squash, 286
  preserves, 290
Spice bag, defined, 28
Spiced Cherries, 103–4
Spoon sweets, 4, 5
Spoon test, 18
Squash, winter
  about, 286–87
  butter, 289
  jam, 287–88
Steam juicer, 13, 46, 80, 101
  described, 14, 28
  for grapes, 172
  for jelly, 13
  for Oregon grapes, 226
  for quince, 293
Sterilizing jars, 24, 29
Storing preserves, 25–26
Strawberry(ies)
  about, 325–26
  freezing, 326
  jam, 183, 327–30
    with kiwis, 183
    main-crop, 328
    with orange, 329
    small-batch, 327
    sun-cooked, 332–33
  juice, in Rhubarb Cordial, 324
  -kiwi jam, 183

-orange jam, 219
preserves, 331
    with rose petals, 331
species of, 325–26
syrup, 333–34
Strawberry tree
. about, 335–36
jam, 336
Sugar, 8–9, 10–11, 29, 44
    caramelization of, 44
    crystallization of, 10–11
    for gelling, 8–9
    in preserves, 19
    warming of, 10
Sunberry, 161. *See also* Garden huckle-
        berry(ies)
Sunshine Strawberry Jam, 332–33
Sweet Orange–Lemon Marmalade,
        217–19
Sweet violets. *See* Violet(s)
Syrup(s), 4
    apple cider, 41–42
    Asian pear, 246–47
    Asian pears in, 250–51
    blackberry, fermented, 72
    blueberry, fermented, 81
    cherry, 99–100, 101, 105–6
    chestnuts in, 208–9
    cider, 41–42
    cranberry, 117
    elderberry, raw, 137
    ginger in, 164–65
    honey, 216–17, 250–51
    huckleberries in, 79
    huckleberry, fermented, 81
    lemon, 195
        with ginger, 195
    of Liège, 250–51
    lime, 194–95
        with ginger, 195
    orange slices in, 216–17
    pear-apple, 250–51
    peaches in, 234, 235
    pineapple, 262–63
    pomegranate, 284–85
    in preserves, 18–19
    quince, 305–8
        with lime, 306
        raw, with honey, 308
        raw, with sugar, 307

rose hip, 158
rose petal, 155
strawberry, 333–34
vanilla-flavored, figs in, 148
violet, 159, 160

T

Thermometer, calibrating, 19
Thread test, 18–19
Tomatillo(s)
    about, 337, 338
    jam, 339
    -lime marmalade, 340
Tomato(es)
    about, 341–42
    -apple butter, 347
    green, preserves, 346
    marmalade, 342–43
    preserves, 344–46
        with pineapple, 344–45
    yellow, preserves, 344–45
Troubleshooting, 30–31

U

United States of Arugula (Kamp), 180

V

Vaccinium, 75–76, 111
    macrocarpon, 110–11
Verjuice, 169
Viburnum trilobum, 114
Vinegar,
    blackberry, 73
        in shrub, 74
    raspberry, 317
        in shrub, 318
Viola odorata, 151–52, 159
Violet(s)
    about, 151–52, 159
    champagne, 151–52
    ice, 160
    syrup, 151–52, 159, 160
    tea, iced, 151
Virginia House-Wife, 341

Vitamin C
  for acidulating water, 231, 292
  in strawberry tree fruit, 335
Vitis, 168–69, 170, 171, 172

W

Walnut(s), Persian
  about, 205
  in *Cogna,* 175–76
  in Fig Conserve, 146
  green, preserves, 207–8
  in Prune Plum Conserve, 277–78
Washington, Martha, 150
Watermelon
  about, 348–49
  molasses, 350
  preserves, 349–50
  rind preserves, 351
  seedless, 348–49
Waters, Alice, 189

White currants. *See* Currant(s), white
Whole Figs in Vanilla-Flavored Syrup,
  148
Whortleberry, 75
Wiegand, Ernest H., 105
Wilson, C. Anne, 219
Winter squash. *See* Squash, winter

Y

Yellow Tomato–Pineapple Preserves,
  344–45

Z

Zest, defined, 29
Zucchini (marrow)
  about, 353
  preserves, 354